Start Here!™

Build Windows 8 Apps with HTML5 and JavaScript

Dino Esposito
Francesco Esposito

Published with the authorization of Microsoft Corporation by:
O'Reilly Media, Inc.
1005 Gravenstein Highway North
Sebastopol, California 95472

ISBN: 978-0-7356-7594-0

1 2 3 4 5 6 7 8 9 LSI 8 7 6 5 4 3

Printed and bound in the United States of America.

Microsoft Press books are available through booksellers and distributors worldwide. If you need support related to this book, email Microsoft Press Book Support at *mspinput@microsoft.com*. Please tell us what you think of this book at *http://www.microsoft.com/learning/booksurvey*.

Microsoft and the trademarks listed at *http://www.microsoft.com/about/legal/en/us/IntellectualProperty/ Trademarks/EN-US.aspx* are trademarks of the Microsoft group of companies. All other marks are property of their respective owners.

The example companies, organizations, products, domain names, email addresses, logos, people, places, and events depicted herein are fictitious. No association with any real company, organization, product, domain name, email address, logo, person, place, or event is intended or should be inferred.

This book expresses the author's views and opinions. The information contained in this book is provided without any express, statutory, or implied warranties. Neither the authors, O'Reilly Media, Inc., Microsoft Corporation, nor its resellers, or distributors will be held liable for any damages caused or alleged to be caused either directly or indirectly by this book.

Acquisitions and Developmental Editor: Russell Jones

Production Editor: Christopher Hearse

Editorial Production: S4Carlisle Publishing Services

Technical Reviewer: Russ Mullen

Indexer: Angela Howard

Cover Design: Jake Rae

Cover Composition: Karen Montgomery

Illustrator: S4Carlisle Publishing Services

To Michela and Silvia, who are stronger and smarter than they think.

—Dino

To Grandma Concetta, for providing free calories through amazing quantities of unbeatable homemade prosciutto.

—Francesco

Contents at a glance

Contents

What do you think of this book? We want to hear from you!

Microsoft is interested in hearing your feedback so we can continually improve our
books and learning resources for you. To participate in a brief online survey, please visit:

microsoft.com/learning/booksurvey

Chapter 14 Publishing an application

What do you think of this book? We want to hear from you!

Microsoft is interested in hearing your feedback so we can continually improve our books and learning resources for you. To participate in a brief online survey, please visit:

microsoft.com/learning/booksurvey

Introduction

For years, programming has been the nearly exclusive domain of people that others typically thought of as super-experts, gurus, or geniuses. The advent of mobile programming, however, changed things a bit because the idea of programming for these devices regained its appeal for youngsters. Today, a teenager appearing suddenly in the spotlight due to his or her ability to build a cool Android or iPhone app is not uncommon. There are a few reasons why this is happening, and why it's happening now.

One reason is certainly that today's teenagers are the first generation of digital natives. You're far more likely to find a few programmers among this group than among the members of previous generations. Another reason is that mobile apps are much easier to write than any other type of modern software. Mobile apps are small pieces of code built around a smart idea. It's one thing to build a mobile app, and quite another to plan and maintain a multitiered enterprise system.

Being mobile added a new dimension to software development. In this context, Windows Phone is not simply yet another mobile platform to code for; It is by far the simplest (and even most pleasant) platform to code for, regardless of background. This makes coding for Windows Phone an excellent way to get started with programming. This is particularly true for the smart kids who constantly hunger after new technology and seek emotional gratification in that technology. I've seen this happen with my 14-year-old son, Francesco—who is the effective coauthor of this book.

Microsoft Windows 8 takes the "programming with pleasure" approach one step further. With Windows 8, you can not only build mobile apps for tablets, but also build standalone applications for yourself, either for fun or to help automate some of the repetitive tasks of everyday life. Windows 8, with its overall simplicity, brings back a dimension of craftsmanship in applications that went missing as the complexity of software architectures and websites increased over the past decade or so. On one hand, Windows 8 is a powerful client front end for rich and sophisticated middleware; on the other, it is simple enough for nearly everybody to program via HTML5 and JavaScript.

This book is intended as a quick (but juicy) beginner's guide for getting started crafting Windows 8 applications, and how to publish and sell them through the Windows Store. The key point of this book is to make it clear that if you have a good idea and are a quick learner, you can create a Windows 8 app regardless of your age or programming background. You'll see how to write functional applications for the new Microsoft operating system and have them run on desktop computers, as well as tablets. As evidence, consider that Francesco is a teenager—and he wrote most of the examples and a few chapters of this book.

After completing the book, you won't be a super-expert, but you'll surely know enough to start writing your own apps, at least for fun.

Who should read this book

This book is a beginner's guide to Windows 8 programming using web technologies, such as HTML5 and JavaScript. But the scope of the word "beginner" needs some further explanation. One definition of a beginner, in a programming sense, is a person who has never learned any serious programming. While this book does target such beginners, it does require some minimal background knowledge about HTML5, JavaScript, and some familiarity with basic concepts of logic and formalism, such as *IF*, *WHILE*, and assignments. Another definition of a beginner, however, would include people who have never learned Windows programming, or people who perhaps wrote COBOL for decades—or even perhaps a person who built and maintained a Visual Basic 6 application for the past 15 years. While this book can also be useful for those more experienced "beginners," people with serious programming experience are not the target audience for this book.

This book attempts to provide a smooth approach to key topics of Windows 8 programming. If you are primarily interested in Windows 8 and are new to Windows Phone, Microsoft Silverlight, or even single-page applications, then you should definitely consider getting this book.

Who should not read this book

This book won't make you a top-notch Windows 8 developer. If you have some solid experience with Windows 8, with Windows Phone or Silverlight, or with other programming languages, then you might want to try another, more advanced book instead, or just rely on online MSDN documentation or StackOverflow links. You should be a true Windows 8 beginner to enjoy this book.

Organization of this book

This book is divided into three sections. Chapters 1-5 cover the basics of acquiring and using Microsoft Visual Studio 2012 Express and also provide a summary of what you need to know about HTML, CSS, and JavaScript. Chapters 6-11 deal with programming Windows 8 apps and cover the foundation of Windows 8 programming while providing step-by-step exercises that help you understand and deal with the user interface of Windows 8 apps, graphics, video, data storage, and Internet calls. Finally, Chapters 12-14 focus on advanced Windows 8 programming, with an emphasis on working with device sensors and accessories (such as printers, GPS, webcams, and so forth), interacting with the system (Live tiles), and publishing your completed application.

Finding your best starting point in this book

Overall, the scenarios for using this book are quite simple. We recommend you read it cover to cover, because it is designed to guide you through the key topics you need to know to program Windows 8 with HTML5 and JavaScript. However, if you already have a solid grasp of the technologies used in this book—Visual Studio 2012 Express, HTML5, CSS, and JavaScript—you may be able to skip Chapters 1-4 without compromising your understanding of the rest of the book.

Conventions and features in this book

This book presents information using conventions designed to make the information readable and easy to follow.

- Each exercise consists of a series of tasks, presented as numbered steps (1, 2, and so on) listing each action you must take to complete the exercise.

- Boxed elements with labels such as "Note" provide additional information or alternative methods for completing a step successfully.

- Text that you type (apart from code blocks) appears in bold.

- A plus sign (+) between two key names means that you must press those keys at the same time. For example, "Press Alt+Tab" means that you hold down the Alt key while you press the Tab key.

- A vertical bar between two or more menu items (such as, File | Close), means that you should select the first menu or menu item, then the next, and so on.

System requirements

You will need the following hardware and software to set up yourself on the various mobile platforms and compile the sample code:

- A PC equipped with Windows 8 and Visual Studio 2012 Express for Windows 8.

Code samples

Most of the chapters in this book are built around exercises that are reflected in the sample code for the chapter. All sample projects in their finalized form can be downloaded from the following page:

http://aka.ms/SH_W8AppsHTML5JS/files

Follow the instructions to download the starthere-buildapps-winjs-sources.zip file.

Installing the code samples

Follow these steps to install the code samples on your computer so that you can use them with the exercises in this book.

1. Unzip the starthere-buildapps-winjs-sources.zip file that you downloaded from the book's website (name a specific directory along with directions to create it, if necessary).

2. If prompted, review the displayed end user license agreement. If you accept the terms, select the accept option, and then click Next.

> **Note** If the license agreement doesn't appear, you can access it from the same webpage from which you downloaded the starthere-buildapps-winjs-sources.zip file.

Errata and book support

We've made every effort to ensure the accuracy of this book and its companion content. Any errors that have been reported since this book was published are listed on our Microsoft Press site at oreilly.com:

http://aka.ms/SH_W8AppsHTML5JS/errata

If you find an error that is not already listed, you can report it to us through the same page.

If you need additional support, email Microsoft Press Book Support at *mspinput@ microsoft.com*.

Please note that product support for Microsoft software is not offered through the addresses above.

We want to hear from you

At Microsoft Press, your satisfaction is our top priority, and your feedback our most valuable asset. Please tell us what you think of this book at:

http://www.microsoft.com/learning/booksurvey

The survey is short, and we read every one of your comments and ideas. Thanks in advance for your input!

Stay in touch

Let's keep the conversation going! We're on Twitter: *http://twitter.com/MicrosoftPress*

Acknowledgements

Dino:

I'll be honest: **Russell Jones**, my editor at O'Reilly Media, convinced me to try this project. If the book is in your hands, both some of the good and some of the bad are on him! When Russell first mentioned this book, when it was still just an idea, I first declined, making the point that I have never written a book for beginners.

But then my son, Francesco (proud and efficient coauthor), made me look at the subject from a different perspective. It was one of those powerful forms of lateral thinking that only young people can sometimes contribute. Francesco said something like, "Dad, I don't think you only admit experts to your software design or ASP.NET MVC classes. If I were a true expert, I'd probably rarely take a class; if I need a class it is because I want someone to show me the way slowly and effectively. If I decide to invest money on a class it is because I feel somehow that I'm a beginner. Why should this be different for a book?"

That message hit home; I found that to be a valuable bit of wisdom; even coming from a 14-year-old boy.

So with that change of heart, I embarked enthusiastically on this project and asked Francesco to cooperate, because he was perfect for testing the material—essentially eating the dog food we were cooking up! Francesco did a truly fantastic job. At one point, I was on a plane about to leave and talking on the phone, giving suggestions on how to improve the gallery of photos and the downloading of JSON data from Flickr. From the outside, that phone call was nothing more than a classic business phone call—the last-minute kind you make just moments before the plane leaves the gate. But I was talking to my son! And, more importantly, he had diligently accomplished all the tasks by the time I got back. Thank you, Francesco!

Francesco:

I love technology and love the Microsoft software platform and tooling. In the beginning, for me, writing the book was primarily a way to get my hands on a Surface device. In the end, though, I spent most of the time working with the simulator and a secondary laptop.

Dad told me that exploring a technology near its birth is usually quite difficult, because you can't always rely on documentation or good examples being available. Frankly, to me that just sounded like one of those excuses that parents trot out when they're unable to do something themselves. Not knowing it might be hard, I just rolled up my sleeves and worked out some examples. And in doing so, I also was able to contribute a list of points for Dad to expand on. I'm not sure this project would have been as pleasant for Dad without my help.

Working on the book was mostly fun, but I do recognize that this book is an important achievement for me. I know I'll feel better if I can share this moment with some people who make my life happier: my mom, my sister, Michela, my friends Francesco and Mattia, and all my waterpolo teammates at UISP Monterotondo. I love you all!

PS: Michela, do you remember that Christmas of 2009 when I was really giving you a hard time and in order to "save" you, Dad decided to initiate (or actually initialize?) me to programming?

Chapter 1

Using Visual Studio 2012 Express edition for Windows 8

Differences of habit and language are nothing at all if our aims are identical.
— *J. K. Rowling*, Harry Potter and the Goblet of Fire

Microsoft Windows 8 marks the debut of a significantly revised runtime platform—the Windows RunTime (WinRT) platform. Like the .NET platform, WinRT supports several programming languages. You will find a pleasant surprise (and an old acquaintance) side by side with the popular .NET languages (such as, C#, Visual Basic, C++, F#)—the JavaScript language.

Note You may not even recall that a decade ago, when Microsoft first shipped the .NET Framework, developers were also given a chance to write applications using an adapted version of JavaScript called JScript .NET. It was not exactly a success; indeed, today you won't even find JScript .NET supported in Visual Studio—the premiere development environment for .NET code. Ten years ago, JavaScript was probably close to the bottom of its popularity. JScript .NET was a dialect of the standard JavaScript, and using JScript .NET didn't mean you could use HTML and CSS to shape up the user interface of the resulting application. This is different in Windows 8.

Building Windows 8 applications with JavaScript means that you define the layout of the user interface with HTML and add style and graphics using CSS. As for the application's logic, you use the standard JavaScript language enriched by any JavaScript libraries you wish (such as the common jQuery library), while you access WinRT system classes using an ad hoc Microsoft-created JavaScript wrapper—the WinJs library.

If you already know a bit of JavaScript development, building Windows 8 applications will not be a huge, new type of adventure. If you are not already a JavaScript developer, the JavaScript route probably represents the shortest path for learning to build Windows 8 applications.

This chapter sets up the preliminary aspects of such a learning path and discusses what you need to install—specifically Windows 8 and Microsoft Visual Studio—and how to configure the environment. In the next chapters you'll first see a summary of HTML (in particular, the latest version of HTML, known as HTML5), CSS, and JavaScript, and then attack the task of building Windows 8 applications with topics more specifically related to Windows 8 programming.

> **Important** If you are already familiar with HTML5, CSS, and JavaScript, you might want to start directly with Chapter 5. If not, at the very minimum I recommend you look carefully at Chapters 2, 3, and 4. Better yet, I suggest you look into specific books for HTML5 and JavaScript, as the chapters you find here represent about 10 percent of the content you would find in a dedicated book. You might want to explore other books in this Microsoft Press series that address these topics directly: *Start Here! Learn HTML5* by Faithe Wempen (Microsoft Press, 2012) and *Start Here! Learn JavaScript* by Steve Suehring (Microsoft Press, 2012).

Getting ready for development

So you want to start building applications for Windows 8 using HTML, CSS, and JavaScript. First, you need to make sure that some software is properly installed on your development machine. The following section discusses the details.

The software you need

As obvious as it may sound, you need to have Windows 8 installed to develop, test, and run Windows 8 applications. The easiest way to develop and test applications for Windows 8 is by using the current version of Visual Studio—Visual Studio 2012.

There are various editions of both Windows 8 and Visual Studio 2012, but for the purposes of this book, you'll need at least the minimal versions of each product: Windows 8 Basic edition and the free Visual Studio 2012 Express edition for Windows 8 applications.

Installing Windows 8

Having a machine equipped with Windows 8 is a fundamental prerequisite to working through the information and exercises in this book. Windows 8 comes in a few flavors, as detailed in Table 1-1.

TABLE 1-1 Windows 8 editions

Version	Description
Windows 8	The Basic edition of Windows 8 is available for both the x86 and x86-64 architecture. It provides a new Start screen and redesigned user interface, live tiles, Internet Explorer 10, and more.
Windows 8 Pro	This edition offers additional features such as booting from VHD and support for virtualization via Hyper-V.
Windows 8 Enterprise	This edition adds IT-related capabilities such AppLocker and Windows-To-Go (booting and running from a USB drive). This version also supports installation of internally developed applications from locations other than the Windows Store.
Windows 8 RT	Only available pre-installed on ARM-based tablets, it also natively includes touch-optimized versions of main Office 2013 applications.

If you don't have your copy of Windows 8 already, you can get a free 90-day trial version from the following location: *http://msdn.microsoft.com/en-us/evalcenter/jj554510.aspx*. Note that this link gets you a non-upgradeable copy of Windows 8 Enterprise. Before you embark on the download, consider that because it is a few gigabytes in size, it may not be quick!

Installing Visual Studio Express

Once you have Windows 8 installed, you can proceed to download Visual Studio 2012 Express edition. (Note that in the rest of the chapter—and the entire book—we'll be using the term *Visual Studio* or *Visual Studio 2012* often just to mean the Visual Studio 2012 Express edition.) As shown in Table 1-2, Visual Studio is available in different flavors.

TABLE 1-2 Visual Studio 2012 editions

Version	Description
Ultimate	The feature-complete version of Visual Studio 2012, offering the top-quality support for every feature.
Premium	Lacks some extensions in the area of modeling, debugging, and testing.
Professional	Lacks even more functionalities in the area of modeling, debugging, and testing but still offers a great environment to write and test code.
Express	Free but basic version of Visual Studio 2012 optimized for specific development scenarios. In particular, it is available for building web applications or Windows 8 applications.

You can read more about and compare Visual Studio features at the following page: *http://www.microsoft.com/visualstudio/11/en-us/products/compare*.

To start downloading Visual Studio Express for Windows 8, go to the Dev Center for Windows 8 applications at *http://msdn.microsoft.com/en-us/windows/apps* (see Figure 1-1).

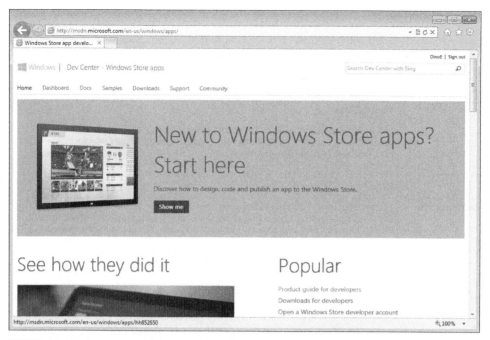

FIGURE 1-1 The home page of the Dev Center for Windows 8 applications.

After clicking the link to download the tools and Software Development Kit (SDK), you will be sent to another page where you can finally start the download process, as shown in Figure 1-2.

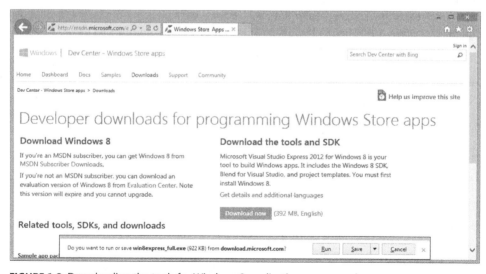

FIGURE 1-2 Downloading the tools for Windows 8 application programming.

Note that you can choose to save the setup program to your local disk or you can run it directly. If you plan to reuse the program on different machines, it could be useful to save it to a known location first.

At various times during the setup, you'll be prompted to accept or modify options. For the purposes of this book, you can simply accept all the default options. The default setup installs the newest .NET Framework 4.5, the Windows 8 SDK, plus a bunch of other tools and project templates. At the end of the installation, if everything worked just fine, you should expect to see the screen reproduced in Figure 1-3. In the unfortunate case in which the software doesn't install correctly, you will get a message with some helpful directions. Please follow them carefully.

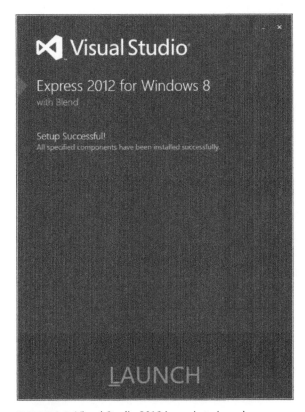

FIGURE 1-3 Visual Studio 2012 is ready to launch.

Now you're ready for some real fun: launching and configuring Visual Studio for your first Windows 8 application!

Configuring Visual Studio 2012

After completing the setup, Visual Studio 2012 Express requires a couple of more steps before it is ready to run.

Getting a product key

Upon launching for the first time, Visual Studio 2012 requires that you activate your copy. This happens through a screen like the one shown in Figure 1-4.

FIGURE 1-4 Product key required for Visual Studio 2012 Express.

Clicking the "Register online" link takes you to a page where you can insert your name, email address, and company details (see Figure 1-5).

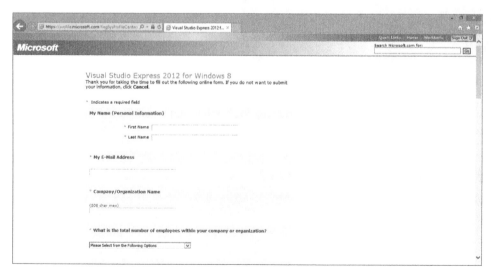

FIGURE 1-5 Registration required for Visual Studio 2012 Express.

You then submit the form. You'll receive an email containing the product key to unlock the current version of Visual Studio (see Figure 1-6).

FIGURE 1-6 Product key retrieval for Visual Studio 2012 Express.

It usually takes only a few seconds to receive an email from Microsoft to your specified address. The email contains the product key as text; copy it to the clipboard and switch back to Visual Studio. In the same window you saw in Figure 1-4, paste the product key you just received.

Creating a developer account

To write and test Windows 8 applications, you need a developer license from Microsoft. The license is free and entitles you to be a registered Microsoft developer. Getting such a license requires only that you sign in using your Windows Live ID, as shown in Figure 1-7. (If you don't have a Windows Live ID, the dialog box that prompts you to enter it provides a quick "Sign Up" link.)

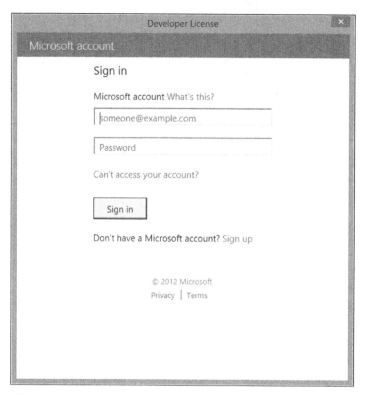

FIGURE 1-7 Creating your developer account.

A developer license successfully installed on a machine enables you to freely create and run Windows 8 applications outside the official Windows Store.

> **Note** A Windows 8 machine can install only *certified applications*, either downloaded from the Windows Store (in much the same way in which it works for Windows Phone applications), or created by registered developers on a "signed" machine, so you'll need the developer license to complete the examples in this book.

You won't receive any further warning from the system until the developer license expires or you remove it from the machine. If your license expires, you can renew it directly from the Visual Studio environment. To renew a license, users of Visual Studio Express click the Store menu and then select Acquire Developer License, as shown in Figure 1-8.

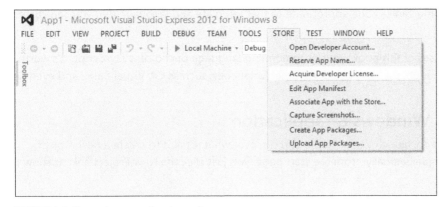

FIGURE 1-8 Renewing your developer license.

You can get as many developer licenses as you need, provided that you have a Windows Live ID account.

Windows Store account

Getting a developer license for Windows 8 is only the first mandatory step in developing and testing Windows 8 applications. Armed solely with a developer account, you can't publish a Windows 8 application to the Windows Store for others to download and install.

There's no direct relationship between developer accounts and Windows Store accounts. Each plays a specific role and you can get one without having the other. However, if you own a Windows Store account and then qualify for a developer license, then the default expiration of your developer license is automatically set to a longer time.

The point to remember here is that before you can publish your Windows 8 application to the Windows Store, you need to get a Windows Store account. You'll see how to obtain a Windows Store account later, in Chapter 14.

Important As a developer and user of a Windows 8 system, keep in mind that your machine can only run Windows 8 applications that have been downloaded from the Windows Store or custom applications for which a developer license has been installed on the machine. Another scenario enables you to host custom applications—when those applications have been "sideloaded" onto the machine by your organization, which in turn holds an enterprise store account.

Start playing with Windows 8 apps

With a developer license installed on your Windows 8 machine, you're now ready to play with Windows 8 applications. When you are about to create a brand new project, you must first choose a project template and a programming language. After you do that, Visual Studio provides some help by generating some vanilla code appropriate to that template and language that you can customize and extend.

For the purposes of this book, your programming language of choice is JavaScript. It's worth remembering, though, that you could use other languages, such as C#, Visual Basic, and even C++.

The "Hello Windows 8" application

Without further ado, launch Visual Studio and discover what it takes to create a new project. It couldn't be simpler, actually; from the start page, you just click the New Project link, as shown in Figure 1-9.

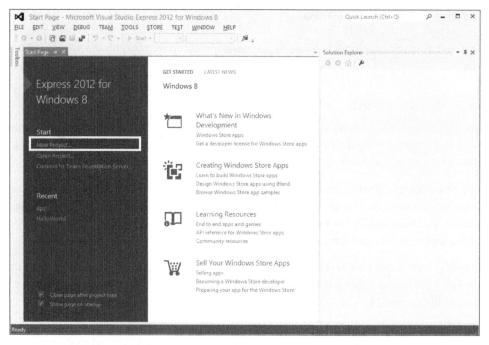

FIGURE 1-9 Creating a new project.

Choosing a project template

Visual Studio offers a few predefined templates for your new project, but choosing the project template only appears to be an easy task. It requires that you have a reasonably clear idea of the final result you want to achieve. The template you truly want to use depends on the interaction model you have in mind, the graphics, and the content you need to work on. Figure 1-10 shows the New Project window you will see after electing to create a new project.

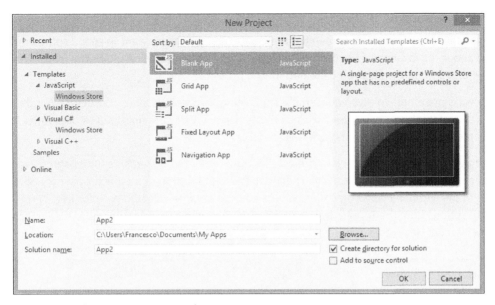

FIGURE 1-10 Choosing a project template.

Templates are grouped by programming language. In the Express edition of Visual Studio considered here, you can create just one type of application—a Windows 8 application for the Windows Store. If you acquire a more advanced edition of Visual Studio, you should expect to see more options available, including web, console, and desktop applications.

So how do you decide which template to use?

Templates have the primary purpose of saving you some work, at least for common application layouts. You are not forced to pick up a specific template, however. If none of the predefined templates seems to be right for you or, more likely, if you don't know exactly which one to pick, then you just select the template for a blank application. Table 1-3 provides more information on the predefined templates for JavaScript.

TABLE 1-3 Predefined project templates for Windows Store applications

Template	Description
Blank App	The application consists of a single and nearly empty page: no visual controls, no widgets, and no layout defined.
Grid App	A master-detail application made of three pages. The master page groups items in a grid. Additional pages provide details on groups and individual items.
Split App	A two-page master-detail application in which the master page shows selectable items and the details page lists related items alongside.
Fixed Layout App	A single-page application whose layout scales using a fixed aspect ratio.
Navigation App	A multipage application with predefined controls to navigate between pages.

For the purposes of this book, the easiest is starting with a brand new blank application. You'll experiment with other types of templates in the upcoming chapters.

Creating the sample project

Before you give Visual Studio the green light to create files, you might want to spend some time thinking about the location of the project. In Figure 1-10, you see Location; that's the place where you enter the disk path to the files being created for the project.

It is always preferable to save your sample applications in a well-organized structure. For the sample code of this book, you'll use a root directory named *Win8* containing *ChXX* directories for each chapter, where *XX* is a two-digit chapter number.

By default, Visual Studio saves your project files right under the *Documents* folder and creates a new directory for each solution. You can change the default location of a project by simply editing the path in the *Location* every time. Alternatively, you can set a new default path for every project by selecting Options from the Tools menu and then picking up the *General* node under the *Projects and Solutions* element (see Figure 1-11).

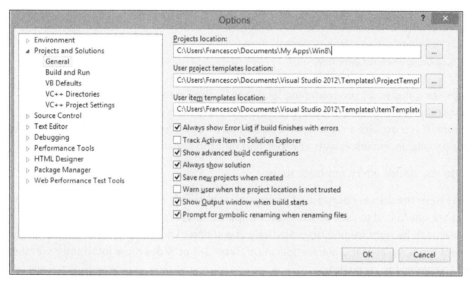

FIGURE 1-11 Changing the default project location.

For the "Hello Windows 8" application, you'll create a new blank application project named **HelloWin8** in the Win8/Ch01 folder, as shown in Figure 1-12.

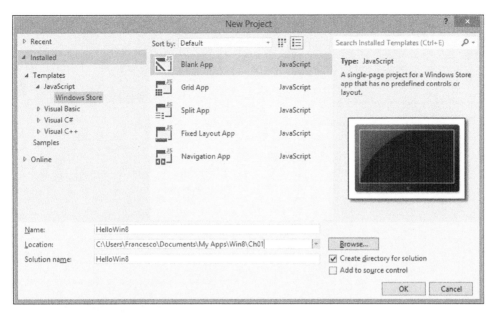

FIGURE 1-12 Creating the HelloWin8 project.

Click OK and you're officially a Windows 8 developer.

> **Note** Visual Studio 2012 comes with a dark theme for windows and controls by default. For the sake of print, we changed it to the light theme which makes for screenshots that render better in print. Anyway, to change the Visual Studio theme, open the Tools | Options menu, and then select Environment from the window shown in Figure 1-11.

Tweaking the sample project

Right after creation, the *HelloWin8* project looks like the image shown in Figure 1-13. It references the Windows Library for JavaScript (under the References folder) and is centered on a HTML page named *default.html*. This page defines the entire user interface of the application and links a Cascading Style Sheet (CSS) file (*css/default.css*) for graphics and a JavaScript file for the logic that loads up the page content and provides any expected behavior (*js/default.js*). Just the *default.js* file is opened in Visual Studio by default.

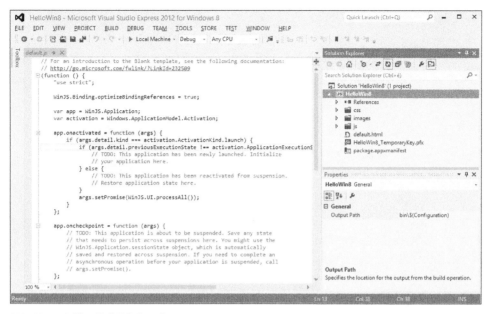

FIGURE 1-13 The *HelloWin8* project.

It turns out that a Windows 8 application written using JavaScript looks like a self-contained web application made of HTML pages properly styled using CSS and powered by JavaScript logic. If you are familiar with the web paradigm and client-side web development, then you only need to make sense of the Windows 8-specific application programming interface (API) exposed to you via a few JavaScript files to link.

Before compiling the project to see what happens, let's make some minimal change: Close the *default.js* file and open up the *default.html* file, which is responsible for the home page of the application (see Figure 1-14). To open a file that is part of the current project, you locate the file by name in the Solution Explorer panel and then double-click it. In general, if you need to open a file that is not included in the project for your reference, then you might want to use the Open item on the File menu.

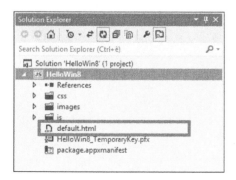

FIGURE 1-14 Opening *default.html*.

The body of the sample HTML page is all here:

```html
<body>
    <p>Content goes here</p>
</body>
```

Let's just replace the placeholder text with some custom text. For example:

```html
<body>
    <p> Hello, Windows 8!<p>
</body>
```

In HTML, the *<body>* element indicates the entire content of a page. The *<p>* element, instead, defines a paragraph of text. The net effect of the change is making the page display the text "Hello, Windows 8."

The next step is building the application and admiring it in action live.

Admiring the app in action

To build the application, you hit F5 or click Build | Start Debugging. *Debugging* is the action of finding and fixing errors in computer programs. However, the sequence Build+Debugging more generally refers to giving the application a try. You launch the application and interact with it to see if it behaves as you expect.

For an even quicker start, you can click the Play button in the toolbar, as shown in Figure 1-15.

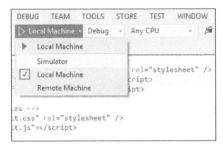

FIGURE 1-15 Starting the debug of the application.

Note that Local Machine is only the default choice where you can choose to run the application. By selecting it, you open up a menu with various options. Running the application on the local machine means switching from the Windows classic desktop mode (where you execute Visual Studio) to the specific UI of Windows 8. If you don't like doing that, you can run applications in a simulator. Using the simulator is helpful for testing the application using various screen orientations and resolutions. Finally, you can even run the application on a remote machine, provided that you have sufficient rights to access that machine.

The Debug option in Figure 1-15 refers to the way in which the compiler produces the code. In debug mode, the binaries include additional information that allows you to set *breakpoints* on specific lines of code and proceed step by step. A breakpoint is a line of code where execution will pause. You typically use breakpoints to stop execution at a given point and investigate the state of the application and its internal data. You can have multiple breakpoints in the program. The Release mode is required for finished applications ready for distribution. In the book, you'll be using the Debug mode predominantly.

Figure 1-16 shows the application in action on the local machine.

FIGURE 1-16 The HelloWin8 app in action.

If you run the application in the simulator, then the application runs in a separate window you can control at will. When you run it on the local machine, then the app runs full screen and it is not immediately apparent what you need to do to get back to Visual Studio to terminate the app. Here's how to exit the application: move the mouse towards the left border until you see a window icon to click to return to the desktop mode. To terminate the app, you then click the Stop button that has replaced the Play button in the Visual Studio user interface.

You're done. But it was way too simple, wasn't it? So let's make the sample application more colorful and add a bit of action too.

Adding a bit more action

Create a new project and name it **HelloWin8-Step2**. First, you'll make it more colorful by simply adding more HTML elements and style information. Next, you will transform it into a simple but fully functional application that generates a random number.

Adding style to the page

Open up the *default.html* page and edit its body tag. The body should now include title and subtitle separated with a line. You use a couple of HTML5 elements for this. Note that in the next chapter you'll learn a lot more about HTML5. Here's the modified body of the page:

```
<body>
   <header>
      Start Here! Build <b>Windows 8</b> Applications with <b>HTML5</b> and
<b>JavaScript</b>
      <hr />
   </header>
   <footer>
      <hr />
      Dino Esposito | Francesco Esposito
   </footer>
</body>
```

Now let's proceed with colors and fonts. The style of the page is defined in the *default.css* file from the CSS folder. By editing a CSS file, you can change nearly everything in a HTML page that has to do with appearance and layout. You'll find a summary of what's important to know about CSS in Chapter 3, "Making sense of CSS."

In the *default.css* file, you initially find something like below:

```
body {
}
```

This code describes the style to be applied to the tag body of any page that links the CSS file. You can edit the CSS file manually or you can create CSS styles using a builder tool available in Visual Studio. To use the tool, right-click a CSS element (that is, *body*) and select Build Style, as shown in Figure 1-17.

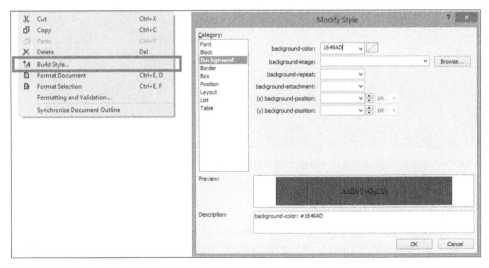

FIGURE 1-17 Editing the style of the page.

Here's a modified style for the page body that changes the background color and adds a bit of space around the content:

```
body {
    background-color: #1649AD;
    padding: 10px;
}
```

You can also customize the header and footer elements slightly to define the color of the text, font size, and a vertical offset, as shown below:

```
header {
    font-size: x-large;
    color: #ffffff;
    padding-bottom: 50px;
}
footer {
    font-size: large;
    color: #eeee00;
    padding-top: 50px;
}
```

Now run the application and be proud of it! (See Figure 1-18.)

FIGURE 1-18 The application running with a modified style.

Generating a random number

So far the application has no behavior at all and is limited to displaying some static text. Let's make it a bit less obvious and add any necessary structure and logic to make it generate and display a random number.

First off, add the following markup to the body of the page in *default.html.* The markup consists of two *DIV* blocks containing the placeholder for generated number and the button to click to get a new number. You insert the following markup between the header and footer elements:

```
<div>
    <label id="numberLabel">?</label>
</div>
<div>
    <input id="numberButton" type="button" value="Get number" />
</div>
```

Next, open the default.js file and add the following JavaScript functions at the bottom of the file:

```
function numberButtonClick() {
    var number = generateNumber();
    document.getElementById("number").innerHTML = number;
}
function generateNumber() {
    var number = 1 + Math.floor(Math.random() * 1000);
    return number;
}
```

The first function is the handler for the click event on the button. The second function just generates and returns a random number between 1 and 1000. The final step consists of binding the click handler to the actual button in the HTML markup. There are a number of ways to do this, the simplest of which is shown below:

```
<input id="numberButton" type="button" value="Get number"
       onclick="numberButtonClick()" />
```

A more elegant way—and the recommended way of doing it in Windows 8 programming— consists of making the binding dynamically as the page is loaded. So open the *default.js* file and modify the code of the *app.onactivated* function, as shown below:

```
app.onactivated = function (args) {
   if (args.detail.kind === activation.ActivationKind.launch) {
       if (args.detail.previousExecutionState !==
           activation.ApplicationExecutionState.terminated) {
           // TODO: This application has been newly launched. Initialize
           // your application here.
           document.getElementById("numberButton").addEventListener(
               "click", numberButtonClick)
       } else {
           // TODO: This application has been reactivated from suspension.
           // Restore application state here.
```

```
        }
        args.setPromise(WinJS.UI.processAll());
    }
};
```

In the end, you just add one line to run when the application has been newly launched. The line just registers a handler for any click event raised by the specified button.

You can give the final touch to the application with a second pass on CSS to adjust the rendering of the label and button. Add the following to the *default.css* file:

```
#numberButton {
    font-size: x-large;
}
#numberLabel {
    font-size: xx-large;
    color: #eeee00;
    font-weight: bold;
}
```

The leading pound (#) symbol indicates that the style applies to any HTML element whose ID matches the name—for example, the style defined as *#numberButton* applies to all elements with an ID of *numberButton*. Figure 1-19 shows the modified application in action.

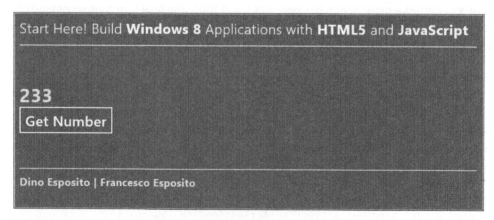

FIGURE 1-19 A Windows 8 application to get random numbers.

Although this is still a fairly simple application, it should be enough to get you started and to give you the overall feeling of how you approach Windows 8 programming with HTML5 and JavaScript. You'll start building more sophisticated applications in Chapter 5, "First steps with Windows 8 development."

Summary

This chapter provided a step-by-step guide to getting ready for Windows 8 programming. You started with the operating system and tools necessary for writing code, then installed and configured Visual Studio 2012 Express edition for Windows 8, and finally played a bit with the simplest type of application.

Before digging into more Windows 8 development, it is necessary to ensure that everybody reading this book is aligned to a minimum level of knowledge of web technologies such as HTML5, CSS, and JavaScript. Therefore, the next three chapters provide a summary of what you need to know about HTML5, CSS, and JavaScript to successfully work through the later chapters. If you feel you already know enough, then feel free to jump directly to Chapter 5. If the later chapters prove too difficult, I recommend you review Chapters 2–4 and/or brush up your knowledge with other resources on HTML5, JavaScript, and CSS.

Chapter 2

Making sense of HTML5

Broadly speaking, the short words are the best, and the old words best of all.

—*Winston Churchill*

HTML5 is the latest version of the HTML language—the popular text-based language used to define the content of webpages. HTML appeared on the scene in the early 1990s. In the beginning it was merely a *markup language* apt at describing simple documents. A markup language is a language based on a set of markers that wrap text and give it a special meaning.

Initially, the set of HTML markup elements, called "tags" or (better) "elements," was fairly limited. It contained elements to define references to other documents and headings, to link to images and paragraphs, and apply basic text styling such as bold or italic. Over the years, however, the role of HTML grew beyond imagination, progressing from being a simple language that described documents to a language used to define the user interface of web applications. That trend continues today with HTML5.

The latest version of HTML5 removes some of the older elements and makes it easier to keep elements that provide style information in one place, and elements that provide text and define the layout of the text, in another place. As you'll see in more detail in the next chapter, style information can be defined through a special distinct file known as a Cascading Style Sheet (CSS). In addition, HTML5 adds some new elements suitable for including multimedia content and drawing, and several new frameworks for manipulating the content of the page programmatically.

With HTML5 alone, you still won't be able to go too far toward building a complete application. However, the union of HTML5, CSS, and JavaScript functions as a close approximation to a full programming language.

- You use HTML5 to define the layout of the user interface and to insert text and multimedia.

- You use CSS to add colors, style, and shiny finishes.

- Finally, you use JavaScript to add behavior by gluing together pieces of native frameworks such as Document Object Model (DOM), local storage, geolocation and, for example, all the specific services of Windows 8 exposed via the Windows 8 JavaScript library (WinJs). The DOM, in particular, is the collection of programmable objects that expose the structure of the current document to coders.

In the rest of this chapter, you'll briefly explore the basics of the HTML5 markup elements, including input forms and multimedia. Neither this chapter nor the rest of the book covers every aspect of the basics of HTML. If you need a refresher on the fundamentals of HTML, you can refer to the book *Start Here! Learn HTML5,* by Faithe Wempen (Microsoft Press, 2012).

Important This chapter and the next two provide an overview of HTML, CSS, and JavaScript. In these chapters, you'll get acquainted with new key elements of HTML5 and CSS3 and receive an end-to-end coverage of common programming techniques you use in JavaScript. The content of these chapters is not specific to Windows 8 apps; it is instead meant to be preliminary to upcoming chapters where you'll be using ad hoc elements from the WinJs library in a basic HTML skeleton, using custom CSS for graphics and custom JavaScript for behavior.

Elements of a webpage

HTML5 comes about a decade after its most recent predecessor (HTML4). Looking at what's new in HTML5, one could reasonably say that all these years have not passed in vain. HTML5 provides a set of new elements that offer several native functionalities that developers and designers used to have to code via artifacts and ingenious combinations of existing elements. Here's a quick look at what's relevant to creating a webpage with HTML5.

Building the page layout with HTML5

In the beginning of the web, most pages were designed as a text documents—meaning that their content developed vertically on a single logical column. Over the years, page layout became more and more sophisticated. Today, two-column and three-column layouts are much more common. In two- and three-column layouts, you also often find headers and footers surrounding the logical columns. Figure 2-1 shows the difference between the layouts at a glance.

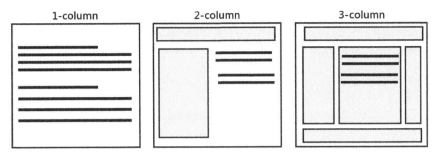

FIGURE 2-1 Different HTML page layouts.

Developers have been smart enough to build such complex layouts using basic HTML block elements such as *DIV.*

Note In HTML, a block element is an element whose content is rendered between two line breaks—one before and one after the content. Therefore, the content displays as a stand-alone "block" of content. One popular block element is *H1,* which renders some text as a first-level heading. The *DIV* element is another popular block element aimed at creating blocks out of any valid HTML content. Block elements are opposed to inline elements, namely elements whose content flows with the rest of the page with no line breaks applied.

Important Note that in this book, as well as in other books and articles, truly common HTML elements, such as *<div>* and *<h1>* often appear in text written without the brackets. However, the use of the angle brackets is mandatory if you are using those elements within HTML itself.

In HTML5, the multicolumn layout is recognized as a common layout and therefore gets full support via several new ad hoc markup elements.

Preparing the sample application

The examples you'll be working with in this chapter are plain HTML pages showcasing some of the features available in HTML5 as supported in Internet Explorer 10. You won't be creating an ad hoc Windows 8 application for each feature, but for this early example—to refresh what you saw in Chapter 1, "Using Visual Studio 2012 Express edition for Windows 8"—go ahead and create a container Windows 8 page that ties together all the links to the various standalone HTML5 pages.

Open up Visual Studio and create a new blank application. Name it **Html5-Demos**. When done, add the following code to the body of *default.html* so that it serves as the main menu for navigating into all of the sample HTML5 pages you'll write throughout the chapter.

```
<body>
    <header>
        Start Here! Build <b>Windows 8</b> Applications with <b>HTML5</b> and
<b>JavaScript</b>
        <hr />
        HTML5 samples
    </header>
    <div id="links">
        <a href="pages/multi.html">MULTI</a>
        <!-- Add here more links to HTML pages as we proceed in the chapter. -->
    </div>
    <footer>
        <hr />
        Dino Esposito | Francesco Esposito
    </footer>
</body>
```

Figure 2-2 shows the aspect of the resulting application. By clicking the links (such as, the MULTI link in the figure below) you force the operating system to open the webpage into Internet Explorer 10—the native browser in Windows 8.

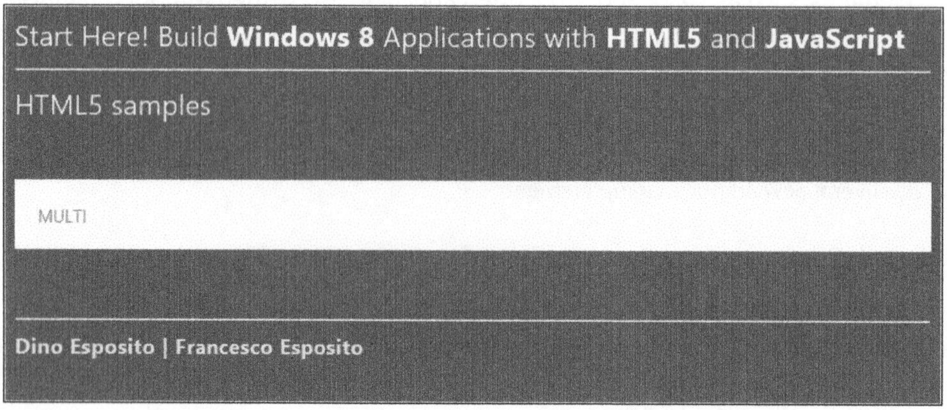

FIGURE 2-2 The home page of the sample application for this chapter.

From now on, you'll be creating plain HTML5 pages and adding an anchor tag *<a>* to the body of *default.html*.

From generic blocks to semantic elements

A large share of websites out there have a common layout that includes header and footer, as well as a navigation bar on the left of the page. More often than not, these results are achieved by using *DIV* elements styled to align to the left or the right.

Let's add a new HTML page to the project: right-click the project node in Solution Explorer and choose Add | New Item from the subsequent flyout menu. What you get next is the window shown in Figure 2-3. From that window, you then choose a new HTML page and save it as *multi.html*.

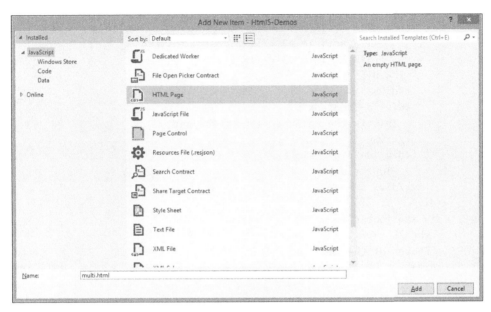

FIGURE 2-3 Creating a new HTML page in Visual Studio.

Next, from within Visual Studio double-click the newly created HTML page and replace the content with the following markup.

```
<!DOCTYPE html>
<html>
    <head>
        <title>MULTI-COLUMN LAYOUT</title>
    </head>
    <body>
        <a href="/default.html">Back</a>
        <hr />
        <div id="page">
            <div id="header">
                Header of the page
                <hr />
            </div>
            <div id="navigation-bar">
```

```
    <ul>
        <li> Home </li>
        <li> Find us </li>
        <li> Job opportunities </li>
    </ul>
</div>
    <div id="container">
        <div id="left-sidebar">
          Left sidebar
          <ul>
              <li> Article #1 </li>
              <li> Article #2 </li>
              <li> Article #3 </li>
            </ul>
        </div>
        <div id="content">
          This is the main content of the page
        </div>
        <div id="right-sidebar">
          Right sidebar
        </div>
    </div>
    <div id="footer">
        <hr />
        Footer of the page
    </div>
    </div>
  </body>
</html>
```

The *id* attribute of the *DIV* elements are given self-explanatory names that help with understanding their intended role. Therefore, the HTML page includes header, navigation bar, footer, and a three-column layout in between the element named container. Figure 2-4 shows how *multi.html* renders on Internet Explorer.

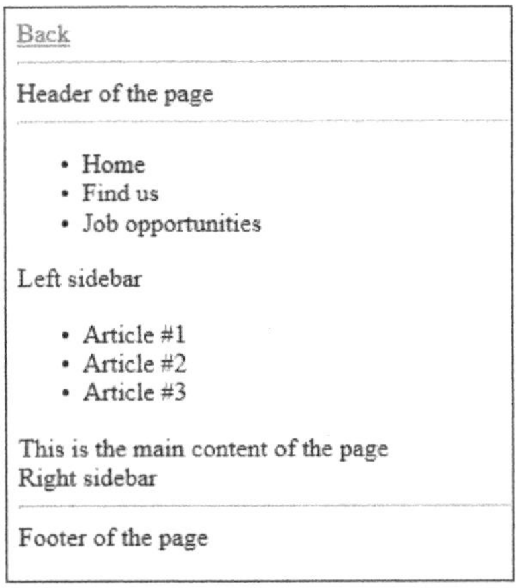

```
Back

Header of the page

    • Home
    • Find us
    • Job opportunities

Left sidebar

    • Article #1
    • Article #2
    • Article #3

This is the main content of the page
Right sidebar

Footer of the page
```

FIGURE 2-4 The *multi.html* page as it is rendered by Internet Explorer 10.

The preceding markup alone, however, doesn't produce the expected results and the page doesn't really show any multicolumn layout. For that, you need to add ad hoc graphic styles to individual *DIV* elements to make them float and anchor to the left or right edge. You add graphic style to an HTML page using CSS markup, placed in a CSS file. The next chapter provides a quick summary of CSS. The real point of this demo is a little different.

As you can see, each *DIV* element is made distinguishable from others only by the name of the *id* attribute. Yet, each *DIV* element plays a clear role that makes it fairly different from others—header is different from footer, and both are different from left or right sidebars.

Header and footer elements

HTML5 brings a selection of new block elements with specific names and clear behavior. The set of new elements was determined by looking at the most common layouts used by page authors. For example, in HTML5 header and footer are new plain block elements you use to indicate a header and footer. Similar elements exist for most of the semantic elements in the previous listing. Here's how you can rewrite the page *multi.html* using only HTML5-specific elements. Name this page **multi5.html**. The listing below shows the content of the body tag for the new page.

```
<header>
      Header of the page
      <hr />
</header>
<nav>
      <a href="..."> Home </a>
      <a href="..."> Find us </a>
      <a href="..."> Job opportunities </a>
</nav>
<article>
   <aside>
      Left sidebar
```

```
    <ul>
      <li> Article #1 </li>
      <li> Article #2 </li>
      <li> Article #3 </li>
    </ul>
  </aside>
  <article>
    <h1>Article #1</h1>
    <hr />
    <section> Introduction </section>
    <section> First section </section>
    <section> Second section </section>
  </article>
  <aside>
    Right sidebar
  </aside>
</article>
<footer>
    <hr />
    Footer of the page
</footer>
```

You can insert header and footer using specific elements with a very simple syntax, as below:

```
<header> Markup </header>
<footer> Markup </footer>
```

It is interesting to notice that you can have multiple header and footer elements in a HTML5 page. The most common use is to give the page a header and footer. However, you should consider these elements as blocks meant to represent heading content of a page or a section of a page and footers.

Section and article elements

HTML5 defines two similar-looking elements to represent the content of a page. The *<section>* element is slightly more generic, as it is meant to delimit a logical section of a HTML page. A logical section can be the content of a tab in a page designed as a collection of tabs.

At the same time, a logical section can also be a portion of the main content being displayed in the page. In this case, the *section* element is likely embedded in an *<article>* element.

```
<article>
   <h1>Article #1</h1>
   <hr />
   <section> Introduction </section>
   <section> First section </section>
   <section> Second section </section>
</article>
```

Note Elements such as *<section>*, *<article>*, *<header>*, and *<footer>* are semantic elements, in the sense that browsers treat them as block elements. If you look at final results, there's nearly no difference between semantic elements and plain *DIV* elements. The most significant difference is in the expressivity of the resulting markup. By using *<section>*, *<article>*, *<header>*, and *<footer>* elements, the resulting markup is much easier to read, understand, and maintain over time.

The *aside* element

A lot of HTML pages display part of their content on columns that lie side by side horizontally. The *<aside>* element has been introduced in HTML5 to quickly identify some content that is related to the content being displayed all around. The syntax of the *<aside>* element is straightforward:

```
<aside> Markup </aside>
```

A very common scenario where you might want to take advantage of the *<aside>* element is to define a sidebar in an *article* element and, more in general, to create multicolumn layouts for the content of the page or sections of the page.

The *nav* element

The *<nav>* element indicates a special section of the page content—the section that contains major navigation links. It should be noted that not all links you can have in a HTML page must be defined within a *<nav>* element. The *<nav>* element is reserved only for the most relevant links, such as those you would place on the main page navigation menu.

The syntax of the *<nav>* element is fairly intuitive. It consists of a list of *<a>* anchor elements listed within the *<nav>* element:

```
<nav>
      <a href="..."> Home </a>
      <a href="..."> Find us </a>
      <a href="..."> Job opportunities </a>
</nav>
```

The *<nav>* element plays an important role in HTML5 because it indicates the boundaries of the section of the page that contains navigation links. This allows special page readers—such as browsers for disabled users—to better understand the structure of the page and optionally skip some content.

Important All semantic elements in HTML5 are important in light of accessibility, and just for this reason, they should be considered for use in any webpage that has chances to be read by disabled users.

Miscellany of other new elements

Semantic block elements represent the largest family of new elements in HTML5. As mentioned, semantic elements are important not so much for the effect they produce in the page but because they increase the readability of the page significantly for developers, software, and especially browsers for disabled users.

Semantic block elements alone do not produce significant changes in the way in which HTML5-compliant browsers render the page. For example, to color and position a sidebar (that is, the *<aside>* element) where you like you still need to resort to CSS settings. However, using semantic elements reduces the noise of having too many generic *DIV* block elements whose role and scope is not immediately clear.

In addition to semantic elements, HTML5 provides a few new elements with an embedded behavior that couldn't be obtained in earlier versions of HTML without resorting to a combination of CSS, markup, and JavaScript. Let's see a few examples.

The *details* element

Many times you have small pieces of content in a page that you want to show or hide on demand. A good example is the title of some news and its actual content. Sometimes you want to display only the title but want to leave users free from clicking to expand the content and hide it to gain more space.

Before HTML5, you had to code all of this manually using a bit of HTML, CSS, and JavaScript code. In HTML5, the entire logic is left to the browser and all you have to do is type the following in an HTML page.

```
<details open>
    <summary>This is the title</summary>
    <div>
        This is the text of the news and was initially kept hidden from view
    </div>
 </details>
```

The *<details>* element is interpreted by the browser and used to implement a collapsible panel. The *open* attribute indicates whether you want the content to be displayed initially or not. The *<summary>* child element indicates the text for the clickable placeholder, whereas the remaining content is hidden or shown on demand. Note that all parts of the *<details>* element can be further styled at will using CSS.

 Important Although the Visual Studio editor recognizes the *<details>* element and even offers IntelliSense for it, the element is not supported by Internet Explorer 10. Other HTML5-compliant browsers, however, do support it—specifically the latest versions of Chrome and Opera.

The *mark* element

HTML5 also adds the *<mark>* element as a way to highlight small portions of text as if you were using a highlighter on a paper sheet. Using the *<mark>* element is easy; all you do is wrap some text in the *<mark>* element, as shown below:

```
The <mark>DETAILS</mark> element is not supported by Internet Explorer 10.
```

The entire text is rendered with default settings except the text enclosed in the *<mark>* element. Most HTML5 browsers have default graphical settings for marked text. Most commonly, these settings entail a yellow background. Needless to say, graphical effects of the *<mark>* element can be changed at will via CSS.

Figure 2-5 shows how the previous text looks using Internet Explorer 10.

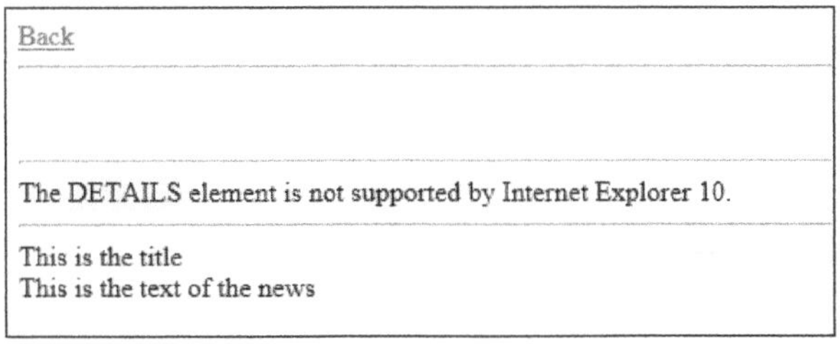

FIGURE 2-5 The *mark* element in action.

The *dataList* element

For a long time, HTML developers asked loudly for the ability to offer a list of predefined options for a text field. The use-case is easy to figure out. Imagine a user required to type the name of a city in a text field. As a page author, you want to leave the user free of entering any text; at the same time, though, you want to provide a few predefined options that can be selected and entered with a single click. Up until HTML5, this feature had to be coded via JavaScript, as HTML provided only two options natively: free text with no auto-completion or a fixed list of options with no chance of typing anything. The new *<datalist>* element fills the gap. Copy the following text to the body of a new HTML page named *datalist.html*.

```
<input list="cities" />
<datalist id="cities">
    <option value="Rome">
    <option value="New York">
    <option value="London">
    <option value="Paris">
</datalist>
```

In the example, the *<datalist>* element is bound to a particular input field—the input field named cities. It is interesting to notice that the binding takes place through a new attribute defined on the

<input> element: the *list* attribute. The attribute gets the name of a <datalist> element to be used as the source of the input options.

When the input field gets the input focus, then the content of the <datalist> element is used to autocomplete what the user is typing. Figure 2-6 shows the element in action on Internet Explorer.

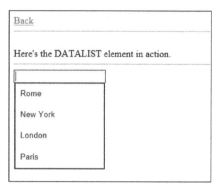

FIGURE 2-6 The *datalist* element in action.

Elements removed from older HTML versions

HTML5 adds some new elements, but also removes a few elements whose presence would only increase redundancy once combined with the new capabilities of CSS and new elements in HTML5.

The list of elements no longer supported most notably includes *frame* and *font* elements. It should be noted, though, that the <iframe> element remains available.

In addition, a few style elements such as <center>, <u>, and <big> are removed. The reason is that this functionality can be achieved easily through CSS. Probably due to the much larger use that page authors made over the years, HTML5 still supports elements such as <b> (for bold text) and <i> (for italic text) that are logically equivalent to the now unsupported <u> and <big> elements.

Collecting data

HTML was originally devised to be a language for creating hypertext documents. Over the years, the language has been enriched with layout capabilities and basic features to collect data. Writing input forms to collect data from users proved to be a nontrivial task. One thing is to collect plain text; it is quite another to collect a date, a number, or an email address.

For too many years, HTML has only offered input text fields completely unable to distinguish numbers, dates, and email addresses from plain text. Subsequently, page developers were responsible for preventing users from typing unwanted characters and for client validation of the entered text.

With HTML5, a lot of this work has been pushed to the browser side. This means that by simply using a slightly more sophisticated set of elements developers can achieve the same level of form validation in a faster and safer way.

Adjusting input fields

In HTML5, you still create an input form by using the same markup elements you used from earlier versions of the language. In other words, the following markup will still give you the opportunity to upload any typed content to the given server.

```
<form action="http://www.yourserver.com/upload">
    <span> Your name </span>
    <input type="text" value="" />
    <input type="submit" value="Save" />
</form>
```

The *<input>* element is the element that inserts a graphical element (such as, an input box or a drop-down list) to collect some input data. You also use the *<input>* element to add a push button to start the submission process to the server. In HTML5, the *<input>* element comes with more options for the type of input boxes. For example, you can have date pickers, sliders, and search boxes offered by the browser. At the same time, the browser provides free form validation for most common scenarios, such as when a field is required and can't be left empty by the user.

New input types

If you look at the HTML5 syntax of the *<input>* element, the major difference with past versions is the list of values now allowed for the *type* attribute. Table 2-1 lists some of the new input types supported in HTML5.

TABLE 2-1 HTML5 specific values for the *type* attribute

Value	Description
Color	Meant to let the browser display any UI that allows entry of a color. Note: This input type is not supported on Internet Explorer 10.
date	Meant to let the browser display any UI that allows entry of a date.
email	Meant to let the browser display any UI that allows entry of an email address.
number	Meant to let the browser display any UI that allows entry of a numeric input.
range	Meant to let the browser display any UI that allows entry of a numeric input.
search	Meant to let the browser display any UI that allows entry of a text to be searched for.
tel	Meant to let the browser display any UI that allows entry of a telephone number.
time	Meant to let the browser display any UI that allows entry of a time.
url	Meant to let the browser display any UI that allows entry of a URL.

Note that the list in Table 2-1 is incomplete and limited to input types that you can really find supported today on some web browsers. Other input types (for example, week) are part of the current HTML5 draft but are not implemented anywhere. You might want to refer to *http://www.w3schools.com/html5* for more details.

Making input fields auto-focusable

HTML5 provides the definitive solution to a couple of common problems that developers faced for years and solved using a bit of JavaScript code. The first of these problems relates to giving the input focus to an input field.

Using JavaScript, you can tell the browser to assign the input focus to a particular input field upon display of the page. In HTML5, you can use a new attribute for the *<input>* element—the *autofocus* attribute. Try placing the following code in the body of a new HTML page named *autofocus.html*.

```
<form>
    <input type="text" value="Dino" />
    <input type="text" autofocus />
    <br />
    <input type="submit" value="Save" />
</form>
```

Save the page and display it in Internet Explorer. As Figure 2-7 shows, the cursor that indicates input focus is on the second field.

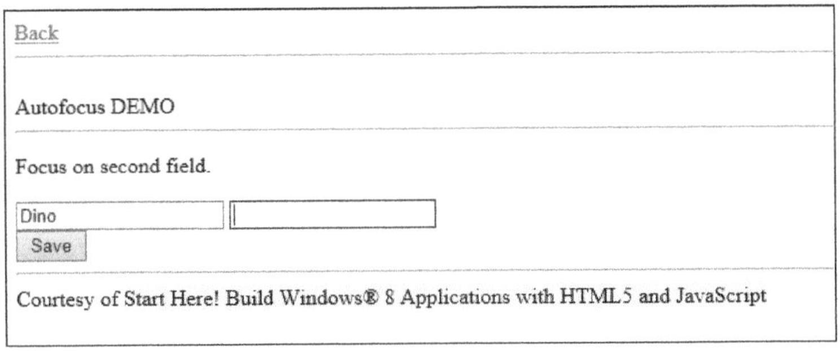

FIGURE 2-7 The *autofocus* attribute in action.

Giving hints to users

Looking at Figure 2-7, it is quite hard to figure out which content goes in which field. Probably in a real-world page, one would use labels and a more sophisticated layout to make it easier for users to understand the expected content for each field. This is *just* the second problem I referred to a moment ago.

Recently, developers got into the groove of displaying a short text message in an input text field to instruct users. Before HTML5, this could only be accomplished by using a bit of JavaScript code. In HTML5, the new *placeholder* attribute makes it a lot easier and even more natural.

Create a new HTML page and save it as *placeholder.html*. Now edit the content of the body, as shown below:

```
<form>
    <input type="text" placeholder="First name" />
    <input type="text" placeholder="Last name" />
    <br />
    <input type="submit" value="Save" />
</form>
```

As Figure 2-8 shows, both empty fields now provide a hint to users about the expected content.

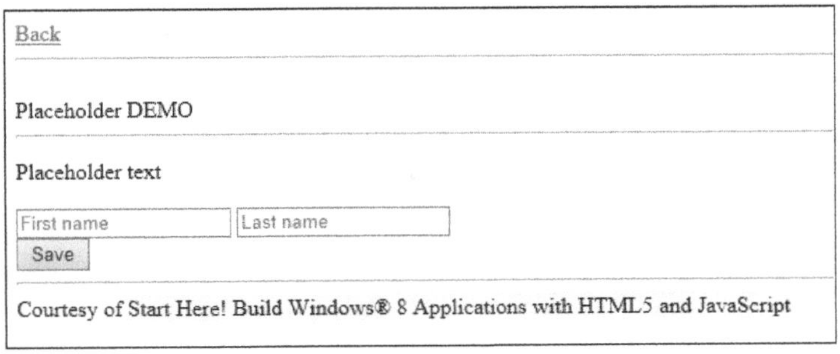

FIGURE 2-8 The *placeholder* attribute in action.

Form submission

Sometimes developers have no other option besides writing the same boilerplate code over and over again, no matter how annoying it is. A good example of boilerplate code that it would be great to stop writing is validation of input forms in HTML pages. Any data collected from an HTML input form should be carefully validated on the server before being used for some business tasks. However, some basic validation tasks can be easily delegated to the browser and commanded by the developers using markup instead of JavaScript code.

HTML5 helps reduce the amount of boilerplate code requested to build effective input forms. I've already mentioned the newest attributes of the HTML5 *<input>* element; the next step is to take a look at other attributes you can leverage to control the whole process of form submission, including ways to ensure that the user has not left required fields blank, and that the user input matches expected patterns. For example, if you ask for a phone number, the user shouldn't be allowed to enter something that couldn't possibly be a valid phone number.

Detecting required fields

By adding the *required* attribute to a *<input>* element, you tell the browser that the input field cannot be blank when the form that contains the *input* element is submitted. You use the required attribute only if the field is not considered optional.

Consider the following content of an HTML page named *required.html*:

```
<body>
<form>
    <input type="text" placeholder="Your PIN" required />
    <br />
    <input type="submit" value="Enter" />
</form>
</body>
```

When the user pushes the submit button and the text field is empty, the browser automatically denies the post and displays an error message. The specific content, form, and shape of the error message may change according to the browser; the overall behavior, though, is similar on all HTML5-compliant browsers. Figure 2-9 shows how Internet Explorer 10 deals with required fields left empty.

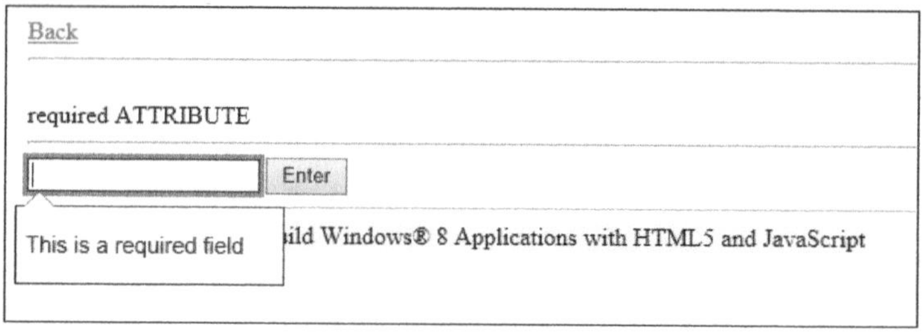

FIGURE 2-9 The *required* attribute in action.

HTML5 browsers allow you to customize the error message by using the *oninvalid* attribute, as shown below:

```
<form>
      <input type="text" placeholder="Your PIN" required
             oninvalid="this.setCustomValidity('PIN is mandatory')" />
      <br />
      <input type="submit" value="Enter" />
</form>
```

 Note In general, you use the *oninvalid* attribute to specify any JavaScript code that should run when the content of an input field is invalid, either when that field value was required and left blank or when its content failed validation.

Validating against regular expressions

Table 2-1 lists popular new types of input fields supported by HTML5-compliant browsers. If your page is expected to collect a date, then you can use an input date field; likewise, you can use a numeric input field if you need to collect a number and so forth. But what if you intend to collect data formatted in a specific way that none of the predefined input types can guarantee? For example, what if you need users to enter a string with two letters followed by exactly six digits?

In HTML5, you can use the *pattern* attribute, as shown in the example below:

```
<form>
      <input type="text"
             placeholder="Your PIN"
             title="2 letters + 6 digits"
             pattern="[a-zA-Z]{2}\d{6}" />
      <br />
      <input type="submit" value="Enter" />
</form>
```

When you use the *pattern* attribute, Internet Explorer 10 requires that you also indicate the *title* attribute—usually used to add a tooltip to most HTML elements. The text of the *title* attribute is combined with a default static message to produce some feedback to the user when the content of the field is invalid.

Figure 2-10 shows how Internet Explorer 10 deals with patterns when the submitted content is invalid.

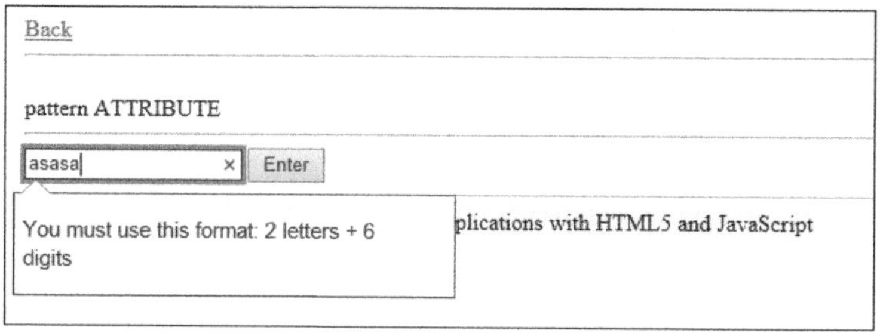

FIGURE 2-10 The *pattern* attribute in action.

The value of the *pattern* attribute has to be a *regular expression*. Regular expressions can get very complex; in fact, they're a topic worthy of a complete book, but learning the basics of regular expression use isn't too difficult. For more information on regular expressions, you can check out *http://www.regular-expressions.info*.

Forms and input validation

Each HTML form should contain a submit button; when the submit button is pushed the browser collects the content of the input fields and prepares to post it to the specified URL. Up until HTML5, the browser was not responsible for validating the content of the form. Developers, though, could hook up validation to the process using a bit of JavaScript code.

Validating a form entails checking that each input field in the form contains valid content. Although the HTML5 standard doesn't mandate browsers to validate the content of a form, this is indeed what happens by default with most browsers. HTML5 browsers give you a chance to disable validation on the entire form, but not on individual fields. You can disable form validation by using the *novalidate* attribute, as shown below in the file *novalidate.htm*:

```
<form novalidate>
      <input type="text" placeholder="Your PIN"
             title="2 letters + 6 digits"
             pattern="[a-zA-Z]{2}\d{6}" />
      <br />
      <input type="submit" value="Enter" />
</form>
```

In this case, the content of the form is submitted to the server regardless of the data held by input fields.

If the form contains multiple submit buttons, you can enable or disable validation on a per-button basis so that validation occurs if users, say, click the first button but not the second. To disable validation when the form is submitted via a particular submit button, you add the *formnovalidate* attribute as follows:

```
<input type="submit" value="..." formnovalidate />
```

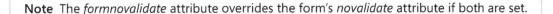

Note The *formnovalidate* attribute overrides the form's *novalidate* attribute if both are set.

Multimedia elements

HTML5 offers two new markup elements that developers can use to play audio and video files from within webpages without resorting to external plug-ins such as Flash and Silverlight. The entire infrastructure to play audio and video (including graphical feedback to users) now is provided natively by the browser.

The *audio* element

To embed audio content into HTML documents, you use the *<audio>* element. The syntax is trivial, as the example below shows:

```
<audio src="/hello.mp3">
   <p>Your browser does not support the audio element.</p>
</audio>
```

Optionally, you can incorporate some markup in the body of the *<audio>* element to be used in case the browser can't deal successfully with the *<audio>* element. Next, you'll explore a bit more about how to embed audio in HTML5 pages.

Using the *<audio>* element

The *<audio>* element supports a variety of attributes, as listed in Table 2-2. Of these, the most important is *src*, which you use to point to the location of the actual audio stream.

TABLE 2-2 Attributes of the *<audio>* element

Attribute	Description
autoplay	Indicates that the audio will start playing as soon as the content is available to the browser.
controls	Instructs the browser to display audio controls, such as the play and pause buttons.
loop	Indicates that the audio will automatically restart after it is finished.
preload Note that the preload attribute is ignored if the autoplay attribute is also present.	Instructs the browser on how to load the audio content when the page loads. Allowed values are none, meaning that no content should be preloaded; auto, meaning that the entire content should be downloaded when the page loads; and metadata, meaning that only content metadata should be preloaded on page display.
src	Indicates the URL of the audio file, whether local or remote.

So far, I have referred to audio content in a rather generic way, without mentioning specific audio formats such as MP3 or WAV. This is a major problem with HTML5-compliant browsers: Not all browsers support the same set of audio formats by default (without resorting to external components).

The problem of codecs

An audio file is a sequence of bytes that codec software decodes for playing. An audio file, therefore, can be encoded in a variety of formats, each requiring an ad hoc codec—MP3, WAV, OGG, and more. More often than not, a codec is a piece of software that implements patented algorithms, so embedding a codec directly in the browser may pose copyright issues.

The current HTML5 standard doesn't make an official ruling about codecs, so deciding on the format to support will remain up to the browser vendors for now.

From a developer's perspective, this is not great news. Different browsers support different audio formats, leaving developers with the problem of working out the most effective way to play audio from the same page on different browsers.

Supported codecs

The simplest way of approaching the problem of multiple codecs is to provide multiple files so the browser can choose the most appropriate for its capabilities. In other words, instead of linking the *<audio>* element to just one audio file and codec, you link it to multiple sources. You no longer use the *src* attribute; instead, you resort to a set of *<source>* elements inside the *<audio>* element. Here's an example of playing an audio file using *<source>* elements:

```
<audio controls autoplay>
    <source src="hello.ogg" type="audio/ogg" />
    <source src="hello.mp3" type="audio/mp3" />
    <p>Your browser does not support the audio element.</p>
</audio>
```

The *<source>* elements link to different audio files. The browser will use the first format it knows how to support. While simple to implement, this approach is not free of issues—in the sense that it requires you to have each audio file available converted into multiple formats and stored on the server in multiple copies.

A basic guideline is that the OGG format is not subject to software patents. OGG will work in Firefox, Opera, and Chrome. To target Safari and Internet Explorer, you need to use MP3 encoding instead.

The *video* element

To embed video content into HTML documents, you use the *<video>* element. The syntax is just as trivial as what you have seen for the *<audio>* element:

```
<video src="/hello.mp4">
    <p>Your browser does not support the video element.</p>
</video>
```

Similarly, you can optionally incorporate some markup in the body of the *<video>* element to be used in case the browser can't deal with video successfully.

Using the *<video>* element

Table 2-3 presents the list of attributes you can use to customize the aspect and behavior of the *<video>* element in HTML5-compliant browsers.

TABLE 2-3 Attributes of the *<video>* element

Attribute	Description
autoplay	Indicates that the video will start playing as soon as the content is available to the browser.
controls	Instructs the browser to display video controls such as the play and pause buttons.
height	Indicates the desired height of the video player in the HTML document.
loop	Indicates that the video will automatically restart after it is finished.
muted	Indicates that the video sound should be muted off.
poster	Instructs the browser to display a specified image while the video content is downloading, or until the user chooses to play the video.
preload Note that the preload attribute is ignored if the autoplay attribute is also present.	Instructs the browser on how to load the video content when the page loads. Allowed values are *none*, meaning that no content should be preloaded; *auto*, meaning that the entire content should be downloaded when the page loads; and *metadata*, meaning that only content metadata should be preloaded on page display.
src	Indicates the URL of the video file to play, whether local or remote.
width	Indicates the desired width of the video player in the HTML document.

It is highly recommended that you always set both width and height in a *<video>* element. This helps the browser to reserve enough space while rendering the page. In addition, you should always set width and height to the real size of the video clip you plan to incorporate. If you downsize the video player, you force the browser to do even more work. Keep in mind that downsizing a video won't save the user any download time. If you have a video that is too large for the page, you should resize it with an ad hoc program first, and then link it using its new size.

Figure 2-11 shows how Internet Explorer 10 renders a *video* element.

Courtesy of Start Here! Build Windows® 8 Applications with HTML5 and JavaScript

FIGURE 2-11 The *video* element in action.

Supported codecs

When it comes to codecs, video suffers from the same issues that audio does. Therefore, it requires the same workaround.

You should not use the *src* attribute unless you are well aware of the concrete risk that the video may not be playable on some browsers. To gain the widest support from HTML5-compliant browsers, you should use the *<source>* element. Here's the rewritten content of the sample *video.html* file:

```
<video controls width="320" height="240">
     <source src="/sample.ogg" type="video/ogg" />
     <source src="/sample.mp4" type="video/mp4" />
     <p>Your browser does not support the video element.</p>
</video>
```

Just as for audio, the *<source>* elements link to different video clips and the browser will use the first format it knows how to support. As a guideline, you should plan to have an MP4-encoded video for Internet Explorer and Safari, and OGG for all other browsers.

Summary

HTML has been around for a couple of decades, but it only recently underwent significant syntax changes. The new HTML5 specification clears out some obsolete elements and adds new markup elements for specific (and common) tasks. New elements have stronger semantics that make it obvious what they are for—such as *header*, *footer*, *menu*, *section*, and more.

These new elements, however, live side by side with older and, semantically speaking, more generic elements such as *DIV*. The result is that sometimes you have two or more ways to achieve the same rendering—using direct HTML5 elements or a combination of more generic elements. If you plan to target HTML5 browsers, using new elements keeps your markup easier to read and understand—in a word, simpler.

The purpose of this book is to build Windows 8 applications, as opposed to classic websites, which makes the differences between older HTML and HTML5 unimportant: this book uses HTML5 all the way through. However, if your goal is to build a website for the general public, then integrating HTML5 in the markup of the pages is much more difficult. For web applications, you will need to deal with browser differences and ensure that the behavior is uniform across major browsers.

Chapter 3

Making sense of CSS

In matters of style, swim with the current; in matters of principle, stand like a rock.
—Thomas Jefferson

As you learned in Chapter 2, "Making sense of HTML5," an HTML page is made up of a bunch of elements that together define the content and layout of what the browser will actually display. Each element of the HTML markup language has its own semantics and syntax. So an *INPUT* element, for example, indicates an input field, and additional attributes specify shape and behavior of the input field. The display of these elements is usually determined by the specific browser.

So far, nothing has been said about how to give these elements a custom appearance. Nonetheless, changing font, colors, margins, and sizes of HTML elements is definitely possible—and to a large extent, even desirable. An acronym for Cascading Style Sheet, CSS is the name of the language used to format the content of HTML pages.

An HTML page results from the combination of three components: content, style, and behavior. Content is expressed via the HTML markup language, as discussed in Chapter 2. Style is managed via CSS, as you'll see in this chapter. Finally, behavior is handled via JavaScript, which you'll learn about in the next chapter.

Styling a webpage

HTML arrived well before CSS in the early 1990s. In the beginning, developers used to tweak the appearance of the page by simply adding ad hoc attributes to markup elements. While initially effective, this approach soon became unmanageable and a significant source of confusion for developers and users.

To acquire larger and larger market shares, vendors began adding new proprietary style attributes with each new release of their browsers. As a side—but not secondary—effect, HTML documents became significantly larger in size and subsequently led to download issues. There was more work for the servers but also more work for client browsers and slower responses for users.

In addition, browsers were often challenged to interpret unknown attributes and tags. It was not an easy choice for architects to decide whether the appropriate reaction to malformed markup was to throw an error to the user or to just silently skip over unknown elements. Most browsers opted for the second option. Although that choice improved the user experience, it made life for developers significantly harder and, in hindsight, it might not be overreaching to say that it delayed the explosion of client-side web developing by a few years.

To find a consistent way to separate content from presentation, back in the mid-1990s the World Wide Web Consortium (W3C) created a committee to give shape to a standard language for styling the content of webpages. That was the beginning of CSS. The very first recommendation came out in 1996. Over the ensuing years, new levels of specifications have appeared regularly, with growing adoption from browser vendors and increasing levels of use by developers. Today, the CSS3 standard is complete and broadly adopted by browsers. A CSS4 standard is in the works.

For the purposes of this book, CSS will refer to CSS3.

Adding CSS information to pages

So CSS is a language that complements HTML and gives page authors the great opportunity to define structure and content in one file and define layout and appearance in another file. Thanks to such a neat separation of concerns, different teams of people—typically web developers and graphical designers—can work in parallel on the same project.

In the rest of this chapter, you'll explore various ways to add CSS styling to HTML pages.

Inline styling

CSS works by adding style information to individual HTML elements. Up until a few years ago, it was fairly common among HTML authors to add style information locally, within the definition of the HTML element. This technique, known as *inline styling*, consists of adding a new *style* attribute to each HTML element you are interested in configuring. Here's an example:

```
<div style=" ... ">
    <!-- some markup goes here -->
</div>
```

The content of the *style* attribute is a semicolon (;) separated string. Each token within that string consists of two parts: a property name and a value separated by a colon (:). Here's a sample *style* string that defines the background and foreground color of any content inside the styled *DIV* element:

```
<div style="background-color:#000000;color:#ffffff">
    <!-- some markup goes here -->
</div>
```

The net effect of the preceding code snippet is that the content of the *DIV* element is given a black background (color #000000), whereas any text it contains is written in white (color #ffffff). That style information is scoped to the specified *DIV* element and doesn't apply to any content outside of it.

This technique has both pros and cons, but the cons likely outweigh any pros. Inline styling just works; it's easy to understand and quick to apply for everybody—experts and novices. But it has critical drawbacks. In particular, the markup of pages gets fat and soon becomes harder to read and understand. In addition, there's the potential for a lot of repetitive style details across the same page and multiple pages. You should avoid inline styling as a bad programming practice or, at the very least, you should limit its use to a small number of places where you want to make exceptions to more general style rules created in CSS.

Embedded styles

Another option is grouping style definitions in a few places within the HTML file. You can use a *STYLE* element, in fact, as the repository of custom styles. Within a *STYLE* element, you first identify the target element and then define attributes that affect its appearance. The *STYLE* element is usually located under the *HEAD* element at the top of the HTML page. You can have multiple *STYLE* elements in any HTML page. Here's an example:

```
<html>
  <head>
    <style>
        body {
            background-color: black;
            color: white;
        }
    </style>
  </head>
...
</html>
```

As you may recognize, the content inside curly brackets describes the style to apply. The expression you find just before the opening bracket—*body* in the previous example—indicates the element (or elements) the style will apply to.

You'll see more detail about this point in just a few moments; for now, it's sufficient to say that the expression that identifies the target of the style is referred to as the *selector* and can be the name of a user-defined CSS class, the ID of a particular element, or the tag name of an HTML element. In the previous example, *body* is the name of the main HTML element; so background and foreground colors set through the style shown will affect the entire body of the page.

Although embedding *<style>* elements in an HTML page makes for a cleaner approach to page authoring than inline styling, it is not a recommended practice. Compared to inline styling, embedded styles promote the reuse of styles across multiple elements within the same page. On the other hand, style information must be incorporated into each page and contributes to making your pages heavier.

The reuse of a style is possible, but only within the boundaries of a single page; to use the same style from within different pages you would have to replicate the style definition in each page.

Using external files

Rather than inline or style tags, the recommended approach for styling HTML elements entails the use of separate CSS files (or *style sheets*) to which each page links autonomously. The browser identifies the CSS content as a single URL and downloads it only once—regardless of how many pages in the website use the styles in that style sheet. Moreover, the downloaded file can be cached at the local computer and reused over and over again until the file expires, with no further download costs for the browser.

Here's a brief example of how to define and link a style sheet to alter the default appearance of a HTML page. From the New File dialog box shown in Figure 3-1, first create a new HTML page and name it **demo1.html**, and then proceed to create a new style sheet named **demo1.css**.

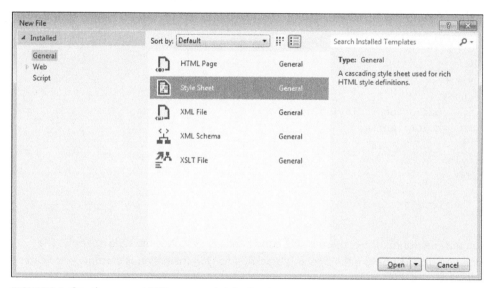

FIGURE 3-1 Creating a new HTML page and style sheet.

Now open the HTML page and edit its content until it matches the code below:

```
<!DOCTYPE html>
<html>
    <head>
        <title>CSS Example</title>
    </head>
    <body>
        <header>This is our header</header>
```

```
        <footer>
            <hr />
            Start Here! Build Windows® 8 Applications with HTML5 and JavaScript
        </footer>
    </body>
</html>
```

You have just given the page a bit of content. You have not yet done anything to link the HTML page with any style sheet. To do so, edit the *HEAD* element of the HTML page as follows:

```
<head>
    <title>CSS Example</title>
    <link href="demo1.css" rel="stylesheet" />
</head>
```

Now when rendering the page, the browser will use the information contained in the style sheet to adjust the appearance of elements.

 Note In the rest of the chapter and the book, you'll always be using style sheets via separate CSS files. Unless otherwise noted, you won't be using any more inline styling or embedded styles.

Selecting elements to style

The next step is learning how to write a style sheet. A style sheet consists of a sequence of commands defined according to the following pattern:

```
selector {property1: value; property2: value2; ...}
```

The *selector* is an expression that identifies the element (or the elements) to be styled. A selector can identify a single element through its unique ID, all elements with a given tag (for example, all *DIV* elements), or all elements sharing the same CSS class. As you'll see in a moment, a CSS class is a named collection of style commands.

The style commands are in the form of

```
property-name: value;
```

Each selector can refer to multiple style commands. Each style command ends with a semicolon (;). A final command that ends without the semicolon is often forgiven by browsers and renders correctly. Anyway, it is preferable to always use the ending semicolon for each style command. Blanks can be used to separate consecutive style commands. Blanks do not affect the way in which browsers parse the style sheet, but they help considerably in reading the content of the style sheet.

The CSS standard defines a long list of property names for you to use in style commands and related feasible values. In addition, some browsers define their own custom properties to add proprietary features.

In this section, you'll review the purpose and syntax of selectors. Then you'll be up to exploring the CSS properties and their values.

 Note The content of an embedded *STYLE* element and a style sheet CSS file is the same. At any time, you can take the content of an embedded *STYLE* element and save it to a linked CSS file to achieve the same graphical outcome.

Referencing elements by ID

In HTML, all elements in a page can (and sometimes should) have a unique ID. Having an ID is not mandatory, but it's the recommended way for a page author to identify (in unambiguous way) a given element. In HTML, you give an element a unique ID by setting the *ID* attribute, as shown below:

```
<div id="header" ... />
```

Multiple elements in the same page shouldn't have the same ID—even though this aspect is sometimes tolerated by browsers and doesn't usually prevent the page from being rendered.

The pattern to refer to an element via ID in a CSS style sheet is expressed as follows:

```
#id {
    ...
}
```

The selector consists of the ID string prefixed by the # symbol. Let's consider the following HTML *button* element:

```
<input id="button1" type="button" value="Say Hello!" />
```

To style the button so that its caption shows in red, you need to have the following command in the style sheet:

```
#button1 {
    color: red;
}
```

You typically reference elements by ID when you don't expect to reuse the style commands for other elements in the pages of the site. Using a selector based on ID is, therefore, a way to style just one specific element.

Referencing elements by name

HTML elements are automatically styled by browsers, and each browser may style these elements differently. For example, a plain *button* element is styled with round corners on, say, an iPhone and with square corners on a Windows Phone.

CSS allows you to change the appearance of standard HTML elements by creating a selector with the name of the element's tag. For example, to style all hyperlink elements—for example, the *A* element—in the same way, you define a selector as below:

```
/* All A elements are yellow and don't render the underline */
a {
   color: yellow;
   text-decoration: none;
}
```

Note that, all in all, styling by tag name may sometimes be too invasive, at least for certain tags. For example, having all links look the same is more acceptable than having all input fields or table elements look the same throughout the whole set of pages of the site.

Referencing elements via custom classes

If you intend to give the same appearance to a variety of elements in one or more pages, then you need to create a CSS class. As mentioned earlier, a CSS class is a named collection of style commands. You define the class in a style sheet by indicating the (arbitrary) name of the class prefixed by the dot (.) symbol. Here's an example:

```
/* This CSS class named "red-button" defines a button with red text */
.red-button {
    color: red;
}
```

In the source code of an HTML page, you assign an element a CSS class using the *class* attribute. Here's an example:

```
<input id="button1" class="red-button" type="button" value="Say Hello!" />
```

What if in the HTML page you assign an element a class name that doesn't exist? Nothing bad will happen; the browser will just ignore the setting.

The cascading model

When rendering any HTML element, browsers expect to find a value defined for each possible CSS property they recognize. This doesn't mean, however, that developers should assign a value to just each possible CSS property for each element in the page. The "C" in the CSS acronym says it all. C stands for *cascading* and all it means is that browsers provide a default value for each property. These values can be overridden by developers.

For each CSS property, the actual value that determines how the element will render is given by the value possibly assigned directly to the element or to its innermost parent element. At the root of the CSS hierarchy there's the default value assigned by the browser. Let's consider the following HTML snippet:

```
<html>
   <body>
     <header>
        <div>
           Hello, world!
        </div>
        <div>
           This is me.
        </div>
     </header>
     This is the body of the page.
   </body>
</html>
```

The text is given a default combination of fonts and colors by the browser. You can override these settings by styling the *BODY* element. If you do so, all settings propagate down the document tree and apply to any text in the page. If you intend to modify the text in *HEADER*, or in just one of the *DIV* elements within the header, you add new style commands only to that element. Any settings that are not explicitly overridden retain the value assigned to them at a higher level of the hierarchy. Figure 3-2 illustrates the cascading model of CSS in which settings applied at a given element affect all the elements found in the subtree rooted in that element.

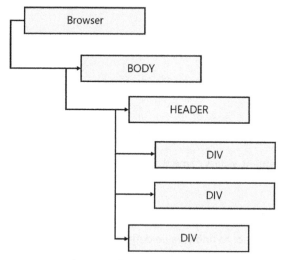

FIGURE 3-2 The "cascading" model.

Basic style commands

The CSS syntax includes several properties that you can use to define nearly every aspect of HTML elements: font, colors, measurement, layout, position, shadowing, and more. Here's a quick summary of the most frequently used properties. If you're seeking a full reference, have a look at *http://bit.ly/Snr6cX.*

Setting colors

Changing the colors of some text is often the first thing that developers try to do to exercise control over a software feature. Let's see the options available to modify colors in a CSS style sheet.

Defining colors

In all the examples so far, you have seen colors referred to by names such as black, red, or white. CSS allows you to express color in other more powerful ways. The HTML and CSS standards define 147 color names, among which you find black, blue, fuchsia, gray, green, purple, red, silver, white, and yellow. The full list of predefined colors can be found at *http://bit.ly/QyqKUx.*

In general, colors are expressed as a triple of integer values (between 0 and 255) for their Red, Green and Blue component. You can use any of the following syntaxes to indicate a custom color:

```
.my-classic-button {
    color: #ff0000;
}
.my-fancy-button {
    color: rgb(255, 0, 0);
}
```

In the former example, you use a hexadecimal expression for the RGB values. Hexadecimal values must be prefixed by #. The first two characters refer to the Red, the second two refer to the Green, and the last two refer to the Blue.

In the latter example, you use the *rgb* function instead, which accepts decimal values. Also in this case, the order of color components is Red, Green, Blue.

Note Browsers also allow you to add a level of transparency to colors. This is achieved by adding a fourth value to the color definition—the alpha channel. In the hexadecimal format, the alpha value ranges from 0 (completely opaque) to 255 (completely transparent). In the RGB format, the alpha value can be expressed as a decimal value (that is, 0.5) or as a percentage (that is, 50%). If you intend to add transparency to colors, you have to use the *rgba* function, as shown below:

```
.my-classic-button-transparent {
    color: #88ff0000;           /* transparency is first value, 88 in this
case */
}
.my-fancy-button-transparent {
    color: rgba(255, 0, 0, 0.5);  /* transparency is fourth value, 0.5 in this
case */
}
```

In general, you should be aware that older browsers may not support transparent colors. However, as a reader of this book, the presumption is that you're mostly interested in Windows 8 programming, and in the context of Windows 8, transparent colors are fully supported.

Changing the foreground color

The color of any piece of text around an HTML page is controlled by the *color* property. By setting the *color* property on the *BODY* element, you give all the text within the page a default color of your choice.

```
body {
    color: black;
}
```

You are not limited to just one color per page; you also can set the foreground color of every single element you have in the page. To select one or more elements, you use ID or class selectors. For example, the aforementioned *red-button* custom class renders text in red for all elements where it is applied.

```
.red-button {
    color: red;
}
```

Changing the background color

The background color of an HTML element plays an important role in HTML design, since it can be used to achieve compelling effects. Each element can have its background painted with a solid color or a gradient of colors. It can also have the background textured with a bitmap. Let's start with the simplest scenario: using a solid color. Here's what you need:

```
.blue-button {
    color: #ffffff;    /* white */
    background-color: #0000ff;   /* blue */
}
```

The *background-color* property accepts a color expression.

Using gradients

To give an HTML element a gradient background, you set the *background* property with an expression that describes the type of gradient you want. Here's how to create a linear vertical gradient that begins with blue, ends with red, and has some white in the middle.

```
.blue-button {
    color: #ffffff;    /* white */
    background: linear-gradient(to bottom, blue, white 80%, red);
}
```

In particular, the white appears towards the end of the gradient (80%) and the red takes the remaining 20% of the background. The keyword *bottom* indicates the direction of the gradient. Similarly, you can create a radial gradient by just using the *radial-gradient* function.

Using a background bitmap

There are several more properties to learn about if you intend to use a bitmap as the background of the element. Consider the following example:

```
.img-button {
    color: #ffffff;    /* white */
    background-image: url(/images/button-bkgnd.png);
    background-repeat: no-repeat;
 }
```

The *background-image* property allows you to link the image for the background. You do that via the *url* function, as you can see in the example. If the image is too small for the background area, you may decide to repeat it vertically and/or horizontally or to render it only once. You control this aspect via the *background-repeat* property, with the values *no-repeat*, *repeat-x* (horizontal), and *repeat-y* (vertical).

Bitmaps are often used to paint the background of the entire page. If the page is rich in content and scrolls horizontally or vertically, what should the image do? Should it scroll with the rest of the page or should it stick to its original position and have the content scroll over it? You can control that; here's how:

```css
body {
    color: #ffffff;   /* white */
    background-image: url(/images/bkgnd.png);
    background-repeat: no-repeat;
    background-attachment: fixed;
}
```

The *background-attachment* property accepts either of the following two values, whose meanings are straightforward: *fixed* and *scroll*.

Controlling text

In any HTML document, the text is the most important part. Hence, choosing the right combination of font and effects is *key* for a successful page. All browsers use a default font for the text and this font (that is, Times New Roman) is often not appropriate for most users. Switching to a different font family couldn't be easier. However, before you learn that, a consideration specific to Windows 8 programming is in order.

Important Windows 8 comes with its own highly specific user interface. The primary font is Segoe UI. Since you may write Windows 8 applications using HTML and CSS, you are allowed to change the font. However, this is not a recommended practice. In some cases, changing font family and size may even give you a hard time uploading the final application to the Windows Store. In general, when it comes to using CSS for Windows 8 applications, changing the font family and font size becomes a delicate point. You should not do this, unless it is necessary and even then possibly only for small portions of the user interface. Instead, you should use the default Windows JavaScript style sheets, as you'll encounter in Chapter 5, "First steps with Windows 8 development."

Choosing the font family and size

In CSS, you use the *font-family* property to indicate one or more families of fonts you would like to use. When it comes to fonts and browsers, it should be clear that the content of the *font-family* property is only a recommendation for the browser. Since the webpage is hosted on a website and viewed on a local computer, it may be that the local computer is not equipped with the requested font. For this reason, it is a good practice to always indicate alternate fonts, as shown below:

```css
body {
    color: #ffffff;   /* white */
```

```
    background-image: url(/images/bkgnd.png);
    background-repeat: no-repeat;
    background-attachment: fixed;
    font-family: "trebuchet ms", helvetica, sans-serif;
}
```

Font families are listed in order of preference. If the first choice is not available, then the browser moves on to the second, and so on. If a font name contains spaces, it is preferable to enclose it in quotes even though this is not always strictly necessary on all browsers.

Years of HTML development have taught developers that Helvetica and Sans-serif as backup fonts are a great choice that ensures at least decent rendering across all browsers.

What about the size of the font? You can indicate the desired font size through relative and absolute lengths and using a number of measurements. For example, you can use keywords like *x-small*, *small*, *medium*, *large*, and *x-large*. These keywords are relative to the standard browser font size, as modified by the user. If you indicate the font size as a percentage, then the actual size is relative to the surrounding text. If you use a number between 0 and 1 with the *em* measure, then the actual size is relative to the parent element. Finally, if you use a number of pixels (*px* is the measure), then the actual size is relative to the screen resolution. Here are a few examples:

```
#footer {
    font-size: 80%;
}
#copyright {
    font-size: 9px;
}
#trademark {
    font-size: .8em;
}
```

Relative lengths are the best possible choice for rendering on a screen. Absolute lengths, such as points (*pt* is the measure) or perhaps millimeters (*mm* is the measure), may lead to text that shows larger or smaller on different computers.

 Important As mentioned, for Windows 8 applications it is preferable that you stick to the classes defined in the standard Windows 8 style sheets.

Styling fonts

More often than not, you want to alter the default style of the font to give some text more relevance. This means making some text italic, bold, or perhaps underlined. Boldness is expressed through the *font-weight* property, whereas styles (that is, italic) require the *font-style* property.

```
#footer {
    font-size: 80%;
    font-weight: 700;
    font-style: italic, underline;
}
```

If you just want to render some text in bold, you can simply set the *font-weight* property to *bold*. If you need more control over the weight of the text, you can choose a value between 400 (normal) and 700 (bold). Higher or lower values are still allowed, and they just decrease or increase the "weight" of the font.

HTML display modes

An HTML page results from the composition of multiple elements. How are these elements actually composed by the browser? Will they just be stacked up horizontally or vertically? Is there blank space that can be configured between them? In this section, you'll learn about the first point before addressing the second point in the next section.

HTML allows two basic display modes: *inline* and *block*. All HTML elements render in one of these ways by default. For example, the *DIV* element is always rendered as a block, whereas the *SPAN* element is rendered inline. You can change display modes via CSS, however. The property to use is named *display*.

Block elements

Block elements are stacked up vertically. Each block element takes up the entire width available and is rendered as if there were a line break before and after. This means that whenever the browser encounters a block element it begins rendering on a new line. When done, it moves to the next line before attacking a new element. Here's how to ensure that a custom CSS class renders out as a block:

```
.headline {
    display: block;
}
```

Common HTML elements that are displayed as blocks by default are *H1* (and other heading elements), *DIV, P, UL, LI, TABLE,* and *FORM*.

Inline elements

Conversely, inline elements don't force the browser to break the flow of HTML when rendering. An inline element just renders side by side with existing content, and strictly takes up necessary space. Here's how to ensure that a custom CSS class renders out content inline:

```
.headline {
    display: inline;
}
```

Common elements rendered inline by default are *SPAN*, *A*, *INPUT*, and *IMG*.

 Note By using the display property, you can turn block elements into inline elements and vice versa. What browsers do normally is simply a predefined setting that can be changed by developers.

Floating elements around

Sometimes blocks and inline display modes are not enough to achieve your graphics goals. Let's consider the following HTML markup:

```
<div id="article">
    <img src="picture.png" />
    <span>Some possibly long text</span>
</div>
```

By default, image and text are rendered side by side, and the text is placed at the bottom of the image, as shown in Figure 3-3.

Some possibly long text

FIGURE 3-3 Basic alignment of image and text.

Via CSS, you can alter the vertical alignment of the text to middle or top. However, none of these tricks will give you what you likely want—text floating around the image, as depicted in Figure 3-4.

Some possibly long text displayed
all around the image in a nice wrap.

FIGURE 3-4 Text floating around an image.

To achieve this effect, you need to deal with the *float* property. The *float* property has the effect of displaying elements next to one floated on a continuous flow that automatically wraps to the next line when the containing box ends. The *float* property uses values like *left* or *right* to denote the direction of the flow. The following CSS applied to the former HTML snippet produces the output of Figure 3-4.

```
#article {
    float: left;
    width: 100px;
}
```

When *float* is used, the elements that follow move up to fill any available space—similar to what happens in a text editor when you remove a carriage return. The *float* property breaks the usual meaning of block and inline. At some point, though, you need to restore things to the natural order and stop floating. The element where floating stops must be styled as below:

```
#stopFloating {
    clear: both;
}
```

The *float stopper* element can be a true element of the page (that is, a paragraph of text) or an empty DIV element only used to stop floating.

> **Note** If you're still a bit confused about the differences between inline and floating, consider that inline is all about having individual elements laid out side by side on the same logical line. Floating, however, is about wrapping elements between a starting and an ending point.

Inline-block elements

Floated elements work well, but they also have some drawbacks when they span over multiple lines and each element is of a different size. When you face this problem, then the third possible value of the *display* property comes to the rescue: the *inline-block* value.

An *inline-block* element is a block element rendered inline with other block elements. Internally, each block element will render as usual with all block, inline, and floating settings it needs. Consider the following HTML snippet:

```
<ul id="container">
    <li>Block #1</li>
    <li>Block #2</li>
    <li>Block #3</li>
</ul>
```

Now style the elements as follows. The results are shown in Figure 3-5.

```
li {
    display: inline-block;
    width: 100px;
    min-height: 100px;
    background-color: green;
    color: white;
    vertical-align: top;
}
```

FIGURE 3-5 *Inline-block* elements.

It should be noted that *inline-block* elements, if aligned vertically to the top, also work well in the case of multiple rows of different heights. When not floating, in fact, the browsers always use a single, logical horizontal line to render on.

The drawback of *inline-block* elements is that they consider any literals in the HTML source. This means that blanks you have in the source (in case of fixed widths) may cause an undesired wrap to the next line. To be on the safe side, you should consider writing your HTML on a single line with no extra blanks or carriage returns. This may be required only for the section of the page that uses elements styled as inline-blocks.

Note As the content of Figure 3-5 may suggest, *inline-block* elements may be very helpful to arrange the style of the Windows 8 user interface using HTML and CSS.

Spacing and the boxing model

CSS builds a relatively rich and articulated infrastructure around each HTML element. This infrastructure is known as the *boxing model* and is featured in Figure 3-6.

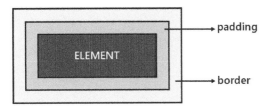

FIGURE 3-6 The CSS box model.

The boxing model defines what browsers expect to find around each single HTML element. The first surrounding box is the padding box, and it is controlled by the *padding* property. Next, there's the border box used to frame an element; border settings are controlled via the *border* property.

In addition, each element can be placed in another larger box, known as the margin box. Margins are controlled by the *margin* property and determine the distance between the boxed element and its neighbors.

Defining padding

The *padding* property defines how many pixels should be added around the element. Additional pixels inherit the same background settings of the element. You typically use padding to add some spacing around the actual content (that is, text) of the element, as shown in Figure 3-7.

padding: 0px;   padding: 10px;

FIGURE 3-7 The effect of padding HTML elements.

If you set the *padding* property, then padding is even all around the element. However, you can set padding for each side of the element. You do that through properties such as *padding-top, padding-left, padding-bottom,* and *padding-right.*

Defining borders

You can control borders of an HTML element through the *border* property. If you set this property, then each side of the element is styled in the same way. To configure each side separately, you use specific subproperties such as *border-top, border-left, border-bottom,* and *border-right.*

While styling a border, you can indicate width, color, radius, and style. Each of these aspects has its own subproperty such as *border-width, border-color, border-radius,* and *border-style.* You express width and radius (for rounded corners) in pixels, while using CSS color strings to express colors. Here's an example:

```
.rounded-button {
    color: #ffffff;    /* white */
    background: linear-gradient(to bottom, blue, white 80%, red);
    border-radius: 5px;
    border-width: 1px;
    border-color: #ffffff;    /* white */
}
```

An element border can be a solid, dotted, or dashed line. Just *solid, dotted,* and *dashed* are feasible values for the *border-style* subproperty.

Defining margins

In HTML, the margin is the distance that exists between a given element and its neighbors. Unlike padding, the space indicated by margins is not rendered as part of the element. That area displays any underlying content belonging to parent elements.

You express margins in pixels, and you can set margins independently through usual subproperties: *margin-top, margin-left, margin-bottom,* and *margin-right.* For example, if you set *margin-bottom* to *10px,* then you are extending the height of the element by 10 pixels. These 10 extra pixels of height are rendered with a transparent background though.

Defining width and height

By default, HTML elements take up just the minimum space they need to render their content. In some cases, you might want to assign them a fixed size, whether absolute or relative. The properties you need to do this are *width* and *height*. You typically set *width* and *height* using pixels or percentages.

```
body {
    width: 100%;
}
```

Here's a more interesting example of CSS settings that produce a layout like the one shown in Figure 3-8. First start from the HTML:

```
<body>
    <header>
        Header of the page
    </header>
    <div id="main">
       main
    </div>
</body>
```

And here's the related CSS content:

```
body {
    margin: 0px;
}
header {
    width: 100%;
    height: 80px;
}
#main {
    width: 930px;
    height: 100%;
    margin: 0px;
    margin-left: auto;
}
```

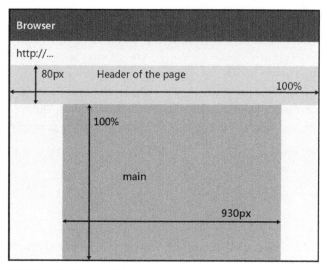

FIGURE 3-8 Width and height used to create a nice (and common) page template.

The *BODY* element sets its margin to 0 pixels, meaning that empty space will be left between the page content and browser's edges. The *HEADER* element takes up the entire width of the screen and just 80 pixels of the height. The *DIV*, with an ID of *main*, gets the entire height of (remaining) screen and limits itself to a fixed 930 pixels width. More interestingly, the *margin* of the *DIV* is first set to 0 and then the left margin is *overridden* to the special value of *auto*, meaning that the margin will be adjusted automatically by the browser to center the content.

> **Note** When it comes to width and height, you also have min/max subproperties to define a minimum/maximum width or height. The properties are *min-height*, *max-height*, *min-width*, and *max-width*. It should also be noted that *width* and *height* properties refer to the size of the content and don't count for padding, borders, and margins.

Advanced CSS scenarios

So far, you have seen only basic CSS selectors—ID, tag names, and custom classes. However, the CSS syntax for selectors is much more rich and sophisticated than this. A bunch of built-in pseudo-classes and operators can be combined together and define a sort of powerful query language. In this way, you can select a very specific set of HTML elements to style.

CSS pseudo-classes

You use CSS pseudo-classes to add special query capabilities to some selectors. The syntax to apply pseudo-classes looks like the following:

```
selector:pseudo-class {
    ...
}
```

Let's review a few examples of common pseudo-classes.

Anchor pseudo-classes

In a nutshell, pseudo-classes are like smart query operators you can use on certain HTML elements to further restrict the application of the style. Some pseudo-classes are generic and can be applied to nearly all selectors; some, instead, only make sense if applied to specific elements. Let's review pseudo-classes that work well with HTML anchors.

> **Note** Anchors are one of the most basic elements of HTML. Anchor is the more technical name used to refer to a hyperlink, and the reason why the *A* is used to identify the element. An anchor is made of two main parts: display text and underlying URL. When browsers encounter anchors, they typically render the display text underlined and show the linked URL in the status bar. When the user clicks the anchor, the browser navigates to the specified URL.

Usually, browsers render any occurrence of the *A* element in different ways depending on the status—the link was visited, is active, or the mouse is hovering. Each state is mapped to a different pseudo-class. Here's how to fully style an anchor:

```
a {
    text-decoration: none;    /* no underlining */
    color: #aaaa66;
    padding: 0px;
}
a:visited {
    text-decoration: none;    /* no underlining */
    color: #aaaa66;
}
a:hover {
    text-decoration: underline;
    background-color: orange;
    color: black;
    padding: 2px;
}
a:active {
    text-decoration: none;    /* no underlining */
    color: #aaaa66;
}
```

The *visited* pseudo-class defines the look and feel of the anchor once it has been clicked at least once. The *hover* class refers to the mouse hovering on the anchor. Finally, the *active* class refers to the look and feel of the anchor when it holds the input focus. The previous example manages to render the anchor always in the same way, and gives it a different color scheme when the mouse is over it.

Pseudo-classes for input elements

Sometimes you just want a different style for input fields (that is, text boxes) that are disabled, checked, or focused. CSS makes it fairly easy to do this through a bunch of ad hoc pseudo-classes. You can use the *checked* class to select all check boxes or radio buttons that are currently checked. Likewise, you can use *disabled* and *enabled* classes to query for related elements. The *focus* class, instead, signals which element is currently holding the input focus.

The following example automatically switches the background color of an *INPUT* text field to reflect the focused state:

```
input[type=text]:focus {
    background-color: orange;
    color: black;
}
```

The previous code snippet contains an interesting construct that you have not met before: an expression in square brackets. That's an attribute pseudo-class.

Attribute pseudo-classes

An attribute pseudo-class applies to an existing CSS selector and restricts the output to only elements that contain a given attribute with a given value. Let's look at the previous CSS snippet more closely.

```
input[type=text]:focus {
    background-color: orange;
    color: black;
}
```

The *[type=text]* selector applies to *INPUT* elements and it restricts the list of *INPUT* elements to only those where a *type* attribute exists and has a value of *text*. Table 3-1 lists the most popular attribute selectors.

TABLE 3-1 Popular attribute selectors

Selector	Description
[attribute]	Elements that contain an attribute with the specified name.
[attribute = value]	Elements that contain an attribute with the specified name and value.
*[attribute *= value]*	Elements that contain an attribute with the specified name whose value contains the specified value.

Selector	Description
[attribute != value]	Elements that contain an attribute with the specified name whose value is different from the specified value.
[attribute ^= value]	Elements that contain an attribute with the specified name whose value begins with the specified value.
[attribute $= value]	Elements that contain an attribute with the specified name whose value ends with the specified value.

Pseudo-classes for retrieving child elements

Sometimes you just want to pick up some child elements of a given selector. The *first-child* pseudo class returns the first child element, whereas *last-child* returns the last one. In addition, you can pick up the *n*th child of a given element using the *nth-child(n)* class, where *n* indicates the index of the child element to select.

Compound selectors

As you may have guessed, in CSS selectors can be composed together to form queries of any reasonable complexity. You can concatenate selectors using a blank, the comma, or other ad hoc symbols to define queries. Table 3-2 illustrates the most common scenarios.

TABLE 3-2 Popular compound selectors

Selector	Example	Description
element element	*div a*	Selects all *A* elements contained in a *DIV* elements.
element, element	*div,p*	Selects all *DIV* elements and all *P* elements.
element > element	*div > a*	Selects all *A* elements directly children of a *DIV* element.
element + element	*div + a*	Selects all *A* elements placed immediately after a *DIV* element.

In addition, consider the following example:

```
div.headline a {
    ...
}
```

The *div.headline* expression indicates all *DIV* elements given a CSS class named headline. The following *a* just restricts the query to all *A* elements contained within any subtree rooted in a *DIV* element with a class of *headline*.

Note When it comes to classes and pseudo-classes, names are case-insensitive.

Media Queries

When you attach a CSS file to an HTML document through the *LINK* element, you also have the option of selecting the medium where the style will be applied. You indicate the medium through the *media* attribute. If no *media* attribute is specified, then browsers understand that the same CSS file should be used in any possible scenario.

In the beginning, the role of the *media* attribute was limited to using different CSS files for viewing and printing a given HTML page. Originally, feasible values for the media attribute were *screen, print*, and *all*.

More recent browsers support a true query language in the *media* attribute that allows you to select the CSS file to apply it to based on the browser's runtime conditions.

Dynamic selection of the CSS file

Here's an example of how to dynamically link CSS files to an HTML page using media queries. The idea is that a page offers a number of choices and the browser dynamically picks up the most appropriate choice given its current status.

```
<link type="text/css"
      rel="stylesheet"
      href="tiny.css"
      media="only screen and (max-width: 320px)">
<link type="text/css"
      rel="stylesheet"
      href="large.css"
      media="only screen and (min-width: 321px)">
```

Interestingly, modern browsers are also able to adjust their selection of the CSS file as dynamic conditions change. With reference to the above code snippet, it means that the browser will automatically apply *tiny.css* when the width of the screen is up to 320 pixels and switch to *large.css* when the window is resized to at least 321 pixels.

The media queries mechanism serves two purposes. On one hand it gives you a chance to make pages that adapt to the current screen size; on the other hand, it represents a simple, but effective, tool to give your pages a mobile interface at nearly no cost. In the simplest case, in fact, a mobile device *is* just a browser with a smaller screen size.

Syntax of Media Queries

As mentioned previously, a browser's runtime conditions can affect the selection of the CSS file. Let's briefly review which runtime information you have access to in order to decide about the CSS file. First and foremost, a media query expression begins as a way to force older browsers to ignore the statement. Table 3-3 lists the main media query properties.

TABLE 3-3 Popular media query properties

Property	Description
width	Returns the width of the current browser view. The property supports min/max prefixes.
height	Returns the height of the current browser view. The property supports min/max prefixes.
orientation	Returns "portrait" when the value of the *height* property is greater or equal to the value of the *width* property. Otherwise, it returns "landscape."

The *orientation* property, for example, allows you to determine (more specifically than with just *width*) whether the page is being viewed in portrait or landscape mode.

In addition, you can use *AND* and *NOT* operators to build up expressions as complex as you like them to be.

Summary

CSS is the language used to add graphical styles to HTML pages. It is based on a collection of commands that select one or more HTML elements and alter their default appearance. You identify target elements via selectors and style them through a collection of property/value assignments.

In this chapter, you learned how to define selectors and explored the most important properties you might want to set in order to achieve great results with your pages.

As a developer primarily interested in Windows 8 applications (as opposed to general web development), you will (probably) be using readymade Windows 8 style sheets and conventions in most of your work. At any rate, the content of this chapter should have given you the basics to understand any further CSS feature you encounter along the way.

To complete the introductory part of the book for web development, let's now have a look at the basics of the JavaScript programming language.

Chapter 4

Making sense of JavaScript

Grasp the subject, the words will follow.

—Cato, the Elder

JavaScript is probably a language with nine (or even more) lives. JavaScript made its official debut in 1996 as part of the Netscape browser and happily survived the first 15 years of the Internet era. It was originally supposed to be a simple language targeted at web authors willing to make their HTML pages more responsive and attractive. JavaScript was never designed to be a full-fledged programming language, but rather something that was easy to work with.

And in the end it worked very well.

JavaScript has a remarkably low barrier to entry and it is flexible enough to enable experts to do nearly anything with it. Today, knowing JavaScript is a critical skill for essentially all developers; it is easy to get acquainted with, but unfortunately, it's also not trivial to master.

With the release of Windows 8, Microsoft makes HTML5 and JavaScript a first-class platform for building applications. Developers use HTML5 to build layout and CSS to style it. Developers also use JavaScript to manipulate page elements. At the same time, though, developers have access to a bunch of system-provided libraries that offer user interface widgets and components that allow developers to access capabilities specific to Windows 8.

It is expected that developers using JavaScript to write Windows 8 applications are primarily interested in binding freshly downloaded data to user interface elements. It doesn't mean, however, that you can't use JavaScript to implement at least a few bits of business logic. In general, though, keep in mind that the more business logic you must express in JavaScript, the less appropriate JavaScript may be as your choice of programming language.

This chapter aims at revisiting the foundation of the JavaScript language, and discusses a few basic patterns for organizing JavaScript code from within a Windows 8 application.

Language basics

The JavaScript language relies on a solid standard, as defined by the ECMA-262 and ISO/IEC 16262:2011 papers. Unlike what happens with other popular programming languages like C#, JavaScript code is not compiled before execution. Instead, JavaScript code is interpreted and then executed on the fly. For this reason, JavaScript programs need a runtime environment (the engine that translates and executes the code you write) in order to run. On the Windows 8 platform, JavaScript is supported by a runtime environment named Chakra that, like the Buddhist force it is named after, pushes vital energy throughout the body of HTML pages.

> **Note** The majority of programming languages (such as C#, Visual Basic, C++, and Java) let developers express an intended behavior by using a high-level syntax. The code expressed in this way, though, must first be "compiled" to a lower-level language that is much closer to the actual behavior of the machine. Put another way, the programming language commonly used by developers is a mere abstraction over the behavior of the machine. A classic compiled language needs a special tool—the compiler—to transform high-level syntax into lower-level syntax. You can't run your program until you have successfully compiled it. Other languages—such as JavaScript—are not compiled. This doesn't mean they don't need any adaptation to run; a non-compiled (interpreted) language simply has its "compilation step" performed during execution just before a given line is executed.

Let's now navigate through the basics of the language, digging out aspects of the type system, the use of variables and functions, and good and bad programming habits.

The JavaScript type system

The JavaScript type system is composed of a few primitive types and a few built-in objects. When you write JavaScript code, however, the range of types you can work with is actually much larger. In addition to built-in objects, you can also rely on objects provided by the host as well as objects you import from externally linked frameworks. For Windows 8 applications, in particular, you need to import the Windows 8 JavaScript (WinJs) library—the gateway to the native Windows 8 application programming interface (API).

This chapter, though, focuses on the native type system as defined in the aforementioned JavaScript ECMA-262 standard definition.

Primitive types and built-in objects

In JavaScript, the primitive types are *number, string, Boolean, undefined, Object* and *Function*. Built-in objects are *Array, Math, Date,* and *RegExp,* plus a few objects that are just functionally richer wrappers for some primitive types. Such wrapper objects are named *String, Boolean,* and *Number,* and they just add more capabilities to the corresponding primitive type.

The type *number* represents floating point numbers with zero or more decimal places. There are no separate types for concepts such as integers, long integers, singles, doubles, or bytes. One special number, *NaN*, is reserved for numbers that don't make mathematical sense—it is a variable that contains the result of a math operation that makes no sense. In fact, the name *NaN* is the acronym of Not-A-Number. The built-in *Number* object just wraps a primitive numeric value and adds a method to convert the number to a string.

The type *string* represents a sequence of zero or more characters. The content of a string is bracketed in matching pairs of single or double quotes. The built-in *String* object adds a few methods, including *substring*, which extracts a segment of the string between two specified indexes, and *toLowerCase*, which converts characters in the string to lowercase.

Table 4-1 summarizes other built-in objects.

TABLE 4-1 JavaScript built-in objects

Built-in object	Description
Array	Supplies a rich programming interface for a collection of JavaScript objects. You can access members by index and also add and remove existing elements.
Date	Supplies a variety of handy methods to work with a date, including getting and setting individual elements such as day, month, or year. It also works to deal with time information.
Math	Supplies an interface to perform a variety of mathematical tasks ranging from getting random numbers to power, and from rounding to min/max and absolute value functions.
RegExp	Supplies regular expressions.

The JavaScript global object

All JavaScript objects inherit from a unique global super object, and subsequently, properties and functions of the global object augment all native and custom objects. In particular, the global object features the following properties:

NaN, which returns the value for Not-A-Number.

Infinity, which returns the value for infinity.

Table 4-2 lists the functions available on the global object.

TABLE 4-2 JavaScript built-in objects

Function	Description
eval	Gets code in the form of a string and executes it on the fly.
escape / unescape	Encodes and decodes special characters in a plain string.
encodeUri / decodeUri	Encodes and decodes special characters in a URI string.
isNaN	Returns *true* if the specified value is Not-A-Number.
isFinite	Returns *true* if the specified value is infinity.
parseInt	Parses a string and tries to extract an integer number out of it.
parseFloat	Parses a string and tries to extract a floating point number out of it.

It should be noted that any object, value, or constant you happen to use in your JavaScript coding that doesn't seem to belong to any objects of yours is ultimately available because it's exposed by the global JavaScript object.

Null vs. undefined

When it comes to null-ness, JavaScript introduces a subtle difference that many higher-level languages such as C# and Java miss. As you'll see more in detail in a moment, a JavaScript variable is not bound to a fixed type. Subsequently, the variable is not bound to any type until it is explicitly assigned a value. At this stage, the type of the variable is said to be *undefined*.

In JavaScript, *undefined* is seen as a special type rather than as a value. If you check the type of an unassigned variable using the *typeof* operator, you get the string *undefined*. If you instead attempt to evaluate the *content* of an unassigned variable, you get *null*. Pay attention to the following code:

```
var x;          // therefore the type of the variable is "undefined"
var y = null;
```

What happens if you compare *x* and *y*?

JavaScript has two equality operators: the double equals sign (==) operator and the triple equals sign (===) operator. If you use the == operator, both expressions are evaluated and the resulting values are compared. However, if you use the === operator, then the types of the values are also compared. In reference to the previous code snippet, if you compare *x* and *y* using the == operator then you get *true,* meaning that the *undefined* value of *x* ultimately evaluates to *null*, which matches the value assigned to *y*.

In contrast, if you compare *x* and *y* using the === operator, then you get *false*: the two variables hold the same value but are of different types.

Dealing with variables

In JavaScript, a variable is simply a storage location and is not restricted to always storing values of a fixed type. When assigned a value, variables take on the type of the data being stored. For this reason, a JavaScript variable may change its type quite a few times during its lifespan, as shown in the following code snippet:

```
var data = "dino";    // now data is of type string
data = 123;           // now data is of type number
```

JavaScript variables spring into existence the first time they're used; until then, they hold a value of *null* and their type is *undefined*.

Local variables

When defining variables, you should always use the *var* keyword as a hint to the parser and yourself. The *var* keyword is not strictly required, but it is highly recommended to keep the scope of the variable under strict control.

Variables defined within the body of a function are scoped to the function—and are therefore local variables—only if they have been declared using the *var* keyword. If you omit *var*, variables are treated as global, but remain undefined until the function executes once.

You should also note that JavaScript lacks the concept of block-level scope that you find in many other programming languages. Consider the following code:

```
function foo(number) {
   var x = 0;              // Variable x is local to the function and not visible
outside

   if (number >0) {
      var y = number;    // Variable y is NOT local to the IF block;
      ...
   }
}
```

The variable *y* is not local to the *if* block, and its content is also accessible from outside the block. However, because it is defined with *var*, the variable is local to the function. It is important to note that if you miss the *var* keyword in the *if* block, what you might expect to be a temporary variable will be promoted to the much higher rank of a global variable!

The same concept just shown for an *if* statement also applies to *for* and *while* loops.

Global variables

Variables declared in the global scope—that is outside any function body—are always global regardless of whether or not *var* is used. Consider the following snippet to experience the subtle differences between local and global, represented by the *var* keyword:

```
var rootServer = "http://www.expoware.org/";   // global variable
section = "mobile";                            // global variable

function doSomething() {
    var temp = 1;                              // local variable
    mode = 0;                                  // global variable, but undefined
until called
}
```

The JavaScript runtime environment stores global variables as properties of a hidden object referenced through the *this* keyword. Note that browsers often mirror the global object via the *window* object.

Protecting the global namespace

In nearly any programming language, coding is (much) easier if you can use global variables. Global variables, however, have downsides too. A critical downside is the risk of name collisions between variables defined in different parts of your code, third-party libraries, advertising partners, and analytics libraries. A name collision combined with the dynamic typing of JavaScript variables may wind up inadvertently modifying the state of the application—with potentially unpleasant anomalies at run time.

Consider how easy it is to unwittingly create global variables: miss a *var* and you get a global; mistype a variable name in an assignment and you get a fresh new global. This latter feature is possible because JavaScript allows you to use a variable without declaring it first.

There is a workaround. When you need to use global variables, a good technique is to create them as properties of a wrapper object. You place code similar to the following in a JavaScript file that you then link from every page:

```
var Globals = (function() { return this; }());
```

Next, you make a point of referencing whatever global object you use via the *Globals.Xxx* expression, where *Xxx* is the name of the global variable you want to use. In this way, at least all of your global variables will stand out in code.

 Note JSLint (*http://www.jslint.com*)—an online tool for static analysis of JavaScript code— does help in catching anti-patterns in your code, including the lack of *var* keywords.

Variables and hoisting

Hoisting is a JavaScript feature that allows developers to declare variables everywhere in the scope and then use them everywhere. In JavaScript, you are allowed to first use the variable and then declare it (such as, *var*) later. The overall behavior is just as if the *var* statement were placed at the top. Here's an example:

```
function() {
    mode = 1;
    ...
    var mode;
}
```

Historically, this feature was introduced to keep the entry barrier to JavaScript for non-expert developers as low as possible. When you use JavaScript to write significant portions of code, however, hoisting is a clear source of confusion and becomes error prone. It's a good habit to place all your variables at the top of each function, even better if you place them in a single *var* statement as shown below:

```
function() {
    var start = 0,
        total = 10,
        index;
    ...
}
```

Note that having multiple *var* statements, instead, is neither bad nor wrong. However, sticking to the single *var* approach helps force you to always define a variable before you use it.

Dealing with objects

JavaScript is not usually catalogued as an object-oriented language, at least not at the same level as Java and C#. The primary reason for this is the definition of an object that you get from JavaScript is different from the commonly accepted idea of an object that you get from classic object-oriented languages.

Structure of JavaScript objects

In JavaScript, an object is a dictionary of name/value pairs. The blueprint of the object is implicit and you have no way to access it. A JavaScript object usually only has data, but you can add behavior. The (explicit) structure of an object may change at any time—for example, you can add new methods and properties at run time. The implicit structure never changes. Here's how you can add a new property to an existing object:

```
var theNumber = new Number();
theNumber.type = "Number";
```

Adding a member to a JavaScript object works only for that particular instance. If you were now to create another instance of the *Number* object, the property *type* would not be available for the new *Number* object. You can work around that problem by using prototypes.

The *prototype* common property

If you want to add a new member to all instances being created of a given type, you have to add the member to the object's prototype. Here's how to add a *type* property to all the numbers so that you gain more control over the effective type of the object.

```
if (typeof Number.prototype.type === 'undefined') {
    Number.prototype.type = "Number";
}
```

Important The example you just examined, and specifically the use of a custom *type* property, is not coincidental. In JavaScript, you can use the *typeof* operator on a variable name to discover the type of an object currently stored in the variable. However, most of the time all you get back as a response is the word "Object." There is no easy way to distinguish between, for example, strings and numbers. For this reason, the use of a custom *type* property makes even more sense.

Creating new object instances

You can use the *Object* type to create aggregates of values and methods, which is the closest you can get in JavaScript to standard object-orientation, such as C#. Here's a possible way to create a new object:

```
var dog = new Object();
dog.name = "Jerry Lee Esposito";
```

In general, the direct use of the constructor of an *Object* is disregarded. A better approach entails using an object literal, as shown below:

```
var dog = {
    name: "Jerry Lee Esposito",
};
```

Using the constructor of an *Object* poses some performance issues to the JavaScript interpreter, which has to resolve the scope of the constructor call and look up a potentially large stack. In addition, using the constructor directly also doesn't transmit the sense of objects as dictionaries, which is a key point of JavaScript programming.

Dealing with functions

In JavaScript, a *function* is a bit of code bundled up into a block and optionally given a name. If a function is not given a name, it is called an *anonymous* function. Functions represent a scope and are treated like objects; they may have properties and can be passed around as arguments and interacted with.

You use functions for two main reasons: for defining repeatable behavior, and for creating custom objects.

Named functions for repeatable behavior

A named (as opposed to *anonymous*) function is defined as follows:

```
function doSomeCalculation(number) {
   ...
   return number;
}
```

Defined in this way, the function is globally visible and is interpreted as a new member added to the JavaScript global object. You can call the function from anywhere in your code, as shown below:

```
var result = doSomeCalculation(3);
```

JavaScript functions can be called with any number of arguments—regardless of the declared number of parameters. In other words, you may have a function like *doSomeCalculation*, which declares just one argument *(number)*, but you can invoke it by passing any (greater) number of arguments.

```
var result = doSomeCalculation(1, 2);
```

Although browsers may tolerate this type of coding, it is still a bad programming practice. However, you can leverage such flexibility to easily define functions that deliberately accept a variable number of arguments.

In JavaScript, a function can access declared parameters by name or by position using a predefined array called *arguments*. This array returns the actual list of parameters passed to the function. In this way, for example, the function below can accept any number of arguments and process them.

```
function doSum() {
    var result = 0;
    for(var i=0; i<arguments.length; i++)
        result += arguments[i];
    return result;
}
```

Both calls shown below are acceptable for the function *doSum*.

```
var r1 = doSum(1, 2, 3);
var r2 = doSum(4, 5);
```

A function that accepts a variable number of arguments is perhaps more clearly defined with no explicit formal parameters. However, you can also have some parameters declared and still accept and process any number. At any rate, the *arguments* array returns the effective list of parameters found in the call—in the order in which they are listed.

Immediate functions and objects

In JavaScript, an *immediate* function represents a piece of code that is defined and executed in the same place. You usually place the definition of a function somewhere (say, in a distinct file) and invocation goes somewhere else. This approach works well when you expect to use the function multiple times and from a variety of places. An immediate function is an excellent trick for defining any work that needs be done only once.

An immediate function has its definition wrapped in parentheses with the list of parameters placed at the end, as shown below:

```
var result = (function() {
    ...
}());
```

An expression where an immediate function is used, indicates that a value—not the function itself—is being returned. If the function needs parameters, the previous code can be rewritten as follows:

```
var result = (function(x, y, z) {
    ...
}(1, 2, 3));          // 1,2,3 are actual values for x,y,z
```

Similarly, you can have *immediate objects*. An immediate object is a function defined in the same place where one of its methods is invoked and executed. An immediate object has its literal-based definition wrapped in parentheses, as below:

```
({
    init: function() {
        // perform initialization tasks
    },
}).init(...);
```

Both immediate objects and functions create a scope sandbox that prevents their local variables from polluting the global namespace.

So should you use immediate functions or immediate objects? That's mostly up to you, but it ultimately boils down to how complex your code is (or that you anticipate it's going to become). For very complex tasks, an immediate object is perhaps preferable because it allows you define properties and split implementation into multiple methods. An immediate function is something simpler that works well for any code expressed as a plain sequence of statements.

Extending existing objects with behavior

Earlier, this chapter discussed how properties can be added to an object's prototype so that each new instance of that object is augmented with those new properties. Nearly the same considerations can be made for functions, which can be used to augment an existing object definition with behavior. As an example, consider the *Number* object again. The following code shows how to add a new *random* member that returns a random number greater than the specified minimum.

```javascript
// This code needs to run once--so we add it as an immediate function.
(if (typeof Number.prototype.random === 'undefined') {
    Number.prototype.random = function(min) {
        var n = min + Math.floor(Math.random() * 1000);
        return n;
    };
}());
```

After this code has run once, you are free to use the following function:

```javascript
function doWork() {
    var n1 = new Number().random(0);
    var n2 = new Number().random(10);
    alert("Numbers are " + n1 + " and " + n2);
}
```

 Note Augmenting the prototype of native objects is considered a bad practice because it makes the code less predictable and may hurt maintainability. This consideration, though, applies mostly to team development. If you're writing code for yourself, this point is less important.

Constructor functions

As mentioned earlier, there are two main reasons for using functions: defining repeatable behavior and creating custom objects. Here, you'll tackle the second scenario, starting with a look at the following code:

```javascript
var Dog = function(name) {
    this.name = name;
    this.bark = function() {
```

```
      return "bau";
   };
};
```

What you have here is a new object named *Dog*. Early on, when talking about objects, you also created something similar:

```
var dog = {
   name: "Jerry Lee Esposito",
};
```

The big difference here is that the latter code snippet represents a snapshot of only data; the former code snippet, instead, is a function with data and behavior.

So how would you use the *Dog* object? To use the *Dog* object, you need to instantiate it using the classic *new* constructor, as shown below:

```
var jerry = new Dog("jerry");
```

What if you miss the new operator and go with something like this?

```
var jerry = Dog("jerry");
```

The tricky thing is that if you forget to use the *new* operator, you won't get any exception and your code will just run. However, any action you perform on *Dog* (for example, setting the *name* property) will be executed on the *this* object. Without the *new* operator in front, that would be resolved as the global JavaScript object. This means that you are polluting the global namespace of the JavaScript interpreter. Here's a safe countermeasure that doesn't create issues whether or not you use the *new* operator:

```
var Dog = function(name) {
   var that = {};
   that.name = name;
   that.bark = function() {
      return "bau";
   };
   return that;
};
```

The difference is that you now explicitly create and return a new object—an object named *that*. This is familiarly known as the "Use-That-Not-This" pattern.

Important This is also the most appropriate way to create your own aggregates of data and behavior (objects) by using an explicit constructor without the need to use the *new* operator. In this way, you get very close to object-oriented components in JavaScript.

Having fun with callback functions

Callbacks are just functions passed as an argument. Code that receives a callback function can call the calling code back when appropriate. For example, suppose you have a generic function that holds a collection of numbers. At various times you need to loop over the collection and perform different operations, such as sum and multiplication. Should you really define two distinct (but fairly repetitive) functions, as shown below?

```
function sumAllNumbers() {
    // STEP 1: COLLECT INPUT DATA
    var numbers = new Array();
    for (var i = 0; i < arguments.length; i++) {
        numbers.push(arguments[i]);
    }

    // STEP 2: PERFORM OPERATION
    var result = 0;
    for (var i = 0; i < numbers.length; i++) {
        result += numbers[i];
    }

    // STEP 3: DISPLAY RESULTS
    alert("SUM result is: " + result);
}

function multiplyAllNumbers() {
    // STEP 1: COLLECT INPUT DATA
    for (var i = 0; i < arguments.length; i++)
        numbers.push(arguments[i]);

    // STEP 2: PERFORM OPERATION
    var result = 1;
    for (var i = 0; i < numbers.length; i++) {
        result *= numbers[i];
    }

    // STEP 3: DISPLAY RESULTS
    alert("MULTIPLICATION result is: " + result);
}
```

Both functions consist of three main steps. The first step is repeated in both functions; the second step is specific to each function; and the third step does the same thing in each case, but with different data. Having functions defined in this way simply works. If getting results is all you are interested in, then feel free to stop here.

The whole point is that a simplistic solution like this may possibly work well in a simple scenario. As complexity grows, you may end up with a great deal of duplicated code—which is bad because it forces you to make changes in several places and if you miss making the change in one place you can introduce bugs that can be truly hard to find and fix. Callback functions help by making the previous code not only smaller, but also far easier to read.

To illustrate the point, you'll start by creating a single function that orchestrates the various steps for both the sum and multiplication; you can call this function *handleNumbers*.

```
function handleNumbers(operationCallback) {
    // STEP 1: COLLECT INPUT DATA
    var numbers = new Array();
    for (var i = 1; i < arguments.length; i++)  // start from 1 to skip callback
function
        numbers.push(arguments[i]);

    // STEP 2: PERFORM OPERATION
    var result = operationCallback(numbers);

    // STEP 3: DISPLAY RESULTS
    alert(result);
}
```

Now define a couple of highly specific functions: one that sums and one that multiplies all received parameters.

```
function doSum(numbers) {
    var result = 0;
    for (var i = 0; i < numbers.length; i++) {
        result += numbers[i];
    }
    return result;
}

function doMultiply(numbers) {
    var result = 1;
    for (var i = 0; i < numbers.length; i++) {
        result *= numbers[i];
    }
    return result;
}
```

At this point, the invocation code becomes:

```
handleNumbers(doSum, 1, 2, 3, 4);
handleNumbers(doMultiply, 1, 2, 3, 4);
```

With this structure in place, adding yet another operation on the array of numbers is simply a matter of creating a function that performs the desired operation. There's no need to worry about collecting numbers or displaying results.

Contract-based callback functions

If you strictly compare the actual effects of the two versions of the code, you should note a difference. In the former version, where repetitive code was used you could output a message saying something like "*SUM result is XXX.*" In the more generic and callback-based solution, all you could show to the user was the bare numeric result.

It may sound like a minor point, but it actually isn't.

The problem is that the output message needs to incorporate some information—the name of the operation—that can be provided only by the injected function. How can you force a function like *doSum* to return two values—the actual result of the operation plus the name of the operation? You need to define a contract for the callback and actually upgrade the callback from the rank of a simple function to the higher rank of an object.

First, you define the contract (or interface) that you expect the callback to have. The contract defines all the information that the caller needs. In this case, the caller probably expects to find a method to calculate a number (call it *execute*) and a string to indicate the name of the operation (call it *name*). Here's how you would rewrite the *handleNumbers* function:

```
function handleNumbers(operation) {
    // STEP 1: COLLECT INPUT DATA
    var numbers = new Array();
    for (var i = 1; i < arguments.length; i++)
        numbers.push(arguments[i]);

    // STEP 2: PERFORM OPERATION
    var result = operation.execute(numbers);

    // STEP 3: DISPLAY RESULTS
    alert(operation.name + " result is " + result);
}
```

You now define two distinct objects—*Sum* and *Multiplication*.

```
var Sum = function () {
    var that = {};
```

```
        that.name = "SUM";
        that.execute = function (numbers) {
            var result = 0;
            for (var i = 0; i < numbers.length; i++) {
                result += numbers[i];
            }
            return result;
        };
        return that;
    }

var Multiplication = function () {
    var that = {};
    that.name = "MULTIPLICATION";
    that.execute = function (numbers) {
        var result = 1;
        for (var i = 0; i < numbers.length; i++) {
            result *= numbers[i];
        }
        return result;
    };
    return that;
}
```

Finally, the code to invoke operations looks like what follows:

```
handleNumbers(new Sum(), 1, 2, 3, 4);
handleNumbers(new Multiplication(), 1, 2, 3, 4);
```

Using objects in lieu of functions gives you a lot more programming power because you are not limited in any way in terms of the contract that you can support.

Anonymous Functions

So far, this chapter has focused mostly on named functions. What about unnamed functions (anonymous functions), instead? In JavaScript, anonymous functions are the pillar of functional programming. An anonymous function is a direct offshoot of lambda calculus or, if you prefer, a language adaptation of old-fashioned function pointers. Here's a simple example of an anonymous function:

```
function(x, y) {
    return x + y;
}
```

The *only* difference between a regular function and an anonymous function is in the name (or lack thereof).

Why are anonymous functions becoming so popular? The primary reason is that anonymous functions allow you to define code in place—without the need to define a named function somewhere. The drawback of anonymous functions is that they are not reusable. As long as you need to pass a one-off piece of code as an argument, then using an anonymous function is more than acceptable. However, if the function might be used more often, a named function is preferable. Just for the sake of illustration, here's a rewrite of the previous code using anonymous functions:

```
// Perform a sum
handleNumbers(function(numbers) {
    var result = 0;
    for (var i = 0; i < numbers.length; i++) {
        result += numbers[i];
    }
    return result;
},
1, 2, 3, 4);
```

Readability is not always ideal; but for very basic code, this approach can still work.

Organizing your own JavaScript code

So far, you have focused primarily on the syntactic aspects of the JavaScript language, and you've explored JavaScript's object-oriented capabilities. It is now about time to shift to how you use JavaScript code from within HTML pages, and specifically, in the context of Windows 8 applications.

Any JavaScript code you use in an HTML page is always invoked in response to an event that is either fired by the browser or fired in response to some user action. Hence, the first point to focus on is how to define event handlers in an HTML page. Next, you need to know a little about how to organize the code.

Linking JavaScript code to pages

First and foremost, an *event handler* is a JavaScript function invoked in response to an event. The event can be fired by the browser—for example, the browser fires an event when the page has fully loaded—or in response to an action by a person—for example, when a user clicks a button. Event handlers must be associated with events to produce any visible effects. HTML defines a number of *onXXX* attributes (where *XXX* is the name of the event, such as *click* or *load*) that you can set in the HTML markup to associate the event with the name of a JavaScript function.

Unobtrusive JavaScript is a pattern that suggests a more effective way of achieving the same result. Unobtrusive JavaScript is also the preferred way of binding code to events in Windows 8. Let's find out more.

Event attributes of an HTML element

For years, it has been common to write HTML pages with input fields and buttons explicitly attached to JavaScript event handlers. Here's a typical example:

```
<input type="button" value="Click me" onclick="handleClick()" />
```

From a purely functional perspective, there's nothing wrong with this code—it works as expected: the *onclick* attribute associates the click action with the *handleClick* JavaScript function, so that function then runs whenever a user clicks the button. This approach, however, is largely acceptable only when you're using JavaScript to spice up simple HTML pages. It becomes unwieldy when the amount of JavaScript code represents a significant portion of the page or the view.

In a way, unobtrusive JavaScript is the script counterpart of CSS classes. With CSS, you write plain HTML without including inline style information. Next, designers style elements using CSS classes. Likewise, for unobtrusive JavaScript, you avoid using the *in-tag* event handler attributes (*onclick*, *onchange*, *onblur*, and the like) and instead use a single JavaScript function to attach handlers when the page is ready for display. By not using event attributes, you keep markup code and JavaScript code separated.

What about the code that is referenced by event handlers? In other words, where would you get the code for functions like *handleClick*?

Embedded JavaScript code

You can embed JavaScript content in an HTML page in a number of ways. The simplest way to have JavaScript code ready to use in an HTML page is placing it in the page within a *SCRIPT* element.

```
<script type="text/javascript">
    ...
</script>
```

As browsers encounter one of these *<script>* sections, they stop page rendering, execute the script, and then proceed. If the *script* element doesn't contain immediate code to execute (for example, suppose it contains only function declarations), then the browser simply takes note of the function and proceeds. A *script* element is therefore an acceptable place to embed the definition of functions invoked by event handlers.

Embedding script code in a page has both pros and cons, but mostly cons. Table 4-3 summarizes both.

TABLE 4-3 Pros and cons of embedding JavaScript code in HTML pages

Pro	Con
The page has no dependencies and is self-contained. As a developer, you don't have to look in several places to find out things specific to a page.	The page is larger and takes more time to download.
	The script code cannot be used outside the page that contains it.
	Restructuring the code to minimize duplicated functionalities is compromised by the fact that no code reuse is possible outside the page.
	Script code cannot be cached by browsers separately from the page.

In addition, there's another point to consider: with embedded code, any changes to the script are immediately visible. You just save the file and refresh the browser. But when the script file is linked as an external resource (more on this in a moment), then you need to play some tricks to ensure that changes are immediately visible and not hidden by cached copies of the same file.

This aspect is certainly important, but it doesn't affect released applications. It is an important aspect, but only during the development phase.

External files

As an alternative to embedding code in a *script* element, you can use the same *script* element to link a JavaScript file as an external resource. Here's how to do it:

```
<script src="http://..." type="text/javascript" />
```

The pros of using externally linked JavaScript files are exactly opposite to the cons of using embedded script. This is the way to go; or, at least, using externally linked files should always be the first option you consider in general web development and in Windows 8 development.

jQuery and Windows 8

At present, most JavaScript development is done with the immensely popular jQuery library. You can download the library from *http://jquery.com.*

Typical web developers use the jQuery library to unobtrusively bind handlers to events and to detect page-level events, such as the event that indicates the page is ready for display. In addition, web developers use jQuery to query for ad hoc subsets of page elements. With reference to the previous chapter on CSS, you could say that jQuery offers a syntax that mimics the syntax of CSS selectors. In reality though, jQuery selector syntax is even richer than CSS standards.

For developers who have a strong web background, the thought of writing HTML pages without using jQuery (or other popular JavaScript libraries, such as, *knockout.js*) may be nonsense.

In Windows 8, using jQuery (and other libraries, other than the WinJs library) may sometimes be problematic, depending on how you use the jQuery library.

The reason why jQuery can sometimes be problematic is the new security model that Microsoft has adopted for Windows 8 applications. According to this model, dynamic manipulation of the page structure done with data that is potentially unsafe (that is, coming from untrusted sources) is prohibited.

If you are familiar with jQuery, you can use it as long as doing so doesn't give you a hard time. If you are not familiar with jQuery, then it is suggested that you avoid using it for Windows 8 applications. For most of the advanced jQuery features (such as plugins), you will find native components in the WinJs library for Windows 8. To query elements in the hosting HTML page, you can use HTML standard functions—such as *document.querySelector*—that supports a CSS-like syntax to select elements.

Practices and habits

JavaScript code is easy to make work, but definitely hard to manage and evolve, unless you set up and adhere to a number of practices. This sole purpose of this section is to summarize the do's and don'ts of plain JavaScript programming. "Plain" JavaScript programming means JavaScript techniques not specifically targeted to Windows 8 development. You'll switch to focusing on specific aspects of Windows 8 JavaScript development in the next chapter.

Group your globals

In this chapter, you learned about the need to make your global data stand out. You can achieve this by using the following code at the top of every JavaScript file you happen to use.

```
var Globals = (function() { return this; }());
```

Suppose you have a global variable that represents the name of the application; for example, this variable is named *AppName*. The purpose of the previous suggestion was so that you can use the variable as shown below:

```
Globals.AppName = "MyApp";
```

It should be noted that *AppName* and *Globals.AppName* would point to the same location, and both can be used in the application with the same meaning. Of course, if you consistently use the version with the *Globals* prefix, you make your global variables stand out in code.

This approach is not free of issues. In particular, it still creates as many entries in the global namespace as there are variables associated with *Globals*. Here's a slightly better approach: first, you place the following code at the top of each and every JavaScript file you define.

```
Globals = Globals || {};
```

Next up, you define your global members as members of the newly created *Globals* object. The difference is that now *Globals* is a brand new global object, and all the members you want to use as global in your application are actually defined as children of *Globals* and are not polluting the JavaScript namespace. Put another way, all your application's global variables are grouped under a single global object that is visible to the JavaScript interpreter.

Keep application state at hand

All applications need to maintain their own state, that way the state can be persisted to disk when the application is closed or, when used on a mobile device, the application is sent to the background.

A good approach is to have some code ready to load the application's state upon application startup. Data can be loaded from a storage location (if available), downloaded from some remote location, or simply initialized to default values. When the application exits, the current state should be persisted to storage to be ready for next use.

For this pattern to work smoothly, it is necessary that you start by defining a JavaScript object whose properties represent the state of the application. Here's an example:

```javascript
var MyAppState = function () {
    var that = {};
    that.init = function () {
        // Take care of initialization and default values
    };
    that.load = function () {
        // Take care of loading from storage
    };
    that.save = function () {
        // Take care of storage
    };

    // Other properties here
    ...

    that.init();
    return that;
}
```

To attach an instance of this object to the *Globals* container, you write code as follows:

```javascript
Globals.Current = new MyAppState();
```

From now on, you can read and write the state of your application via highly readable statements such as *Globals.Current.Xxx*, where *Xxx* is the name of a property or member defined on *MyAppState*.

Be ready for localization

Having the application ready for international markets may be a key to your success (or it might be just for your own enjoyment if you're approaching Windows 8 development with a light spirit). In general, localization is an important factor for applications published to a public store, as is the case with Windows 8 applications.

In JavaScript code for web applications, you don't get a lot of built-in help with localization issues. Thankfully, in Windows 8 development, you get significant support from the WinJs library. At the end of the day, all you need to do is mark any elements whose content you want localized with a special attribute. Next, you need only add a localized resource file to the application for each language you intend to support.

The Windows 8 runtime will take care of automatically selecting the right content from the right resource file according to the currently set locale.

 Note If you are at all familiar with C# and general Windows development, this overall pattern should be nothing new. It's precisely the old good pattern of Windows localization, just adapted to the new Windows 8 API.

Summary

This chapter offered a quick tour of the JavaScript language and discussed taking an approach unbiased by Windows 8 or web slants (to the extent that's possible). You reviewed the basics of the language and outlined a few common-sense patterns for effective development.

Quite honestly, this chapter, as well as the preceding two chapters on HTML and CSS, can only serve the purpose of refreshing or perhaps clarifying some existing knowledge of the subjects. HTML, CSS, and JavaScript each deserve a book of their own to be fully explained and learned step by step. In case you feel you need a more specific resource, seek out the following Microsoft Press books.

For rank beginners:

- *Start Here!*™ *Learn HTML5* by Faithe Wempen (Microsoft Press, 2012)

- *Start Here!*™ *Learn JavaScript* by Steve Suehring (Microsoft Press, 2012)

For those with some experience, or as a more in-depth follow-up to the previous books:

- *HTML5 Step by Step* by Faithe Wempen (Microsoft Press, 2011)

- *JavaScript Step by Step* by Steve Suehring (Microsoft Press, 2013)

It is key to note that this chapter covered mostly plain JavaScript. And JavaScript is, for the most part, a language used in HTML pages. And HTML pages are essentially web-based resources.

Starting with the next chapter, that all changes. You'll see that coding Windows 8 with JavaScript is inherently a somewhat different experience than coding JavaScript for the web. A Windows 8 application is primarily an application written against the Windows 8 API. JavaScript is just the means by which you express logic and orchestrate calls to the underlying API.

In this context, HTML and CSS are just UI languages through which you design and express the user interface. More than HTML5 elements and custom CSS, you'll be focusing on Windows 8 HTML attributes and style sheets. Everything you have learned in these early chapters will turn out to be helpful in later chapters. But there's a lot more to learn about HTML, CSS, and JavaScript that hasn't been mentioned yet.

Chapter 5

First steps with Windows 8 development

Success is counted sweetest by those who ne'er succeed.

—*Emily Dickinson*

In Chapter 1, "Using Visual Studio 2012 Express edition," you had a first short glimpse of the Microsoft Windows 8 programming style. You created a simple application directly from one basic template offered by Microsoft Visual Studio, then turned that into a slightly more functional and significant application capable of displaying a random generated number on demand. As proverbial wisdom reminds us, every journey—even the longest—begins with a small step.

To go beyond the basic level of getting and displaying a random number, you need to acquire some command of HTML and CSS, and get the hang of the JavaScript language. The former will help you imagine and create the graphical part of any applications you intend to try out. The latter will help you organize the code to ward off unexpected results, so that you can translate your ideas into instructions for the operating system more easily.

Now you're ready to take the plunge into the Windows 8 Runtime (WinRT) environment. A runtime environment is the collection of Windows 8 programs and components that interact with any applications and make them run. Such an environment provides services and data to any applications, but also requires that applications comply with some rules and constraints.

This chapter has three main objectives:

- Exploring the Windows 8 runtime environment

- Reviewing graphics requirements for Windows 8 applications

- Understanding the basic stages of the lifecycle of any Windows 8 application.

To meet these objectives, you'll build another sample application that employs a fundamental service of the runtime environment—the data binding service. The data binding service offers an easy way to display data to the users of your application. You'll be using the data binding service quite often in the upcoming chapters.

The Windows 8 Runtime (WinRT)

It's fairly rare for a new version of an operating system to introduce a new type of application that is completely incompatible with older versions of the same system. Sometimes a newer operating system offers a few new functions that tease companies to update existing programs. However, in Windows 8, there's a completely new segment of applications, named Windows Store apps. Not only do these applications run only on Windows 8, but they also have a brand new look and feel, can be offered for free or for sale through the Windows Store, and last, but certainly not least, are not limited to classic personal computers but instead can also run—unchanged—on a variety of Windows 8-compliant devices, most notably Microsoft Surface devices. In addition, Windows Store applications can only be developed on machines running Windows 8.

Note Just to cool down some possibly premature enthusiasm: no, there's no way for you to run your handmade Windows 8 application on an iPad. Any Windows 8 application can run on devices as long the device is compatible with Windows hardware and software requirements.

Windows Store apps and other apps

Windows 8 has two working modes that you can switch on and off—the standard Windows mode and the new Windows 8 mode. When configured for the standard Windows mode, your machine looks not so different from an old-faithful Windows 7 machine. In this mode, you can seamlessly run all of your existing Windows applications, since backward compatibility is fully guaranteed. As a user, in the end, you won't really experience a huge difference.

When a machine equipped with Windows 8 starts up, however, it is configured to operate in the new Windows 8 mode. This brings up a brand new dazzling user interface and makes available a different set of applications. In this mode, you won't find any of your old applications; however, all of your handmade, new Windows Store apps will be listed here (see Figure 5-1, for example).

Note Here's another way of looking at the two souls of Windows 8: You can consider the classic Windows desktop interface as just another application available in Windows 8 mode, except that this built-in application will offer you a view of your machine with the eyes of the Windows 7 operating system.

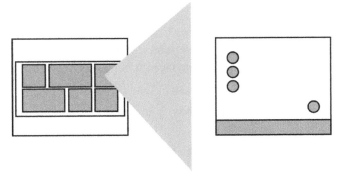

FIGURE 5-1 From Windows 8 back to the classic Windows user interface.

Fate of old-fashioned Windows applications

Windows applications that previously ran on Windows 7 can only be run in standard Windows mode for Windows 8. To have them available in the default Windows 8 user interface, they must be rewritten as Windows Store apps. For example, you can't use any of the Microsoft Office applications without getting and installing a Windows Store version of Microsoft Office. Similarly for browsers, both flavors of Windows 8 have their own version of Microsoft Internet Explorer.

In the end, Windows 8 doesn't break compatibility with the millions of applications available out there. It simply makes it clear that the future of the Windows platform goes in another direction.

Supported programming languages

You can write Windows Store applications in three main ways. You can use HTML and JavaScript, as you'll see in this book. In addition, you can write applications using the C# or Visual Basic programming language and the XAML markup language to specify the user interface. Finally, you can use the C++ language with XAML as the markup language to express the user interface.

All approaches deliver the same programming power. You can build the same application regardless of the language and markup you choose. For a number of reasons, JavaScript and HTML form the approach that makes it easier (but equally effective) for most developers, and especially for beginners.

 Note The fact that any supported programming language for the Windows 8 platform can be used to build any type of application is not a secondary point, and it stems from the overall architecture of the Windows 8 platform.

An overview of the WinRT API

With Windows 8, Microsoft makes an important move. This move is ultimately the reason for the two souls of Windows 8 and the need to distinguish between Windows Store applications and all other applications. Microsoft Windows 8 replaces the underlying layer through which the core of the operating system functions and is exposed to user applications.

The new infrastructure that backs up Windows Store applications is known as the Windows Runtime.

The Windows 8 stack

In Figure 5-2, you see the Windows 8 Runtime stack at a glance. The diagram shows how two parallel stacks can live side by side to support two different application development models—one centered on JavaScript and HTML and one on XAML and C# or Visual Basic. Notably, for clarity reasons the figure omits the third stack we mentioned earlier that is centered on C++ and XAML.

It is key to notice that both stacks rely upon the services of the WinRT application programming interface (API) which, in turn, is serviced by the operating system kernel. The kernel of an operating system is the core engine that provides basic functionality. To use a car analogy, if the WinRT API is the engine, then the kernel can be assimilated to the collection of essential components the engine is made of.

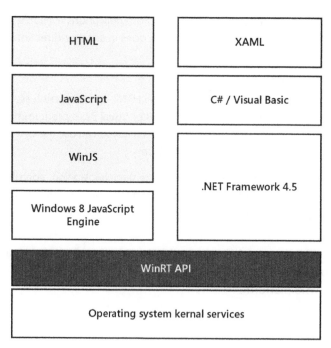

FIGURE 5-2 The Windows 8 stack.

The gray boxes indicate which parts of the stack are interesting for the scope of this book. You'll use HTML (and possibly CSS) to style the user interface and JavaScript to make it behave the way you like. Your interaction with the underlying operating system will actually be mediated by the WinJS library. Any Windows 8 application written with JavaScript will include the WinJS library and use its API to access functions such as storage, networking, graphics, and more.

Any code you write is compiled by the Windows 8 JavaScript engine and then run. Access to the WinRT subsystem occurs dynamically as the user interacts with the application. As you can see from Figure 5-2, WinRT supports all stacks: that's why there's nearly no functional difference between what applications written with JavaScript and C# can do.

Capabilities of the WinRT API

Figure 5-3 expands the black box labeled with the WinRT API name that you saw in Figure 5-2. Also, Figure 5-3 lists the classes of functions available to Windows 8 programmers.

To use a particular class of functions—for example to set up a network connection and download some RSS data from a remote URL—you just reference the appropriate JavaScript file in your application and start using the related functions.

The DirectX block refers to the underlying API that backs up advanced graphic capabilities of upper layers in the Windows 8 stack. Media and presentation blocks provide the infrastructure for image processing and manipulation, and multimedia and visual elements. Networking refers to the communication layer—most notably HTTP connections. Finally, storage is about the reading and writing of files and data, and the Devices block indicates the set of functions to control sensors and locally connected devices, such as printers.

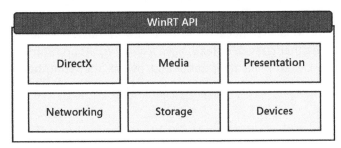

FIGURE 5-3 Class of functionality available in WinRT.

In the upcoming chapters, you'll take a tour of the various classes of functions and see how to take advantage of them in sample applications.

Aspects of the WinRT API

Any code that you write on top of the WinRT API using any of the supported development stacks (that is, HTML+JavaScript) will have some common aspects. These common aspects descend from the design and implementation of the underlying WinRT API and strongly characterize function calls you make through WinJS—your gateway to the low-level WinRT API.

For example, any functions expected to perform for longer than just a bunch of milliseconds have been designed to be asynchronous. This is a huge change for developers with some experience in

Windows development. An asynchronous function is a function that begins execution when invoked but has no well-defined timeline for termination.

In other words, an asynchronous function right after launch proceeds in parallel with any subsequent code. So a developer who needs to execute some code with the results of the asynchronous operation now has the problem of where to place this code. The shift towards asynchronous programming, however, is significantly mitigated by some new facilities available at the language level. In the end, all that you, as a beginning Windows 8 developer, need to learn is how to make a function call and how to grab its results. For former .NET developers, though, the asynchronous nature of the WinRT API might be an issue.

Another area of the WinRT API that deserves some early thoughts is storage and file access. In Windows Store applications, direct file access is restricted in the name of security. That doesn't mean, however, that you cannot permanently store data in a Windows Store application. More simply, the storage API that WinRT makes available doesn't give developers full control over the disk—as it is always the case for classic Windows applications. To open and save documents and files, you also have new file picker components that replace the standard common dialogs of Windows.

Note Developers of Windows Store applications find an overall programming framework (for example, WinJS for those who chose the HTML+ JavaScript stack) that looks a lot like the popular .NET Framework, but still has some key differences. These differences are clear signs of the overall commitment made by Microsoft to rework and reimagine the programming framework that Windows 8 developers deal with. As a result, some of the classes in the WinJS library are functionally identical to .NET Framework classes; some have only minor differences. Some other classes, instead, have a counterpart and some are just unavailable. Finally, some new classes make their debut and, overall, they contribute to making the developer's arsenal powerful enough to build effective and functional applications.

The Windows Store app user interface

Far beyond functionality, what really identifies an application as a Windows Store application is its user interface and the resulting user experience. The new user interface of Windows Store applications is known as the Windows 8 UI. This new revolutionary user interface results from the combination of features specific to the Windows 8 operating system with some innovative design principles. Let's find out more.

Aspects of the Windows 8 UI

If you stop at appearances, then the Windows 8 UI guidelines are just for new Windows Store applications and can't be adapted to Windows 7, web, and mobile apps to new Windows applications, even if developed and run specifically for Windows 8.

If you take a second, deeper look at the Windows 8 UI initiative, you can't help but recognize a bunch of universal design principles that describe concisely and precisely the vision behind software applications of the next years. You can conclude that there's substance behind the new look and feel.

The Windows 8 UI at a glance

Here's a quick list of aspects that strongly characterize the user interface of a Windows Store application. First and foremost, a Windows Store application is touch-enabled, but it is not limited to touch as the sole source of input. Support for touch is an aspect that enables the application to work smoothly on a tablet but also on a regular laptop or on a desktop computer equipped with a touch screen.

Second, a Windows Store application displays in a single, plain borderless window devoid of any adornment such as resizable borders, caption bar, and icons. This is definitely a breaking change with any previous version of Windows. At the same time, a Windows Store application adapts to the effective size and shape of the screen and can offer a fluid rendering experience. The content adapts intelligently to whatever layout the physical screen may have.

Finally, a Windows Store application integrates smoothly with the surrounding environment and will leverage new facilities, such as the App bar, Live tiles (a smart replacement for old-fashioned desktop icons), and the Charms bar (quick buttons to interact with other apps through well-known contracts). A Live tile, in particular, is a square block displayed in the Start screen of Windows 8 that references an installed application. What makes a tile "live" is the ability to display a little animation and content based on the data the application holds or the current state. Figure 5-4 displays the Charms bar; Figure 5-5 shows live tiles; and Figure 5-6 illustrates the App bar.

Charms bar

FIGURE 5-4 The Windows 8 Charms bar.

Live tiles

FIGURE 5-5 Examples of Windows 8 Live tiles.

FIGURE 5-6 The App bar of a Windows Store application.

Device-centric design

A Windows Store application presents itself fused to the design of the operating system and fully immersed in the surrounding environment. You can legitimately think that the design principles applied are then specific of the Windows 8 platform. It is instead a set of principles that, while developed to be applied to Windows 8 applications, are general enough to become source of inspiration for any software and platform that needs be device-centric.

Device-centric is a relatively new term that essentially revolves around the idea that design and functionality of an application should be based on the assumption that the application will run on a variety of different devices—different for screen size, memory capabilities, and programming power.

Inspiring principles of the Windows 8 UI

The Windows 8 UI is inspired by the following seven principles:

- Design for touch and intuitive interaction.

- Be responsive to user interaction and always ready for the next interaction.

- Reduce redundancy in your user interface.

- Fit into the existing UI model.

- Don't reinvent the wheel.

- Collaborate with other applications via contracts.

- Be aware of the clouds.

Extensive application of these principles can really make any applications—and not just upcoming Windows Store applications—much more virtuous and attractive.

> **Note** To understand why Windows 8 UI design principles are important, just consider that for too many years users of software applications have been forced to think and act following the rules of the application design. Regardless of best intentions, software did not take care of end users often enough. This is going to change, though; youngsters are going to be a much less forgiving generation of users than the current one. Be prepared to design applications that are fluid in the design—both graphical design and logical design. That's probably the only software that makes sense shortly. Thanks to the native user interface, Windows 8 is probably really making this easy.

So the question becomes: How would you turn these guidelines into concrete action?

Design for touch

Touch is what makes an application immediate to use, and it is the primary factor that sets the success of smartphones and tablets. Touch is, however, also a divider. If you invest in a user interface that's touch-based, then your software may not be able to run as smoothly on a non-touch device. So it is key that you never consider touch as the only source of input.

This means, for example, offering the mouse or keyboard to classic users and a touch screen to younger (or just more immediate) users. In this way, users may, say, pinch and stretch to zoom on some content on tablets and just click (or perhaps double-click) to get the same effect on laptops.

Be responsive and ready

Touch has been a quantum leap for user experience. It has had the side effect of making another aspect of user experience even more important—responsiveness. As the user taps and "touches" visual elements, she expects them to react quickly, such as other objects in the real world. Try lightly tapping an object on the edge of the table; if the touch was perceived and detected, well, the object falls down immediately: it doesn't display an hourglass and then fall down a few seconds later.

Beyond touch and responsiveness, intuitiveness of the interaction is also critical. A goal of the application should be making it clear for users at any stage what the next operations are. This apparently basic point has nontrivial implications on design of the user interface and organization of the data and logic.

Zero redundancy

For many years, redundancy in the user interface of an application has been considered a good thing. You define a user interface as redundant if it allows performing the same task in more than one way. Keyboard and mouse navigation, slightly different menu items (such as, Save, Save All, Save As), and keyboard shortcuts all produce the same result in many applications you may use currently.

In a user interface that is essentially touch-based, all these methods have no reason to exist. Subsequently, the zero redundancy policy is a great virtue of Windows Store applications.

This is a design consideration that also emerges quite clearly in many successful mobile applications and is tightly connected to a growing need for simplicity and effectiveness—like being able to do more things (or just the same things) with less options and less tools.

Do as Romans do

Another pillar of software development of the past that the Windows 8 UI brings into question is the overall user interface model. For various reasons, some applications made a point of providing a custom user interface. Sometimes this has happened to make the application shine in comparison to other applications of the same type. Sometimes, instead, it came as the result of trying to make the application in some way more usable and enjoyable.

Any application in Windows 8 should take its own space in the context of the user interface model dictated by the platform. For this reason, the fourth principle of Windows 8 applications can be summarized with the old proverb that suggests doing as Romans do, at least when you're in Rome. Also, this principle is nothing new to anybody with a bit of experience in mobile application development.

Especially in iOS and Windows Phone markets, applications may be rejected if they provide a user interface that clashes with guidelines. You take the same risk with Windows Store apps.

Do as Romans do (and don't reinvent the wheel)

The fifth principle of Windows Store applications is a tricky corollary of the fourth. It just strengthens the importance of giving applications a user interface that fits well with the system's user interface. Not only do you want to make apps consistent with the system, but you also want to achieve that by using tools and templates offered by the Windows 8 stack of choice.

For this reason, you'll be using extensively the aforementioned WinJS library in the upcoming chapters. WinJS is the repository of the native tools for building Windows Store applications with HTML and JavaScript. You'll find an introduction to the library in the next section.

Collaborate (and don't reinvent the wheel)

Full integration with the host platform is a winning point of any Windows Store application, as it allows users to feel at home with just about any application. Furthermore, it also enables distinct applications to interact and exchange data.

The sixth principle can then be summarized by saying that applications may rely on public services exposed by other applications in order to implement their functionality. Windows Store applications may import functions from other applications via contracts. A *contract* is a formalized API for applications to invoke functions from other applications. This saves you from rewriting the same functions over and over, and at the same time, it brings users to the same action in mostly the same way.

For example, Windows Store applications can support the system-defined *Search* contract to retrieve information from other applications and implement the *Share* contract to expose their content publicly.

Above us only cloud

Finally, the seventh principle probably needs no further explanation. Local disks are no longer and not necessarily the only place to save and read data. To ensure a continuous feel between the user and the application, for years developers used to save personal data to cookies and local settings. The cloud just adds another dimension by publishing personal data and making that information available to others for social software interaction. Here the cloud indicates user-specific or even application-specific storage that lives on some remote server that is publicly accessible.

Components for the presentation layer

The WinJS library is a library made of JavaScript objects expressly designed to provide easy access to core Windows 8 features and subsequently simplify the development of Windows Store applications with JavaScript.

WinJS consists of two main parts: a collection of behavioral objects to deal with core tasks such as storage, networking, multimedia, and application lifecycle, and a set of widgets for user interface arrangements. You'll use both parts of the WinJS library in the rest of the book. Anyway, it is helpful to have an overall vision of the visual widgets you can quickly incorporate in your applications as building blocks.

Visual elements of WinJS

Table 5-1 provides a view of the visual elements you find in the WinJS library. You will compose the user interface of your future Windows Store applications by integrating one or more of these components in an HTML template.

TABLE 5-1 WinJS widgets

Widget	Description
AppBar	Displays a horizontal command bar that is usually placed at the bottom of the window.
DatePicker	Pops up a calendar and enables the user to pick up a date.
FlipView	Displays a collection of items and allows a user to flip through them, displaying one at a time. A typical example can be displaying pictures and captions with the ability to flip through them horizontally.

Widget	Description
Flyout	Displays a simple popup message that disappears only when the user touches (or clicks) anywhere on the screen.
ListView	Arranges a collection of items in a variety of layouts; for example, as a grid or as a list.
HtmlControl	Displays any content provided in the HTML format.
Menu	Displays a flyout that looks like a standard menu list.
PageControl	An aggregate of HTML, JavaScript, and CSS that can be embedded as in a view or navigated to as an external page. You use the PageControl element to define the aggregate.
SemanticZoom	Enables the user to zoom between two different views of the same content. One view is the zoomed-out representation of the content; the other instead provides the zoomed-in view.
TimePicker	Enables the user to select a time in a graphically appealing way.
ToggleSwitch	Displays a standard user interface for users to turn an item on or off.
Tooltip	Displays a pop-up view that can incorporate rich content, such as images and formatted text. The purpose of a tooltip is to provide additional but optional information over a data element in the view.
ViewBox	Elements displayed within a ViewBox automatically scale to fill the available space. The ViewBox widget also reacts to changes in the size of the container, such as after a screen rotation or a window resize.

These visual components cover a good number of common scenarios; you can expect to find more readymade Windows Store visual components from third-party vendors, open-source projects, and blog posts. As you get more and more familiar with Windows 8 development, you can even start creating your own widgets. Having a widget to provide a given functionality just makes it far easier to reuse it across multiple pages and applications.

Important You mostly write Windows Store applications using HTML and CSS to define the user interface. Anything you can do with HTML and CSS is fine. Stock visual elements listed in Table 5-1 just help you in making available useful components and in giving your applications an overall consistent look and feel.

On-demand user interface

It should be clear by now that Windows 8 provides a few standard ways for users to access features in an application. There are static commands bound to fixed elements in the user interface (such as, buttons) and dynamic commands that become available on demand.

By using the principle of on-demand UI, you aim at leaving the real estate of the application as clean and tidy as possible and not at all overloaded with visual items. At the same time, items required to trigger commands and start operations show up on demand when the user seems to need them. The App bar and the system's Charms bar are the mechanisms provided by Windows 8 for on-demand UI. The App bar is a repository of an application's commands that pops up as the user moves towards the bottom of the screen. The Charms bar slides in from the right edge.

Charms provide a common way for users to get to the features of nearly every application; for example, search, share, and access to files. The App bar, instead, contains application-specific commands and is expected to list commands that make sense for the current view only.

Creating a sample app bar

To get familiar with WinJS programming, here's a quick taste of what it means to create an *AppBar* in a Windows Store application. As first step, you need some HTML markup to host the *AppBar*. Most WinJS visual components just take an HTML segment and transform it into something else. You can create a new blank project and edit the *default.html* page to contain the following code:

```
<!DOCTYPE html>
<html>
<head>
    <meta charset="utf-8" />
    <title>My AppBar</title>

    <!-- WinJS references -->
    <link href="//Microsoft.WinJS.1.0/css/ui-dark.css" rel="stylesheet" />
    <script src="//Microsoft.WinJS.1.0/js/base.js"></script>
    <script src="//Microsoft.WinJS.1.0/js/ui.js"></script>

    <!-- MyAppBar references -->
    <link href="/css/default.css" rel="stylesheet" />
    <script src="/js/default.js"></script>
</head>
<body>
    <h1 id="header">
        Sample page using an app-bar.
    </h1>
    <hr />
    <div id="yourAppBar" data-win-control="WinJS.UI.AppBar" data-win-options="">
        <button data-win-control="WinJS.UI.AppBarCommand"
                data-win-options="{id:'cmdAdd',label:'Add',icon:'add'}">
        </button>
        <button data-win-control="WinJS.UI.AppBarCommand"
                data-win-options="{id:'cmdRemove',label:'Remove',icon:'remove'}">
        </button>
        <hr data-win-control="WinJS.UI.AppBarCommand"
            data-win-options="{type:'separator',section:'global'}" />
        <button data-win-control="WinJS.UI.AppBarCommand"
                data-win-options="{id:'cmdDelete',label:'Delete',icon:'delete'}">
        </button>
        <button data-win-control="WinJS.UI.AppBarCommand"
                data-win-options="{id:'cmdCamera',label:'Camera',icon:'camera'}">
        </button>
```

```
            </div>
        </body>
    </html>
```

The body of the previous page includes a plain *DIV* and a few *BUTTON* elements. The magic that transforms this markup into an *AppBar* in pure Windows 8 style is the *data-win-control* attribute.

Applied to the *DIV* tag, the attribute transforms it into a *WinJS.UI.AppBar* object—namely an AppBar. Likewise, applied to a *BUTTON* element it makes it a button on the AppBar or an object of type *WinJS.UI.AppBarCommand*. The *data-win-options* attribute contains settings for control. For example, an *AppBar* button is assigned a unique ID, a label, and an icon. To display an AppBar, you either swipe up from the bottom of the screen or right-click the application's screen. Finally, you can achieve the same outcome by pressing the Windows button and Z.

What about some action to be performed when the user clicks a button?

The HTML for the layout you have just entered serves the purpose of defining the layout of the bar. To add a behavior, you also need some JavaScript. You edit the *default.js* file in the project, as shown below:

```javascript
(function () {
    "use strict";

    WinJS.Binding.optimizeBindingReferences = true;

    var app = WinJS.Application;
    var activation = Windows.ApplicationModel.Activation;

    app.onactivated = function (args) {
        if (args.detail.kind === activation.ActivationKind.launch) {
            if (args.detail.previousExecutionState !==
                activation.ApplicationExecutionState.terminated) {
                // Load application state if needed
            } else {
                // Restore application state here.
            }
            args.setPromise(WinJS.UI.processAll()
                .then(init()));
        }
    };

    app.oncheckpoint = function (args) {
        // This application is about to be suspended.
    };

    app.start();
})();
```

```
// Button functions
function doClickAdd() {
    var alertDialog = new Windows.UI.Popups.MessageDialog("Add button clicked!");
    alertDialog.showAsync();
}

function init() {
    var page = WinJS.UI.Pages.define("default.html", {
        ready: function (element, options) {
            document.getElementById("cmdAdd").addEventListener("click", doClickAdd,
false);
        }
    });
}
```

Expressed as an immediate function, the code defines a page and a few event handlers for it. When the page is ready for user interaction, for example, the code associated with the *ready* event runs. All it does is add a handler to the click event of each of the previously defined buttons. Let's examine, in detail, the code for the click event:

```
document.getElementById("cmdAdd").addEventListener("click", doClickAdd);
```

First, the code retrieves the HTML element in the page whose ID equals the string *cmdAdd*. This HTML element is added as an event listener for the "click" event. An *event listener* is a piece of JavaScript code that is automatically run when the user triggers the specified event—for example, clicks or taps the button. In this case, the click of the button labeled "Add" runs the *doClickAdd* function. In particular, the *doClickAdd* function displays a message, as shown in Figure 5-7.

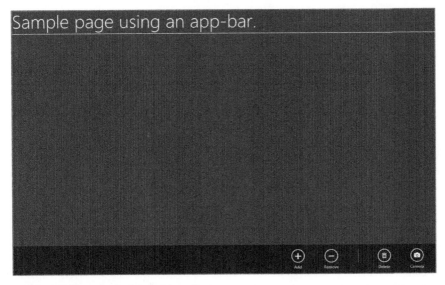

FIGURE 5-7 The sample App bar in action.

> **Note** In its simplicity, this example is quite illustrative of the patterns you'll be applying in all of the remaining chapters. Each of the upcoming chapters, in fact, will provide a list of exercises through which you will practice the various aspects of Windows 8 programming using HTML and JavaScript.

Data binding

In Chapter 1, you built your first Windows 8 application and had it generate a random number. At some point, once the number was generated, you had the problem of displaying the number to the user. When it comes to this, a first option is using the WinJS logger through the *WinJS.log* method, as shown earlier. The WinJS logger, however, is good for testing but not for real applications, since it shows the output only within Visual Studio.

Another option is using a message box, namely a pop-up window that shows some text and needs to be closed manually by the user by clicking one of the displayed buttons. Although sometimes effective, this approach is also much too obtrusive for the user. It is good for asking questions; rarely for showing data. Most of the time, you just want the application to generate some output values and silently display them through the existing user interface. In other words, you want data bound to the existing user interface.

Programmatic manipulation of the HTML page

A Windows Store application written with HTML and JavaScript is primarily an application that consists of webpages—just processed in a slightly different manner from what a classic browser would do. Because of this, a Windows Store application can contain any JavaScript-related code that would make sense to have on a webpage.

When a browser renders a webpage, it creates an in-memory representation of the content so that each and every HTML element turns out to be a programmable object. The in-memory representation is known as the *Document Object Model,* or DOM for short.

You retrieve objects within an HTML page using the following line of code:

```
var element = document.getElementById("id-of-the-element");
```

The parameter passed to the method *getElementById* is the unique ID of the element to retrieve. More complex query expressions can be arranged using the syntax for CSS selectors, as you learned in Chapter 3, "Making sense of CSS." In this case, the code to use looks like the one shown below:

```
// Query for multiple elements
var elements = document.querySelectorAll("your-css-expression");

// Query for just one element by stopping at first match
var element = document.querySelector("your-css-expression");
```

Once you have found the element to update, you can change its content by setting the *innerHtml* property to any string that can optionally contain HTML markup. The code below retrieves an element named *header* and sets its content to the string "Hello," which will be rendered as bold text.

```
var element = document.getElementById("header");
element.innerHtml = "<b>Hello</b>";
```

This pattern represents a programmatic way to update the user interface with calculated data. The approach that is based on direct updates of the DOM is extremely fast, but works well only if you want to update specific elements. Scenarios where you have multiple elements to display—for example, a list—or multiple pieces of data to display on different elements are not served well by this approach.

Note By using the *innerText* property, instead of *innerHtml*, you just set the plain text of the HTML element without touching any markup or style. In a way, using *innerText* is safer, since with it you don't take any risk of altering the existing graphical structure.

Declarative manipulation of the HTML page

The WinJS library also supports a declarative form of updating HTML elements, known as data binding. Let's see how it works. Create a new blank Windows 8 project and edit the *BODY* of the *default.html* page to make it look like the code below:

```
<!DOCTYPE html>
<html>
<head>
    <meta charset="utf-8" />
    <title>DataBinding</title>

    <!-- WinJS references -->
    <link href="//Microsoft.WinJS.1.0/css/ui-dark.css" rel="stylesheet" />
    <script src="//Microsoft.WinJS.1.0/js/base.js"></script>
    <script src="//Microsoft.WinJS.1.0/js/ui.js"></script>

    <!-- DataBinding references -->
    <link href="/css/default.css" rel="stylesheet" />
    <script src="/js/default.js"></script>
</head>
<body>
    <header>
        <h2>Start Here! Build <b>Windows 8</b> Applications with <b>HTML5</b> and
            <b>JavaScript</b></h2>
        <hr />
        <p>Random number displayed via data-binding.</p>
    </header>
```

```
    <div class="center">
        <span id="numberContainer" data-win-bind="innerText: generatedValue"></span>
    </div>

    <div class="center">
        <input id="numberButton" type="button" value="Get Number" />
    </div>

    <footer>
        <hr />
        Dino Esposito | Francesco Esposito
    </footer>
</body>
</html>
```

The *SPAN* element is decorated with the *data-win-bind* attribute. Properly interpreted by the Windows 8 runtime, this attribute does the magic of setting the content of the element via the *innerText* property. What is the *generatedValue* string you see in the code snippet then? The idea is generating a random number and displaying it through the user interface.

Even though you can bind any kind of data to an HTML element, including single pieces of data such as a string or a number, it is likely that you will need to do that for compound objects resulting from a mix of text, numbers, and dates. Let's then assume you have a JavaScript object to describe the data to bind. Add the following script to the bottom of *default.js* file:

```
// Gets an object embedding a random number between 1 and 100
function displayGeneratedNumber() {
    var randomNumber = { generatedValue: Math.floor((Math.random()*100)+1) };

    // more code needed here
}
```

You now have a JavaScript object with a property name *generatedValue* that contains a random generated number comprised between 1 and 100. In light of this, the following markup gets a bit more significance:

```
<span id="numberContainer" data-win-bind="innerText: generatedValue"></span>
```

The string *generatedValue* is an expression that refers to the value you intend to assign to the *innerText* property. But there's one more aspect to clarify: How can the Windows 8 runtime know about the object that exposes the *generatedValue* property? You need to get back to *default.js* and rework the *displayGeneratedNumber* function a bit:

```
// Gets an object embedding a random number between 1 and 100
function displayGeneratedNumber() {
```

```
    var randomNumber = { generatedValue: Math.floor((Math.random()*100)+1) };

    // Enable binding on the HTML element of choice
    var bindableElement = document.getElementById("numberContainer");
    WinJS.Binding.processAll(bindableElement, randomNumber);
}
```

The two lines you added tell the Windows 8 runtime environment that the element named *numberContainer*—the *SPAN* element—should be processed and bound to any content it can get from the object *randomNumber*. At this point, the markup below now has full significance:

```
<span id="numberContainer" data-win-bind="innerText: generatedValue"></span>
```

The property *innerText* of the SPAN element named *numberContainer* will display the value assigned to the property *generatedValue* of bound object *randomNumber*. Is that all? Well, not yet.

The missing link is when the code written in *default.js* will actually run. For this, you need one more edit to *default.js*. You edit the line that calls *setPromise*, as shown below:

```
app.onactivated = function (args) {
    if (args.detail.kind === activation.ActivationKind.launch) {
        if (args.detail.previousExecutionState !==
            activation.ApplicationExecutionState.terminated) {
            // Initialize your application here.
            document.addEventListener("DOMContentLoaded", displayGeneratedNumber);
        } else {
            // Restore application state here.
        }
        args.setPromise(WinJS.UI.processAll()
            .then(init()));
    }
};
```

Next, you also add a new custom function called *init* at the bottom of the *default.js* file.

```
function init() {
    document.getElementById("numberButton").addEventListener("click",
numberButtonClick);
}
```

Are there any lessons you can learn from this example?

First and foremost, data binding is a powerful mechanism that unfolds all of its power when you really manage enough complexity. Using declarative data binding when you only need to display one piece of data is probably overkill. In this case, direct use of *innerHtml* is preferable. When you have a list of items or multiple pieces of a single data item, then declarative data binding is preferable because all you do is manage your variegated data as an object, add an attribute to markup, and adjust a few lines of code to trigger binding.

Important Windows 8 data binding is just one of the services you get out of the box with the WinJS library. You are not forced to use the Windows 8 framework for data binding. It is probably easiest if you have no knowledge of web development. However, if you are already familiar with web development and libraries, such as Knockout (or some jQuery plugins), then you can just import these libraries and do data binding through their infrastructure. In summary, any approach you may know for data binding works in WinJS. If not, you can always use the excellent WinJS native data binding infrastructure.

Note In this chapter, you only scratched the surface of data binding and barely explored a very basic scenario. In the upcoming chapters, you'll learn how to bind complex objects and a list of items to the user interface through the WinJS rich infrastructure.

Understanding the application's lifecycle

Any application in Windows 8 is characterized by a sequence of events that signal start, load and finish of the application. Knowing more about these events that collectively form the application's lifecycle is key, since it may lead to introducing optimizations in the code and producing a better behavior, especially when your Windows 8 application runs on devices. A device, in fact, is hardly as powerful as a laptop in terms of processing power, battery, and memory.

States of a Windows Store application

As Windows 8 is an operating system also devised to run on mobile devices, it can't just ignore a basic rule of mobile operating systems. On mobile devices, the user launches an application but never terminates it. Once launched, the application is kind of owned by the operating system and its lifetime is managed by the operating system.

All Windows Store applications can be in one of the following four states: running, suspended, terminated, or just not running. Transitions between these states are determined by the user and system activity, as illustrated in Figure 5-8.

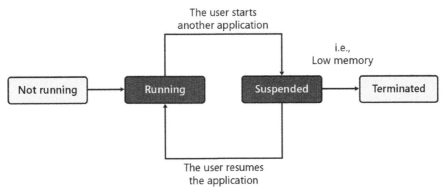

FIGURE 5-8 States of a Windows Store application.

Launching an application

There are quite a few ways for the user to launch the application. The most common way is that the user launches the application from a tile—the Windows 8 counterpart of an icon or shortcut. Another possibility for the application to be launched is when the user searches for some data that the application has exposed or when the user shares data with the application. Both tasks are usually accomplished through items in the Charms bar. Finally, yet another possibility is that the application gets launched because the user opened a file associated with the application.

Starting an application always causes an *activated* event to be fired by WinJS that you can handle through the aforementioned *onactivated* event:

```
app.onactivated = function (args) {
  ...
}
```

Most of the time, you need to do some work during the *activated* event. For example, you check the application's previous state and take appropriate actions. The following code is part of any WinJS-based application and provides a placeholder where you then add any initialization code you may have. Upon launch, you typically load default data.

```
app.onactivated = function (args) {
    if (args.detail.kind === activation.ActivationKind.launch) {
        if (args.detail.previousExecutionState !==
            activation.ApplicationExecutionState.terminated) {
            // Initialize your application here.
        } else {
            ...
        }

        // Trigger data binding (if any) throughout the page
        args.setPromise(WinJS.UI.processAll());
    }
};
```

A short note is worth mentioning about the *setPromise* method you see in the code snippet. The method informs the application that some asynchronous work is in progress. The method that hosts *setPromise* can't then be exited until the pending work is completed. However, processing continues up to the end of the containing method. This creates the problem of how you can reliably decide what to do once the pending work—also referred to as the promise—has terminated. The promise object in WinJS has the *then* method that you use to specify any work to do upon completion of the promise. Here's an example:

```
args.setPromise(WinJS.UI.processAll()
    .then(function() { ... })
);
```

Another similar method also exists, named *done*. The difference between *done* and *then* is only that *then* returns another promise object, whereas *done* doesn't return any value.

```
args.setPromise(WinJS.UI.processAll()
    .then(function() { ... })
    .then(function() { ... })
    .done(function() { ... })
);
```

In summary, they do the same work but *done* can only be used at the end of a chain of actions.

Suspending an application

In Windows 8, only one application at a time can be active in the foreground. If the user switches to a new application, then Windows 8 suspends the currently running application and moves it to the background. The suspended application remains in memory even though its code doesn't run. The checkpoint event is fired to the application when it is about to be suspended. Here's how you can handle the event:

```
app.oncheckpoint = function (args) {
  // Save app data in case of termination.
  WinJS.Application.sessionState["location"] = ...;
};
```

During suspension you want to save any data that can help later to reconfigure a state of the application very closely, if not identical, to the state when the application was suspended. You use the *sessionState* dictionary to save values. The *sessionState* dictionary has a list of named entries—for example, location, and takes string values. The name of entries is arbitrary, but usually an indicator of the role of the saved data.

The user can switch back to a suspended application at any time; when this happens Windows just wakes up the application, which regains the foreground at the expense of the current application.

A suspended application is cached in memory for as long as it is possible, but it is not guaranteed to stay in memory indefinitely. It may happen that, perhaps running short of memory, Windows terminates suspended applications. In this case, the user can only restart the application from the tile if she wants it back.

Resuming an application

There's a simple way for a developer to detect whether the application is being run from a tile or a charm or if it is resumed from a suspended state. The *activated* event is fired and the *ActivationKind* property is set to *launch*. In addition, if the *previousExecutionState* is set to *terminated*, then the application has been reactivated from suspension. When recovering from suspension, you might want to retrieve and restore any saved state. The saved state is commonly retrieved from the *sessionState* dictionary or from wherever it was stored during suspension. The code below shows where you insert code during resumption.

```
app.onactivated = function (args) {
    if (args.detail.kind === activation.ActivationKind.launch) {
        if (args.detail.previousExecutionState !==
            activation.ApplicationExecutionState.terminated) {
            // Initialize your application here.
    } else {
            // Restore application state here.
            var data = WinJS.Application.sessionState["location"];
            ...
    }
        args.setPromise(WinJS.UI.processAll());
    }
};
```

Using the *sessionState* dictionary to save data is not mandatory. You can save session data to some persistent store or you can just find it acceptable that the application restarts with a fresh state every time. It is mostly up to you, but saving to session state is the most common approach.

Background tasks

In Windows 8, as well as in other mobile platforms, you can have background tasks to perform non-UI related tasks, such as transfer of data.

A background task is a lightweight class that is associated with a given application and runs periodically while the application is not running. A background task can be linked to a condition and will not run until the condition is met.

A background task is also able to display information on the Lock screen. The Lock screen of a Windows 8 application contains a background image and some information is rendered over that such as the current time, the network status, and battery power. In addition, a background task can write some specific text to the lock screen just to provide a quick update about its status.

Summary

This chapter ends the first part of the book, where you essentially built the base groundwork for the rest of the book and for your journey toward Windows Store applications. Now you should be familiar with HTML and CSS, and know enough of the JavaScript language to make sense of the WinJS specialized components you meet in the next chapters.

Chapter 6

The user interface of Windows Store applications

Be great in act, as you have been in thought.

—William Shakespeare

With this chapter, you enter a section of the book that focuses on concrete examples and exercises of Windows 8 programming. You'll see how to use specific components and functions of Microsoft Windows 8, and also explore a few techniques for producing code that not only "just works," but is also easy to read and well structured. In this chapter, you'll focus primarily on presentation—the user interface—and related aspects, such as visual components, input forms, pop-up windows, and the overall layout of the pages.

> **Important** Readability is an attribute of code that's not just reserved for experts—it is, instead, an attitude that you can learn to adopt right at the beginning of your programming career. Keeping all your code readable will help you immediately, as you'll see the first time you return to your code after a break of a few days or weeks.

Foundation of Windows Store applications

When you open up Microsoft Visual Studio with the intention of creating a new Windows Store application, you must first decide on the type of project you want to create. Visual Studio provides a range of choices, called "templates." Templates, among other things, provide a basic layout for your application (see Figure 6-1).

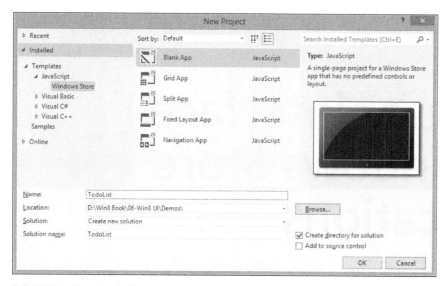

FIGURE 6-1 Choosing the layout of a new application.

Choosing the project type is important, but it is not an essential step. The template basically serves the purpose of giving you (for free) the skeleton of an application with the layout that you are looking for. Most of the project choices come down to whether you want to build a single page or a multiple page application.

For all the sample applications you've built so far, you have used the Blank App template. The Blank App template just gives you an empty HTML page that you can fill up with whatever content and behavior you like. In this regard, the Blank App is the most flexible approach. It doesn't give you a complex page layout, but it does give you a fully functioning project, ready to compile and run.

Defining the layout of the application

Nearly any Windows Store application requires users to navigate between pages. Sometimes, the application explicitly provides a navigation menu so users can find and return to a list of available pages quickly. The Navigation App template that you see in Figure 6-1 addresses that scenario.

In other cases, an application doesn't have a clearly visible navigation bar but still sets up a form of navigation as the user clicks to expand an item from a list into a more detailed view. This is the type of application skeleton you get if you opt to use the Split App or the Grid App template. In upcoming chapters, you'll work on examples using the Grid App template, but for now you'll stick to the Blank App project template.

Examining the project structure

Open up Visual Studio and create a new Blank App project; name it **TodoList**. The main purpose of the exercise is to create an input form to collect information about an activity to track. Figure 6-2 shows the entire content of the newly created project in Solution Explorer.

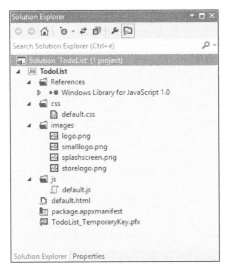

FIGURE 6-2 The files that form the *TodoList* project.

The *References* folder contains the list of libraries required to compile the application. In this case, the only library you need is the by-now-familiar WinJS library.

The *Css* folder contains the style sheets for styling the various HTML pages you use in your application. You can expect to have one CSS file per each page you add to the project.

The *Images* folder is the repository for all image files you need. This includes images you display to the user that are part of the interface, as well as images required to integrate the application into the Windows 8 and Windows Store environments. Table 6-1 explains what each of the *.png* image files in Figure 6-2 are used for.

TABLE 6-1 Purpose of the images in the default project template

Image file	Purpose
Logo.png	This is the image that appears in the tile that is reserved for the application in the Start screen. You can provide this image in either *.png* or *.jpg* format. The recommended size is 150 x 150 pixels. Windows usually overlays the name of the application onto the image; so you might want to consider not including the application's name in the image.
SmallLogo.png	This is the image used to represent the application in search results. The format can be either *.png* or *.jpg*, and the recommended size is 30 x 30 pixels.
SplashScreen.png	This is the image displayed for a relatively short period of time while the application loads after having been launched by the user. The format can be either *.png* or *.jpg*, and the recommended size is 620 x 300 pixels.
StoreLogo.png	This the image used to represent the application in the Windows Store. The format can be either *.png* or *.jpg*, and the recommended size is 50 x 50 pixels.

You may wish to provide additional images as well, such as a *WideLogo.png* image, to provide a larger logo file—up to 310 x 150 pixels. Finally, the *BadgeLogo.png* file is a small image (usually 33 x 33 pixels) displayed on the Lock screen of a Windows 8 device to identify pending notifications from your application.

The *Js* folder contains the JavaScript files that contain any logic required by the application. You usually have one JavaScript file per HTML page in the project, but you may also have additional JavaScript files shared by multiple pages in the project.

The root folder of the project contains three files, as summarized in Table 6-2.

TABLE 6-2 Purpose of the files in the root folder of the project template

File	Purpose
default.html	This HTML page is expected to define the home screen of the application.
Package.appxmanifest	This file contains all the information required to package your Windows Store application for distribution.
Xxx_TemporaryKey.pfx	This file represents a temporary certificate automatically issued for testing the application on your development machine. The *Xxx* in the name is actually a placeholder for the real name of the application. The certificate is used to sign any executable resulting from the project. When the application is complete, you will need to replace this test certificate with a real one obtained from your Windows Store account. Getting a real certificate is a required step for publishing your application to the public store.

These files form the bare minimum set of files you need in a Windows Store application. As you build the application, you will typically create custom folders in the project and add more files of all the types you'll need: more HTML pages, more style sheets, more JavaScript files, and more images.

The next step of the exercise consists of making some changes to the basic user interface to obtain a form for defining the items that will go in the to-do list.

Examining standard style and script references

If you double-click the *default.html* file and open it for editing, you will notice the following markup:

```
<!- WinJS references ->
<link href="//Microsoft.WinJS.1.0/css/ui-dark.css" rel="stylesheet" />
<script src="//Microsoft.WinJS.1.0/js/base.js"></script>
<script src="//Microsoft.WinJS.1.0/js/ui.js"></script>
```

As the comment at the top seems to suggest, these are not usual references to external resources you find in nearly any HTML page. These are special references to style sheet and script files natively embedded in the WinJS library. You will not have any of those files available as source code in your project; yet these files are extracted at run time from the resources of the WinJS library.

It should be noted that you can give your Windows Store application an overall light theme by simply replacing the *link* element in the code above with the following:

```
<link href="//Microsoft.WinJS.1.0/css/ui-light.css" rel="stylesheet" />
```

Any additional CSS or script file you want to reference will go under the next section.

```
<!- TodoList references ->
```

```
<link href="/css/default.css" rel="stylesheet" />
<script src="/js/default.js"></script>
```

In this case, /css and /js refer to the physical folders in your current project.

Adding fixed user interface blocks

The sample application you get from the Blank App template has a dark background and simply displays some placeholder text. You might want to customize your application in a number of ways—for example, by adding a header and footer bar. Here are the header and footer that you used in previous examples:

```
<header>
  Start Here! Build <b>Windows 8</b> Applications with <b>HTML5</b> and
<b>JavaScript</b>
  <hr />
</header>

<footer>
  <hr />
  Dino Esposito | Francesco Esposito
</footer>
```

As an exercise, let's make these components reusable so that you can save them in a page and reference the page wherever needed without worrying about the internal details.

The first step consists of creating a new custom folder in the project. You right-click the project node (named *TodoList*) and from the subsequent menu select the Add | New Folder option. Name the new folder **Pages.**

 Note When creating a new folder, if you accidentally miss editing the folder name, then you likely find a new folder in the project named "New Folder." No worries; you just click it for a while (sort of a long click where you hold the mouse button down for about a second). That will switch the project item into edit mode again, at which point just type **Pages,** and click outside the text box to save your change.

To add a reusable block of HTML, you now right-click the *Pages* node in the Visual Studio Solution Explorer and select Add | New Item from the context menu. From the window shown in Figure 6-3, you then select HTML Page and name it **header.html.** Next, repeat the steps and create a second HTML Page named **footer.html.**

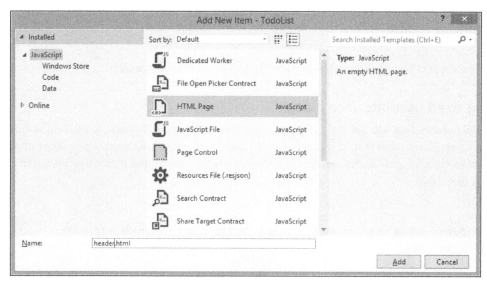

FIGURE 6-3 Adding a new HTML Page component.

Both newly added HTML files have the same content, as shown below:

```
<!DOCTYPE html>
<html>
    <head>
        <title></title>
    </head>
    <body>
    </body>
</html>
```

Edit the content of *header.html,* as shown below:

```
<!DOCTYPE html>
<html>
    <head>
        <title></title>
    </head>
    <body>
      <header>
        Start Here! Build <b>Windows 8</b> Applications with <b>HTML5</b> and
        <b>JavaScript</b>
        <hr />
      </header>
    </body>
</html>
```

Then edit the content of *footer.html*, as shown below:

```html
<!DOCTYPE html>
<html>
    <head>
        <title></title>
    </head>
    <body>
    <footer>
        <hr />
        Dino Esposito | Francesco Esposito
    </footer>
</body>
</html>
```

Save your changes.

The next step consists of referencing your new header and footer elements from the main page—*default.html*. So open *default.html* for editing and modify the *BODY* tag, as shown below:

```html
<body>
    <div data-win-control="WinJS.UI.HtmlControl"
        data-win-options="{uri:'/pages/header.html'}"></div>
    <h1>TO-DO List</h1>
    <div data-win-control="WinJS.UI.HtmlControl"
        data-win-options="{uri:'/pages/footer.html'}"></div>
</body>
```

The *data-win-control* attribute transforms the *DIV* into an HTML control that simply shows the content of the referenced file, namely *header.html*. The same happens for *footer.html*.

Back in Chapter 1, "Using Visual Studio 2012 Express edition," you added a bit of color and style to *default.css*; do the same here, and edit the *default.css* file, as shown below:

```css
body {
    background-color: #1649AD;
    padding: 10px;
}
header {
    font-size: x-large;
    color: #ffffff;
    padding-bottom: 50px;
}
footer {
    padding-top: 50px;
    font-size: large;
    color: #eeee00;
```

```
        font-weight: bold;
}
```

The *default.css* file contains the style information for the *default.html* page. If you want to reuse the same style settings in another page—for example, *mypage.html*—then you could copy *default.css* settings to a new file called *mypage.css*. That works, but there should be a better way of achieving the same results (and there is).

As in Figure 6-4, right-click the *Css* project folder and select Add | New Item. From the next window, select the Style Sheet item and name it after the project—in this case, name it **todolist.css**. Copy the content of the *body, header,* and *footer* CSS classes to your new *todolist.css* file.

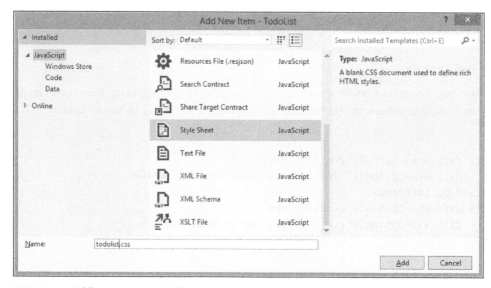

FIGURE 6-4 Adding a custom CSS file.

At this point, you have a global CSS file where you plan to store all global style sheet settings; in addition, you have a page-specific CSS file where you need only those CSS styles that affect elements in that specific page. To make the global CSS file visible to any page, you need to add an extra line in all the pages that represent an application screen. So far, you just need to do that for *default.html*.

```
<!- TodoList references ->
<link href="/css/todolist.css" rel="stylesheet" />
<link href="/css/default.css" rel="stylesheet" />
```

You can run the application now and it should look similar to Figure 6-5. Admittedly, this is still a fairly scanty application, but at least you have learned a couple of very useful techniques for reusing markup and style.

Start Here! Build **Windows 8** Applications with **HTML5** and **JavaScript**

TO-DO List

Dino Esposito | Francesco Esposito

FIGURE 6-5 The current stage of the TodoList application.

Application attributes

Before adding some interaction to the sample application, you need to dedicate a few moments to some configuration steps that are simple but required for any Windows Store applications—review your manifest, logos, and splash screen.

The manifest file

Visual Studio creates an application manifest file automatically when you create a new Windows Store project. The file contains the application's name and description, logos, and other basic information—such as the start page of the application. The manifest file is initially set to some default values that you might want to change at some point. Visual Studio provides a convenient editor so you can make the required changes easily. Figure 6-6 shows the editor; to enable it, you just double-click the *package.appxmanifest* file in the project folder.

The attributes you can specify are grouped by functional areas. For now, focus on the Application UI tab. The display name is the official name of the application as it will be displayed in the store and within Windows 8 menus—for example, the Start screen. The start page is set to *default.html* by default; to change it you just create a new page or rename the existing page and then edit the manifest accordingly. Along with the default language and description, you can also select which rotations are supported (for when the application is running on a tablet) and logo images.

In addition, the manifest file contains some technical information about the application's requirements, such as whether it needs to access local storage or a webcam. You manage these additional settings via the other tabs you can see in Figure 6-6, such as Capabilities, Declarations, and so on. You'll visit these more advanced aspects in later chapters as you build development features that require specific manifest settings.

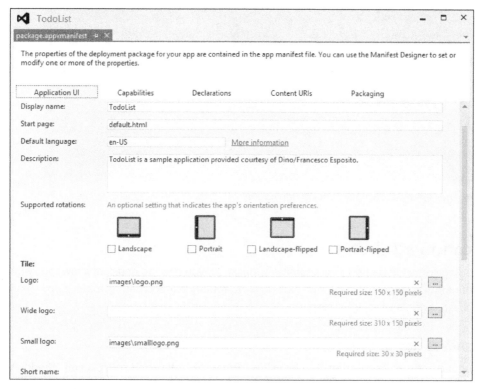

FIGURE 6-6 The editor of the manifest file.

Adding logo images

Any Windows Store application needs a set of images that are used in various scenarios to quickly and easily identify the application. At the very minimum, a Windows 8 application needs the four images discussed earlier in this chapter and summarized in Table 6-1. Some recommendations apply, though, when it comes to creating these images.

First and foremost, a Windows 8 logo has a transparent background. It means that the actual logo consists of a drawing placed on a rectangular area. The background area is made transparent by using ad hoc graphical tools such as Paint.NET. Paint.NET is a free photo editing tool you can get at *http://www.getpaint.net*. Figure 6-7 shows the logo of the sample TodoList application placed on a transparent background.

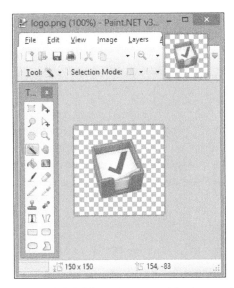

FIGURE 6-7 Adding a transparent background to the logo image.

The checkered texture you see in the figure is the Paint.NET way of telling you that your image has a transparent background. Giving logo files a transparent background is not *mandatory*, but it helps keep your logo images more consistent with the overall user interface of Windows 8 (and anyway, makes them look nicer).

Another little trick you might want to apply to logo images to make them more similar to some Windows 8 native applications consists of flattening the drawing and reducing it to a single color—white. In the end, the logo will be white on a transparent background. It doesn't look that great when you edit the image; but it definitely looks better when you install the application in the Windows 8 environment. Figure 6-8 shows the TodoList application installed with a white-transparent logo.

FIGURE 6-8 The TodoList logo in white on a transparent background. Windows 8 adds the name of the application automatically.

The final point to consider regards the background color of the application's tile in the Windows 8 Start screen. As mentioned, the image comes with a transparent background but you can configure the color of the tile. You do that by entering colors in HTML format in the manifest file. If you scroll down a bit in the window shown in Figure 6-6, you will find a Background input field. As you learned in Chapter 2, "Making sense of HTML5," HTML colors are expressed in the format *#rrggbb* where *rr*, *gg*, and *bb* indicate the hexadecimal values of the red, green, and blue color components. To get a nice light blue color, enter **#2eccfa**.

Adding a splash screen

Every Windows Store application should have a splash screen. A *splash screen* is an image that displays right after the user launches the application and remains visible until the application is ready for interaction. Any Visual Studio project template offers a free splash screen that developers have only to edit with a graphical tool such as Paint.NET. Figure 6-9 shows a reworked splash screen for the TodoList app.

FIGURE 6-9 The splash screen of the TodoList sample application.

There are a few guidelines to keep in mind that apply to splash screens. To begin with, the only purpose of a splash screen is giving users immediate feedback about the application. Windows 8 guidelines recommend that you provide extremely simple images that basically consist of the application's logo placed at the center of the logo surface—620 x 300 pixels.

Ideally, the logo has a transparent background and uses colors that blend well with the selected background color for the splash screen. You can set the selected background color for the splash screen in the manifest editor. You should also avoid showing advertisements and versioning information in the splash screen.

Getting serious with the TodoList application

The next step in the process of building the TodoList application consists of adding an interactive form for the user to enter information about and keep track of a task. In doing so, you'll get familiar with some of the input controls available in Windows 8, as well as some of the HTML5 elements you encountered in Chapter 2.

Building an interactive form

The input form is divided into four sections, each represented with a *div* element. Open the *default. html* file in Visual Studio and make sure the *body* element contains the following markup:

```html
<body>
    <div data-win-control="WinJS.UI.HtmlControl"
        data-win-options="{uri:'/pages/header.html'}"></div>
    <h1>TO-DO List</h1>

    <div class="form-container">
        <div class="form-section"> ... </div>
        <div class="form-section"> ... </div>
        <div class="form-section"> ... </div>
        <div class="form-section"> ... </div>
    </div>

    <div data-win-control="WinJS.UI.HtmlControl"
        data-win-options="{uri:'/pages/footer.html'}"></div>
</body>
```

The *div* block with a CSS class name of *form-container* is just the block of markup you'll be writing in the rest of the chapter. In the *default.css* file, add the following code to style the container *div* elements:

```css
.form-container {
    border-radius: 10px;
    background-color: #99e;
    color: #eee;
    padding: 20px;
    margin: 5px;
    width: 600px;
}
.form-section {
    margin-top: 10px;
}
.block-element {
    display: inline-block;
    vertical-align: top;
}
```

In the topmost *div*, you place controls to capture the description of the task and the due date. The second *div* indicates the priority of the task, and the third allows the user to set the task status. Finally, the fourth *div* contains a button to save the task.

Defining the task object

Most of the JavaScript code inserted in HTML pages deals with updating elements. Data binding is a powerful technique to keep this necessary code to a bare minimum, assigning the burden of doing most of the work to the underlying framework. For data binding to work seamlessly, you should create an object that closely matches the data you plan to read and write through the form. In this case, you need a *Task* object. To create it, add a new JavaScript file to the *Js* folder of the project. You may name it after the application—**TodoList.js**.

Before you get to edit the *todolist.js* file, a small change is required in the *default.js* file to take control of the loading phase of the application. It's the same change you made in the data binding example discussed in the previous chapter. In general, this change is required in any Windows Store application. You locate the *app.onactivated* function and just replace the line that calls into the *setPromise* method with the code below:

```
args.setPromise(WinJS.UI.processAll()
                .then(TodoList.init())
);
```

The effect of this code is yielding control to the function named *TodoList.init* after the activation phase has completed.

Now, turn your attention to the newly created *todolist.js* file and add the following code to it:

```
var TodoList = TodoList || {};

TodoList.init = function () {
    TodoList.performInitialBinding()
}

TodoList.Priority = {
    VeryLow: 1,
    Low: 2,
    Normal: 3,
    High: 4,
    VeryHigh: 5
};

TodoList.firstOfNextMonth = function () {
    var d = new Date();
    d.setDate(d.getDate() + 31);
    var year = d.getFullYear();
    var month = d.getMonth();
    var day = 1;
    var newDate = new Date(year, month, day);
    return newDate;
}
```

```
// Define the Task object
var Task = WinJS.Class.define(function () {
    var that = {};
    that.description = "This is my new task";
    that.dueDate = TodoList.firstOfNextMonth();
    that.priority = TodoList.Priority.Normal;
    that.status = "Not Started";
    that.percCompleted = 0;
    that.minPriority = TodoList.Priority.VeryLow;
    that.maxPriority = TodoList.Priority.VeryHigh;
    return that;
});
```

Now you have a global object named *TodoList* that contains all of the JavaScript functions and objects being used by the application. In addition, you have a *Task* object with a few properties, such as description, due date, priority, status, and percentage of work completed. The next step is editing the user interface so that you can collect data for populating a new *Task* object. At the same time, you might want to use an existing instance of the *Task* object to initialize the input fields.

Collecting text and dates

In the top-most *div*, you place a multiline text editor and a date picker. The multiline text editor requires the *textarea* HTML element. For the date picker, you have two options. You can use the HTML *input* element or you can use a Windows 8 date picker component. Using the Windows 8 date picker makes things far easier for the user. Here's the markup you need to insert in the first *div* of class *form-section*:

```
<div class="form-section">
    <div class="block-element">
        <h3>DESCRIPTION</h3>
        <textarea id="taskSubject" required
                data-win-bind="innerText: description"></textarea>
    </div>
    <div class="block-element">
        <h3>DUE DATE</h3>
        <div class="block-element" id="taskDueDate"
            data-win-control="WinJS.UI.DatePicker" />
    </div>
</div>
```

Let's ignore for a moment the *data-win-bind* attribute and the whole theme of data binding. Let's pay attention instead to the *data-win-control* attribute used on the *div* tag with an ID of *taskDueDate*. The *data-win-control* transforms a plain *div* element into a Windows 8 date picker component. So you see a plain *div* element in the markup, but you actually get a much more sophisticated tree of elements at run time.

Setting the task priority

The task priority is expressed as a number that ranges from one (very low) to five (very high). You can have users just type the number in a text box. This would simply require an *input* field. In Windows 8, you can use one of new input types introduced by HTML5. The hosting environment will then automatically render that as a touch-enabled slider. The following markup is all you need. This markup fills the second section of your input form.

```
<div class="form-section">
    <div class="block-element">
        <h3>PRIORITY        (1=VERY LOW - 5=VERY HIGH)</h3>
        <input id="taskPriority" type="range"
               data-win-bind="value: priority; min: minPriority; max: maxPriority"
    </div>
</div>
```

The *type* attribute on the *input* element set to the *range* string does the magic of giving your users a nice slider. The initial value of the slider, as well as its minimum and maximum values, is set via data binding. You'll see more on data binding in a moment.

Setting the task status

The third section of the form contains information about the current status of the task. The status is expressed with a string picked up from a drop-down list. In addition, you can indicate the percentage of work already done in a numeric input field. Here's the markup you need:

```
<div class="form-section">
    <div class="block-element">
        <h3>STATUS</h3>
        <select id="taskStatus">
            <option>Not Started</option>
            <option>In progress</option>
            <option>Completed</option>
        </select>
    </div>
    <div class="block-element">
        <h3>% COMPLETED</h3>
        <input id="taskPercCompleted" type="number" min="0" max="100"
            data-win-bind="value: percCompleted" />
    </div>
</div>
```

Windows 8 doesn't offer any special facilities for a drop-down list. The plain *select* HTML element works just fine. By setting the *type* attribute of the *input* element to *number,* you force the input box to only accept numbers. Note, though, that Windows 8 still allows you to type non-numeric characters—except that they are discarded when the actual value is read back for further processing.

Adding a button and tooltips

The final section of the form contains a button through which the user collects all the entered data and triggers an operation that physically persists that data somewhere. You won't do anything to save the data in this exercise, but you'll see how to collect data and summarize it for the user. The following markup from the fourth section contains two interesting things: a push button and a tooltip. (A tooltip is a small pop-up window shown when the mouse hovers over a control with the purpose of displaying useful information to the user.)

```
<div class="form-section">
    <div>
        <button id="buttonAddTask"
            data-win-control="WinJS.UI.Tooltip"
            data-win-options="{innerHTML: '<b>Purpose</b><hr>Add the <i>newly
                                        created</i> task to the list.'}">
            Add Task
        </button>
    </div>
</div>
```

Important In the example above, the content of the *innerHTML* property has been split on two rows for readability purposes. If you're typing this code right into a Visual Studio editor, then make sure that you type it as a continuous string; otherwise your code won't compile.

Note In this book, you write Windows 8 applications using HTML and other web-related technologies, such as CSS and JavaScript. In this regard, it might be surprising for any developer with a bit of web development experience to arrange a web form without using the HTML *form* element and submit buttons. In Windows 8, you just don't need any *form* element since there's no server-side component to receive the post of the form's content. On any form intended to collect input data, all you need to have is one or more buttons to trigger actions. You can render these buttons using the plain *button* element.

In Windows 8, you can add a tooltip to any HTML element by simply adding a *data-win-control* attribute set to *WinJS.UI.Tooltip*. You also use the *data-win-options* attribute to initialize the new control. In this case, you pass the *innerHTML* property the markup text to be displayed when the user hovers over the button.

Buttons aren't useful unless they have an associated click event. It is a good programming practice to associate event handlers to HTML elements during page initialization. In this case, you go back to the *todolist.js* file and edit the *TodoLit.init* function, as shown below:

```
TodoList.init = function () {
    document.getElementById("buttonAddTask")
```

```
        .addEventListener("click", TodoList.addTaskClick);
    TodoList.performInitialBinding()
}
```

Now, when the user clicks the *Add Task* button, the code defined in the function *TodoList.addTask-Click* runs. This code needs be added to the *todolist.js* file as well.

```
TodoList.addTaskClick = function () {
    TodoList.alert("Add Task button clicked");
}

TodoList.alert = function (message) {
    var alertDialog = new Windows.UI.Popups.MessageDialog(message);
    alertDialog.showAsync();
}
```

For now, clicking on the button only shows the user a message box; later on, you'll be rewriting this code to display a summary of the task being saved.

What if you want to add a tooltip to an element that is already being transformed into a Windows 8 component via the *data-win-control* attribute? For example, how would you add a tooltip to the date picker component? Here's some example code:

```
<div data-win-control="WinJS.UI.Tooltip"
    data-win-options="{innerHTML: 'Specify the due for the task'}">
    <h3>DUE DATE</h3>
    <div class="block-element" id="taskDueDate"
        data-win-control="WinJS.UI.DatePicker" />
</div>
```

As the preceding markup illustrates, all you need to do is use a wrapper *div* properly configured so it will transform into a tooltip component at run time.

Putting data into the form

So far, you have defined the layout of the form, and with that task complete, it's time to think about how to bind it to data.

Initializing the input form

In the page initialization, you already have a call to a function called *performInitialBinding*. You need to add some code to the body of this function. The expected behavior is fairly simple: the function needs to get a new *Task* object and bind its content to the elements of the user interface. When the purpose of the application form is to add a *new* task, you can pass a newly created (in other words, blank) instance of the *Task* object, which is filled with default values.

However, if the form is being used to edit existing, previously created tasks, then your code must first retrieve the task to edit, load that data into a fresh instance of the *Task* object, and then display it through the user interface.

```
TodoList.performInitialBinding = function () {
    // This may also be a Task object retrieved from some storage
    var task = new Task();

    // Enable binding on the HTML element(s) of choice
    var bindableElement = document.getElementById("form-container");
    WinJS.Binding.processAll(bindableElement, task);

    // Set the date on the date picker
    var datePicker = document.getElementById("taskDueDate").winControl;
    datePicker.current = task.dueDate;

    // Select the status on the drop-down list
    var dropDownList = document.getElementById("taskStatus");
    dropDownList.selectedIndex = TodoList.getIndexFromStatus(task.status);
}
```

Data binding works in a cascading manner, in the sense that you attach a data source object to a container element and then use the WinJS library to resolve *dependencies* for you. You establish a dependency between a user interface element and a property in the data source through the *data-win-bind* attribute. You can do that through markup attributes, in which case the data binding is called *declarative data binding*. You'll see how to create a declarative binding first. (You can also create bindings programmatically rather than declaratively, as you'll see shortly.)

The preceding code shows how to link a data source—the newly created *Task* object—to the *div* element that contains the entire form. This *div* is the element you are binding. The creation of the link passes through the *processAll* function.

Unfortunately, in WinJS, not all components fully support declarative data binding. Data binding works great as long as you want to bind data to plain HTML elements. If you have more ambitious goals, such as binding the due date of a *Task* object to the displayed date of a date picker component, then declarative data binding is not fully supported. Likewise, declarative data binding is not supported on plain HTML drop-down lists and Windows 8 doesn't offer any alternative to plain drop-down lists.

What does this mean to developers?

Quite simply, developers must write some extra lines of code to programmatically bind data to user interface elements. The lines below, excerpted from the *TodoList.performInitialBinding*, show how to programmatically force the date picker to display a particular date and how to programmatically select an element on a drop-down list using the *selectedIndex* property.

```
// Set the date on the date picker
var datePicker = document.getElementById("taskDueDate").winControl;
```

```
datePicker.current = task.dueDate;

// Select the status on the drop-down list
var dropDownList = document.getElementById("taskStatus");
dropDownList.selectedIndex = 1;  // Select the second element
```

You're all set now, and ready to build and debug the application. You should get what is shown in Figure 6-10. If not, carefully check the error messages you may receive from either the compiler or the run time environment.

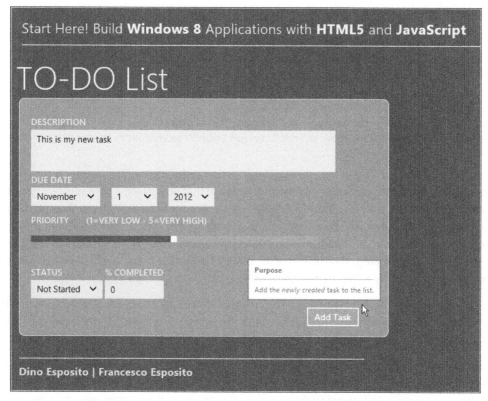

FIGURE 6-10 The TodoList application in action. Note the tooltip on the *Add Task* button.

Building and debugging an application

You write the source code for an application in the context of a Visual Studio *solution*. A solution is the repository of all resources required for the application to work: source files, images, style sheets, manifest, and so forth.

Having a solution is *not the same* as having an application; but you can create an executable application from a solution by successfully "building" (compiling) the solution. To build the current solution in Visual Studio, press F7 or select the Build Solution option from the Build menu, as shown in Figure 6-11. During the build, the Visual Studio environment invokes the compiler and processes your source code. If everything is OK and no syntax errors are detected, you wind up with an executable application that you can launch.

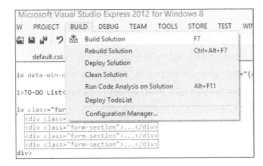

FIGURE 6-11 The Build menu.

When Visual Studio discovers errors during the build step, it lists them for you in a window at the bottom of the Visual Studio environment. However, when you build a JavaScript application (as in this book), it's unlikely that you will get errors during the build process. It's much more likely that you will get *run time errors*.

Run time errors show up during the debugging phase. The debugging phase is all about running the application to see if it does what it is supposed to do. You start debugging the application by hitting F5 or selecting the Start Debugging option from the Debug menu.

Figure 6-12 shows the effect of a syntax error: a comma is missing right before the highlighted line. Note that the message you receive may be a bit misleading about the real causes of the problem. In the figure, Visual Studio seems to indicate that the code is missing a closing bracket. That is definitely a possibility, but it is not the real issue with the code in the figure. The point is that, in general, while you must pay attention to the fact that there is an error, you should take the specific error messages that appear with a grain of salt, because they are "automatic guesses" that the software makes, and don't always reflect the true underlying problem.

```
TodoList.Priority = {
    VeryLow: 1,
    Low: 2,
    Normal: 3,
    High: 4
    VeryHigh: 5
};

// Define the Task
var Task = WinJS.Cl

TodoList.performIn
    var task = new

    // Enable bind
    var bindableEl
    WinJS.Binding.

    var dp = docume
    dp.current = t
    var select = d
    select.selecte
}
```

Microsoft Visual Studio Express 2012 for Windows 8   ?   ×

JavaScript critical error at line 22, column 5 in ms-appx://372c89f5-
a0c2-4f46-95d2-7335ab20a28f/js/todolist.js

SCRIPT1009: Expected ')'

Stop Debugging   Continue

FIGURE 6-12 A syntax error detected.

Another common situation you may face during debugging is the occurrence of an *exception.* An exception is different from a syntax error: in this case, the code is syntactically correct, but the logic is incorrect, so the program fails at run time when processing actual data. An exception is often due to data that is either entered incorrectly by the user or generated by code. Figure 6-13 shows an exception due to an attempt to use an undefined variable.

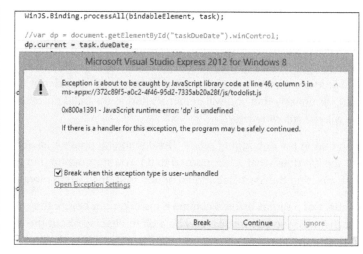

```
WinJS.Binding.processAll(bindableElement, task);

//var dp = document.getElementById("taskDueDate").winControl;
dp.current = task.dueDate;
```

Microsoft Visual Studio Express 2012 for Windows 8

! Exception is about to be caught by JavaScript library code at line 46, column 5 in
   ms-appx://372c89f5-a0c2-4f46-95d2-7335ab20a28f/js/todolist.js

0x800a1391 - JavaScript runtime error: 'dp' is undefined

If there is a handler for this exception, the program may be safely continued.

☑ Break when this exception type is user-unhandled
Open Exception Settings

Break   Continue   Ignore

FIGURE 6-13 A run time error.

Pop-up windows (like the one in Figure 6-13) appear when the system detects the exception. You stop execution by clicking *Break*; by clicking *Continue* you instruct the application to try to carry on. Most of the time, you just want to break execution, figure out what went wrong, and fix the code. The Debug output window—usually located at the bottom of the Visual Studio window—allows you to access the report about what was detected as wrong in the application at any time (see Figure 6-14).

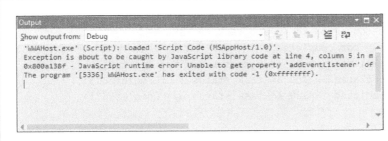

FIGURE 6-14 The Debug window.

As you can see in the figure, the Output window offers a drop-down list for you to pick up the report you need, whether it is about debug or build.

Validating input data

The final step of the TodoList application is to collect input data and summarize that for the user, which allows them to be able approve the result before opting to save the changes. When the user clicks the *Add Task* button, the program should validate and then process the data. In this example, you won't be doing any work yet on storage, so the task the user has defined will not be saved anywhere. However, validation and summary of the information are two features worth discussing right away.

Open the *todolist.js* file and edit the code of the *TodoList.addTaskClick* function, as shown below:

```
TodoList.addTaskClick = function () {
    var currentTask = TodoList.getTaskFromUI();
    if (!TodoList.validateInput(currentTask)) {
        TodoList.alert("There is something wrong with the data you entered.");
        return;
    }
    TodoList.displaySummary(currentTask);
}
```

For now, focus on the *TodoList.validateInput* function. The function receives a *Task* object that has been created and populated with the data entered through the user interface. You also add the following code to the *todolist.js* file:

```
TodoList.validateInput = function (task) {
    // Check description is NOT empty
    if (task.description.length == 0)
        return false;

    // Check date is a future date
    if (task.dueDate <= new Date())
```

```
        return false;

    // Check if perc-completed is >0 and task not started
    // or 100 done but not completed
    if ((task.percCompleted > 0 && task.status == "Not Started")  ||
        (task.percCompleted == 100 && task.status != "Completed") ||
        (task.percCompleted != 100 && task.status == "Completed"))
        return false;

    return true;
}
```

The function returns a Boolean answer to the question: *Is the passed Task object valid for the purposes of the application?* The code ultimately consists of a list of *if* statements that check business rules you want to apply.

Summarizing results

Before you can validate a task, you need to collect the actual data and copy that into a *Task* object. In WinJS, you can't rely on the system doing most of the work for you. If you use C# and XAML to write Windows Store applications, then you can force the system to take the original *Task* object you provided to initialize the form and update it with any changes the user makes through the user interface widgets. This feature is known as *two-way data binding*, but is not supported in WinJS. As a result, you need to introduce a function like the one below. You can copy the code below in *todolist.js*.

```
TodoList.getTaskFromUI = function () {
    var task = new Task();

    // Read the subject of the task
    var taskSubject = document.getElementById("taskSubject");
    task.description = taskSubject.value;

    // Read the due date of the task
    var taskDueDate = document.getElementById("taskDueDate").winControl;
    task.dueDate = taskDueDate.current;

    // Read the priority of the task
    var taskPriority = document.getElementById("taskPriority");
    task.priority = taskPriority.value;

    // Read the status of the task
    var taskStatus = document.getElementById("taskStatus");
    task.status = taskStatus.options[taskStatus.selectedIndex].value;

    // Read the percentage of the task completed
    var taskPercCompleted = document.getElementById("taskPercCompleted");
```

```
        task.percCompleted = taskPercCompleted.value;

        return task;
}
```

When an *INPUT* element is used, you read its current content—whether text or numbers—using the *value* property. If you have drop-down list, then you need to retrieve the *selectedIndex* property of the list first and then map the index to the collection of list items—this collection is referred to as *options*. Finally, if you used a WinJS component (such as, the date picker), then you first need to retrieve its instance via the *winControl* property.

At this point you have retrieved the *Task* object given by the data the user has entered and this object can be validated. If validation is successful, then you can proceed and display a summary of the data (or just save it somewhere). To top off this exercise, you now use a *FlyOut* component to display the task information in some formatted way.

In *default.html*, you add the following markup just before the footer. The markup defines a *FlyOut* component but just leaves it empty.

```
<div data-win-control="WinJS.UI.Flyout" id="flyoutSummary"></div>
```

In *todolist.js*, you now add a final piece of code—the *TodoList.displaySummary* function. This function will retrieve the reference to the *FlyOut* component, fill it up with task data, and show it to the user.

```
TodoList.displaySummary = function (task) {
    var description = "<p><span>DESCRIPTION</span>: " + task.description + "<p>";
    var dueDate = "<p><span>DUE DATE</span>: " + task.dueDate + "<p>";
    var priority = "<p><span>PRIORITY</span>: " + task.priority + "<p>";
    var status = "<p><span>STATUS</span>: " + task.status + "<p>";
    var percCompleted = "<p><span>% COMPLETED</span>: " + task.percCompleted +
                        "<p>";

    // Build the entire content string and attach it to the flyout
    var summary = description + dueDate + priority + status + percCompleted;
    document.getElementById("flyoutSummary").innerHTML = summary;

    // Display the flyout
    var anchor = document.getElementById("buttonAddTask");
    var flyoutSummary = document.getElementById("flyoutSummary").winControl;
    flyoutSummary.show(anchor);
}
```

The preceding code first prepares a bunch of individual strings that correspond to the various properties of the task object you want to summarize. Next, you create a comprehensive string from all the individual strings, and programmatically attach this new comprehensive string to the body of the

FlyOut component by setting the *innerHTML* property on the *flyoutSummary* element of the page. Finally, you show the *FlyOut* component. Note that a *FlyOut* component needs an anchor element that determines where the fly out will display—in this case, you can use the *Add Task* button element as an anchor. Figure 6-15 provides a view of the summary fly out.

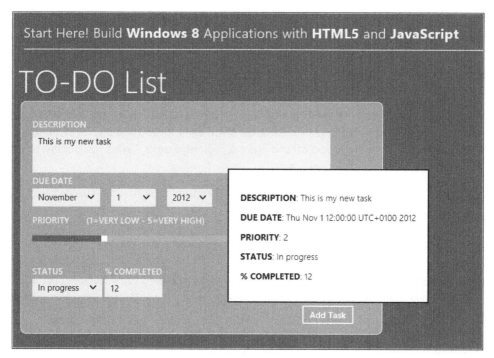

FIGURE 6-15 Summarizing work done to the user.

Summary

Although incomplete—you didn't do anything to save the task—this exercise showed you several aspects of Windows 8 applications. You managed the user interface using a mix of HTML elements and native Windows 8 components. You employed data binding techniques and learned how to structure the JavaScript code you need to have in any solution. In the following chapters, you'll return to the TodoList application to add some more features, such as storing tasks and reading them.

In the next chapter, you'll go through some basic (but still effective) exercises involving images and media content.

Chapter 7

Navigating through multimedia content

The greatest challenge to any thinker is stating the problem in a way that will allow a solution.

—Bertrand Russell

In this chapter, you'll explore the capabilities of the Windows 9 JavaScript (WinJS) library—as far as the display of multimedia content is concerned. You'll see how to build a gallery of images, how to zoom them in and out, and investigate ways to watch YouTube videos from within a Windows Store application.

Foundation of page navigation

So far in this book, all the applications you have created have used the Blank App template. That template is fine for applications that consist of a single page. But what if you want to build an application that displays multiple pages and requires users to navigate between them? Before you start with the nitty-gritty details of getting pictures and video clips into your apps, a brief exploration of the framework that provides navigation is in order. Next, armed with this knowledge, you can start planning a gallery where users can scroll images and click them to perform additional tasks.

The navigation model of Windows Store applications

To jump from one page to another is no big deal; you just invoke a specific piece of code that links to another page. Or, easier still, you just use an HTML hyperlink element.

While both of these approaches work well, you should note that WinJS has a richer set of functionalities available. These functionalities not only let you display a different page, but also track the user's navigation history, letting you provide a better user experience as you merge new pages into the existing layout.

Jumping to a different page

The benefit of using the native Windows Store navigation model is well illustrated by the diagram in Figure 7-1.

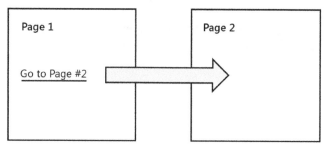

FIGURE 7-1 Jumping from one page to another using the classic HTML hyperlink element.

After clicking the link (or some button), the user sees a completely different page. It is your responsibility to ensure that the user experiences a strong feeling of continuity. You typically achieve that by giving both pages the same layout, using a common color scheme, and fonts. In addition, you should provide users with links to return to the previous page, since you won't get any browser-like Back button automatically from the system.

Displaying a different page

The idea behind the Windows Store application navigation model is that the application consists of a single main page and a number of *page fragments*. The main page contains the header, footer, menus, and other shared parts of the user interface. In contrast, a page fragment just provides new content to replace the content in the main page. In this way, all common parts of the UI remain unchanged during navigation, so the user has the feeling of having changed only context, rather than having jumped to an entirely new place. Figure 7-2 illustrates the Windows Store application navigation model.

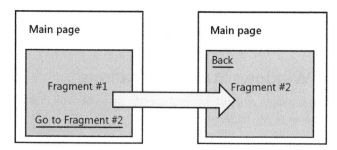

FIGURE 7-2 Displaying different content within the same container.

In the start fragment, you may have buttons and controls through which you control navigation. You are in no way forced to have hyperlinks. When you navigate away from a page fragment, the system does all the work that is required to display the new content effectively to the user. At the same time, the newly displayed page is only responsible for displaying a Back button. The logic to navigate back is gently offered by the WinJS framework.

Inside the Navigation App template

The first example you build in this chapter is an extension of the sample application you got by creating your Windows Store application project from the Navigation App template in Microsoft Visual Studio. Let's then get familiar with the programming model.

Creating a navigation app

You open Visual Studio and create a brand new project using the Navigation App template. You call this project **Gallery**, as shown in Figure 7-3.

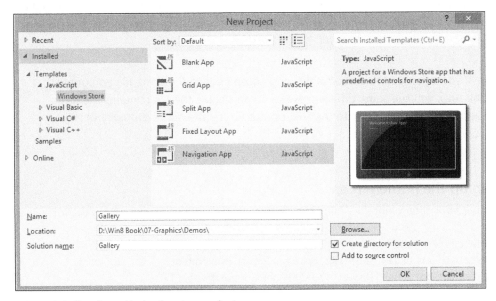

FIGURE 7-3 Creating a Navigation App project.

The project contains a few more files than the Blank App template that you're used to. The familiar *default.html* page plays the role of the main page of Figure 7-2. Companion files *default.css* and *default.js* just provide style sheets and scripts for elements within the main page.

In Figure 7-4, you also notice a brand new *pages* folder. This is the folder where you will group all of your fragment pages, each in a separate subfolder. By default, the *pages* folder has one subfolder named *home*; this is also the name of the only fragment available initially. The *home* folder contains *home.html*, *home.css*, and *home.js*. This is a standard pattern: The CSS file contains all style sheets used by the HTML file and the JS file contains all the required script.

FIGURE 7-4 The Navigation App project.

Another difference from the Blank App template is the *navigator.js* file. The file contains the implementation of the *Application.PageControlNavigator* object. You can consider this file as an extension of the native WinJS library.

 Note If you open up the *default.js* file, and compare it to the same file you get with a Blank App, you see some differences too. In particular, the file contains the logic that automatically navigates to the URL pointed to by the *home* property of the *PageControlNavigator* object.

Setting up the home screen

The *default.html* determines the main user interface of the application. It contains the following code:

```
<div id="contenthost"
     data-win-control="Application.PageControlNavigator"
     data-win-options="{home: '/pages/home/home.html'}">
</div>
```

This code sets up the navigator and makes it point to *home.html* as the provider of the fragment for the initial screen. To arrange the home screen, you make changes to *default.html*. For example, you can add the same *header.html* and *footer.html* files that you created in the previous chapter to the *pages* folder. Next, you edit the *BODY* of *default.html,* as shown below:

```
<div data-win-control="WinJS.UI.HtmlControl"
     data-win-options="{uri:'/pages/header.html'}"></div>

<h1 class="title">My Pet Gallery</h1>
<div id="contenthost"
```

```
        data-win-control="Application.PageControlNavigator"
        data-win-options="{home: '/pages/home/home.html'}">
</div>

<div data-win-control="WinJS.UI.HtmlControl"
        data-win-options="{uri:'/pages/footer.html'}"></div>
```

When the user navigates to another page fragment, only the content of the *contenthost* element will be replaced—everything else will remain unchanged. Figure 7-5 shows the home screen; the dashed area indicates the area reserved to the *contenthost* element, where each successive page will be loaded and displayed.

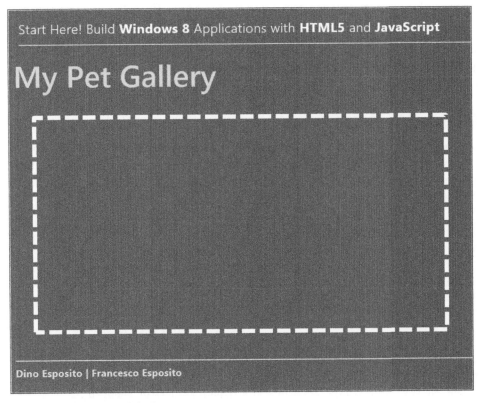

FIGURE 7-5 The layout of the home screen.

With this infrastructure set, you are now ready to build the picture gallery.

Building a gallery of pictures

How would you lay out a gallery of pictures? That mostly depends on your creativity and preferences. In general, a gallery should provide a scrollable list of small images—ideally thumbnails—and give the user a chance to click one image to see it in a larger format and possibly zoom on it. To build the gallery of pictures, you focus on the content of the *home.html* file.

Introducing the *FlipView* component

WinJS comes with a readymade component that is perfect to build a gallery of pictures. This component is *WinJS.UI.FlipView*. A flip view displays as a scrollable list—either vertical or horizontal. The list is arranged in such a way that only one item is displayed at a time. The native user interface of the component also provides navigation buttons for the user to move to the next or the previous item.

The item can have any representation that makes sense for the application. It doesn't have to be an image and it doesn't have to be some plain text. In general, along with a flip view, you define the blueprint of the item to display and define a graphical template for it.

Defining the item to display

As a first step, you define a model for the item you want to display through the flip view. Because you want the flip view to implement a gallery of images, the item is well represented with the URL of the physical image and a caption. You create a new JavaScript file and add it to the project in the *Js* folder. Let's call this file *gallery.js* and add the following code to it:

```
var GalleryApp = GalleryApp || {};
var Photo = WinJS.Class.define(function (img, title) {
    var that = {};
    that.imageUrl = img;
    that.title = title;
    return that;
});


GalleryApp.init = function () {
    var photos = [
        new Photo("images/data/german-sheperd.png", "German sheperd"),
        new Photo("images/data/tiger.png", "Just bigger than a cat"),
        new Photo("images/data/lion.png", "Just hairier than a cat"),
        new Photo("images/data/leopard.png", "Running as a leopard"),
        new Photo("images/data/dane.png", "Hungry from Denmark")
    ];
}
```

The *Photo* object will represent the item displayed through the flip view. In this basic example, you can safely assume that all the images are packaged with the application. In a more realistic application, you might want to get all pictures from the local disk or perhaps from Flickr. For the exercise to work, you need to have five .png image files ready and add them under the *images* folder of the project. To keep these images distinct from all other images you usually have in the project (logo files, for example), it is advisable that you also create a *data* subfolder under images and copy the files there.

> **Note** There is no special reason why the images are .png files. You can use .jpg or .gif images as well. If you use .png files, however, then you can give them a transparent background with some ad hoc tool such as Paint.NET, which produces a much nicer graphical effect. Also, note that when you build galleries of pictures you might want to ensure that all the pictures are the same size. In the example, they're all 250 x 250 pixels.

Creating the *FlipView* component

To add the *FlipView* component, you open the *home.html* file and make sure it contains the following code in the *BODY* element:

```
<div class="fragment homepage">
  <h1>My Pet Gallery</h1>
  <div id="gallery"
       data-win-control="WinJS.UI.FlipView">
  </div>
</div>
```

This code just gets you a new instance of the *FlipView* component. The next step consists of binding it to some photos. You open the *gallery.js* file and add the following code to it:

```
var Gallery = WinJS.Class.define(function (arrayOfPhotos) {
    var that = {};
    that.photos = new WinJS.Binding.List(arrayOfPhotos);
    return that;
});
```

Next, you edit the previously created *Gallery.init* method, as shown below:

```
GalleryApp.init = function () {
    var photos = [
        new Photo("images/data/german-sheperd.png", "German sheperd"),
        new Photo("images/data/tiger.png", "Just bigger than a cat"),
        new Photo("images/data/lion.png", "Just hairier than a cat"),
        new Photo("images/data/leopard.png", "Running as a leopard"),
        new Photo("images/data/dane.png", "Hungry from Denmark")
    ];
    GalleryApp.Gallery = new Gallery(photos);
```

```
        var flipView = document.getElementById("gallery").winControl;
        flipView.itemDataSource = GalleryApp.Gallery.photos.dataSource;
}
```

At this point, the *FlipView* component is bound to the array of photos. If you run the application now, it works and the *FlipView* performs its tasks really well. Unfortunately, the resulting application is neither attractive nor useful for the user. The *FlipView* scrolls through the bound list of *Photo* objects but it can only render them as plain text. Figure 7-6 shows what you get at this point.

There's one more piece of code that needs be explained. You open the *home.js* file and add a call to *GalleryApp.init* in the *ready* event handler so that the *FlipView* can be initialized when the home page is loaded.

```
(function () {
    "use strict";

    WinJS.UI.Pages.define("/pages/home/home.html", {
        ready: function (element, options) {
            GalleryApp.init();
        },
        unload: function () {
        }
    });
})();
```

The *unload* event handler is empty now, but you'll be using it in a moment.

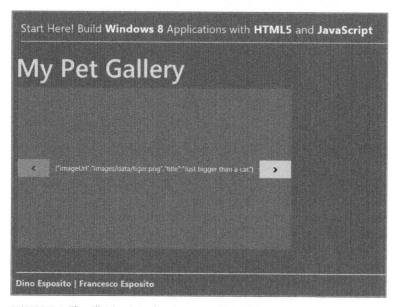

FIGURE 7-6 The *FlipView* just showing some bound data.

Adding a template for the item

The next step is adding a template so that the *FlipView* can render the bound *Photo* objects in a nicer way. You go back to *gallery.js* and add the following line to *GalleryApp.init*:

```
flipView.itemTemplate = document.getElementById("gallery-template");
```

You also need to define the template *gallery-template* in the *home.html* file. You add the following to the *BODY* of the *home.html* file:

```html
<div id="gallery-template" data-win-control="WinJS.Binding.Template">
  <div id="template-container">
    <img class="image" alt="" src="#" data-win-bind="src: imageUrl" />
    <div class="overlay">
        <h2 data-win-bind="innerText: title"></h2>
    </div>
  </div>
</div>
```

The item template is made of an *IMG* element and an *H2* element. These elements are bound to the properties of the *Photo* object. You also need to add a few styles to *home.css*:

```css
#gallery {
    width: 600px;
    height: 350px;
    border: solid 4px #5a12f3;
    background-color: #2c668d;
}
.image {
    width:100%;
    border: solid 1px #fff;
}
#template-container {
    display: -ms-grid;
    -ms-grid-columns: 1fr;
    -ms-grid-rows: 1fr;
    width: 350px;
    height: 300px;
    background-color: #2faee6;
}
.overlay {
    position: relative;
    background-color: rgba(0,0,0,0.5);
    -ms-grid-row-align: end;
    height: 30px;
    padding: 10px;
    margin: 3px;
```

```
    overflow: hidden;
}
```

The first step of the exercise is now complete: run the application and you should see what's in Figure 7-7.

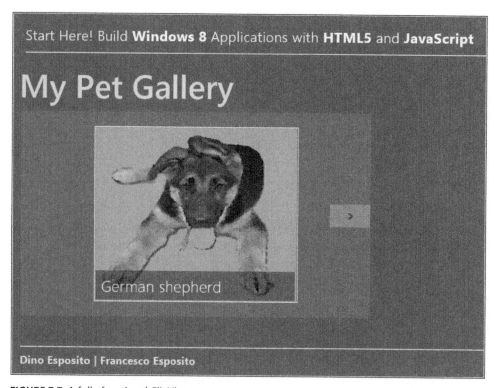

FIGURE 7-7 A fully functional *FlipView* component.

Navigating to a detail page

A gallery of images wouldn't be a gallery if it didn't allow users to click displayed items and navigate to a detail page. This is precisely what you are going to do as the second step of the exercise.

Retrieving the bound item

As a first step, you add a click handler on the *DIV* element that contains the item template. You just add the *onclick* attribute to the *DIV* element, as shown below. In this way, any time the user clicks (or taps) the *DIV*—basically the entire area of the image—she triggers the handler.

```
<div id="template-container" onclick="GalleryApp.showDetails()">
   ...
</div>
```

In the click handler, you need to do a couple of things. First, you retrieve the index of the selected item and from there the bound photo. Second, you navigate to the detail page. Open the *gallery.js* file and add the following code:

```
GalleryApp.getCurrentPhotoIndex = function () {
    return document.getElementById("gallery").winControl.currentPage;
};
GalleryApp.showDetails = function () {
    var currentIndex = GalleryApp.getCurrentPhotoIndex();
    var photo = GalleryApp.Gallery.photos.getAt(currentIndex);
    WinJS.Navigation.navigate("/pages/details/details.html", photo);
};
```

The *currentPage* property of the *FlipView* component returns the index of the clicked item. You use the *getAt* method of the binding list to retrieve the actual *Photo* component that the user clicked. A binding list is just a wrapper around an array of objects that is created only for data binding purposes.

Defining the detail page

Now that you hold the selected *Photo* object, you can think of the detail page. The purpose of the detail page is simply to show more information about a particular *Photo* object. As shown in Figure 7-8, you add a new *Page* control under the *pages/details* folder. The *details* folder should be created before you try to add the *details.html* page.

The Visual Studio wizard adds three new files to the project: *details.html*, *details.css*, and *details.js*.

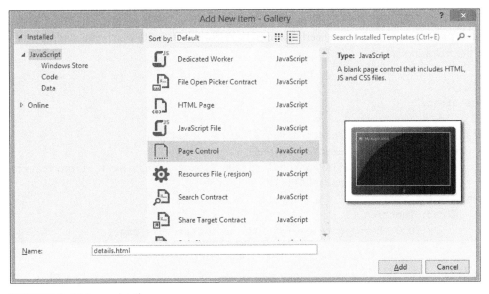

FIGURE 7-8 Adding a detail page.

The *BODY* element of the *details.html* page should contain the following markup:

```
<div class="details fragment" type="button" />
    <header aria-label="Header content" role="banner">
        <button class="win-backbutton" aria-label="Back" disabled type="button"></button>
        <h1 class="titlearea win-type-ellipsis">
            <span class="pagetitle"
                  data-win-bind="innerText: GalleryApp.DetailsPageModel.currentPhoto.title">
            </span>
        </h1>
    </header>
    <section aria-label="Main content" role="main">
    </section>
</div>
```

The most important thing in this page is the *HEADER* element. It contains the Back button that the internal navigation system will use to let users return to the previous page. The CSS style *win-back-button* does the trick of styling the button and it allows the system to retrieve the button wherever you place it in the page.

The *details.html* page is bound to some data. Its model is represented by the *GalleryApp.Details PageModel* object. You declare this object in *gallery.js*:

```
GalleryApp.DetailsPageModel = {};
```

When is this object actually initialized? It happens in the *details.js* file which you slightly edit to contain the following code:

```
(function () {
    "use strict";

    WinJS.UI.Pages.define("/pages/details/details.html", {
        ready: function (element, options) {
            GalleryApp.DetailsPageModel.currentPhoto = WinJS.Navigation.state;
            WinJS.Binding.processAll();
        },
        unload: function () {
            // TODO: Respond to navigations away from this page.
        }
    });
})();
```

You define a page object and also specify a couple of lifecycle events: *ready* for when the page is loaded, and *unload* for when the page is navigated away and then unloaded. In the *ready* event you complete initialization by retrieving any passed data and binding it to internal data structures.

The detail page may receive optional information from the caller page. In this case, the detail page receives information about the photo to display. Any cross-page information is retrieved via the *state* property of the *WinJS.Navigation* object. This remark introduces another whole point to consider about navigation: how to share data between pages.

Passing data between pages

In *gallery.js*, the code that navigates to the detail page is shown below:

```
WinJS.Navigation.navigate("/pages/details/details.html", photo);
```

What's the role of the *photo* argument? The answer is any parameter(s) you want to pass to the destination page. It can be any JavaScript object and the actual content is up to you. Put another way, you are free to give this object any shape that suits your needs. This value is retrieved by the destination page through the *state* property of the *WinJS.Navigation* object.

With this code in place, try running the application.

You navigate to, say, the third photo in the flip view, click the photo, and go to the detail page. The detail page just shows the title of the photo; everything is working as expected in Figure 7-9.

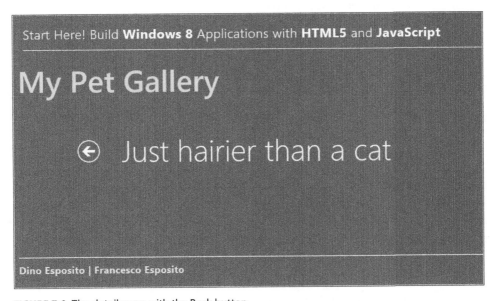

FIGURE 7-9 The detail page with the Back button.

Now try hitting the Back button. Quite surprisingly, you are *not* returned to the photo where you navigated from. You are, instead, returned to the first photo of the flip view. To complete this part of the exercise, therefore, you have two more steps to accomplish: find a way to persist the index of the last photo visited in the flip view and give a richer template to the detail page.

Persisting information across page navigation

When you navigate from one page to the next, the context of the application changes and existing controls are dismissed. The flip view is then dismissed when you jump to the detail page, and it is re-created when you return to the home page. The index of the photo that was visible at the moment of navigation is just lost. To fix things, you need to accomplish three steps:

1. Store the index of the currently visible item in some store that survives the change of page.

2. Instruct the flip view to accept an extra parameter that indicates the starting item.

3. Retrieve the last-visited index from the store and pass it to the flip view; if no index can be found, then tell the flip view to start from the first item in the bound list of items.

For the first step, you go back to *home.js* and add a line to the *unload* event handler.

```
(function () {
    "use strict";

    WinJS.UI.Pages.define("/pages/home/home.html", {
        ready: function (element, options) {
            GalleryApp.init();
        },
        unload: function () {
            WinJS.Application.sessionState.currentPhotoIndex = GalleryApp.
            getCurrentPhotoIndex();
        }
    });
})();
```

The *unload* event handler responds to navigations away from the page. From within this event handler, you can save the index of the current photo to the application's session state. The *sessionState* property of the *WinJS.Application* object is the system-provided container where developers should save any information that may be used to restore the application's state after the application has been suspended and then resumed. The *sessionState* object is a plain dictionary and can be shaped up at will. In other words, if you need to add a custom property to the *sessionState* object, you just add it and go—as you did with *currentPhotoIndex* in the preceding code snippet.

In this case, the application is not going to be suspended—the application is simply navigating to another page—but the *sessionState* is still working and, better yet, you end up having a flip view that can display its original state also when resumed from suspension.

Note Application suspension hardly applies to applications running on a laptop or PC. It is a scenario that applies to applications running on mobile devices. For example, the application is suspended on a tablet when another application is run in the foreground or when the screen gets engaged.

Let's see how to instruct the flip view to retrieve information from the *sessionState* and how to start from a given item. You open *gallery.js* again and add the following lines at the end of the *GalleryApp. init* function.

```
var startIndex = WinJS.Application.sessionState.currentPhotoIndex;
flipView.currentPage = startIndex;
```

If there's no information saved to the *sessionState,* the *startIndex* variable is set to *undefined*. However, the *FlipView* component is smart enough to start anyway from the first element if the value set to its *currentPage* property is not a valid index.

Zooming the image in and out

To complete the exercise, you now need to add some template and behavior to the detail page. The idea is to display the same image the user clicked in the flip view and enable some zoom capabilities.

Defining the template for the detail page

First, you write some additional markup for the detail page. Open *details.html* and fill up the *SECTION* element you find already in the body of the page with the following:

```
<section aria-label="Main content" role="main">
    <img id="zoomable-image" src="#" alt=""
        data-win-bind="src: GalleryApp.DetailsPageModel.currentPhoto.imageUrl" />
</section>
```

The same image you picked up in the flip view is now displayed in the detail page. As a user, how would you like to zoom on the image? This is a point that deserves some attention.

On a classic PC application, a typical user would probably find it natural to click the image to zoom in and click with the right button to zoom out. A Windows Store application, though, is designed to be used on a PC as well as touch-enabled devices, such as a tablet. The ideal gesture to zoom for the user of a tablet would be "pinch-and-zoom." Implementing pinch-and-zoom is definitely possible in WinJS but a lot is left to you. In addition, it wouldn't solve the problem of zooming where a non-touch device is available. For the sake of simplicity, you can opt for yet another approach that works great for both touch and non-touch devices.

Note WinJS provides the *GestureRecognizer* class to give you information about touch manipulations being performed by the user. You can use this class to know about the distance between start and final position of the fingers during a pinch movement. If the distance is positive you zoom in; otherwise you zoom out.

Adding a slider to select the zoom level

A trick to set a zoom level on an image (but more in general on any zoomable content) that works great on any sort of device is using a slider. The slider, in fact, can be easily manipulated through the mouse and through the finger. To add a slider component to the detail page, you need the following markup in *details.html*:

```
<section aria-label="Main content" role="main">
    <input id="zoom-slider" type="range"
           min="1" max="5" value="1" step="0.1" onchange="GalleryApp.zoomImage()" />
    <bZoom level:</b>
    <span id="zoom-level">1</span>
    <div id="zoomable-image-container">
        <img id="zoomable-image" src="#" alt=""
             data-win-bind="src: GalleryApp.DetailsPageModel.currentPhoto.imageUrl"
/>
    </div>
</section>
```

The slider is given by an *INPUT* element with the *type* attribute set to *range*. The *min* and *max* attributes indicate the range of values the user can select via the control. The *step* attribute indicates the step of increment or decrement. As you are using the slider to set a zoom level, overall 1 and 5 form a good interval, and 0.1 as a step provides a pleasant experience.

By default, the WinJS slider displays a tooltip to give visual feedback of the value being set. For some reason, the tooltip appears only for integer values. This forces you to introduce some other way to let the user know about the zoom level being set. At the same time, you probably want to dismiss tooltips in total. It only requires a small edit in *details.css*:

```
.details input[type=range]::-ms-tooltip {
    display: none;
}
```

Note that the *.details* token in the style sheet expression indicates that tooltips are suppressed only for slider components within an element marked with the *details* class. The *details* class is used to mark only the body of the *details.html* page. You can cross-check this looking at the full source code of the *details.html* page.

Manipulating the image

The slider features a handler for the *onchange* event. Such a handler is required to give you a chance to do some work whenever the selection on the slider changes. In particular, you might want to update the text near the *Zoom level* label, and zoom the image accordingly. The code required is added to the *gallery.js* file:

```
GalleryApp.zoomImage = function () {
    var container = document.getElementById("zoomable-image-container");
    var slider = document.getElementById("zoom-slider");
    var img = document.getElementById("zoomable-image");
    var label = document.getElementById("zoom-level");

    // Do some calculation
    var w = container.clientWidth;
    var h = container.clientHeight;
    var zoom = slider.value;
    var offset = ((w * zoom) - w) / 2;

    // Refresh the user interface
    img.style.zoom = zoom;
    container.scrollLeft = offset;
    container.scrollTop = offset;
    label.innerHTML = zoom;
}
```

The zoomable image lives in a *DIV* container, as styled below. The style should be added to *default.css*.

```
#zoomable-image-container {
    width: 250px;
    height: 250px;
    border: solid 1px #fff;
    position: relative;
    overflow: scroll;
}
```

The value of the zoom level is saved to the *zoom* variable and used to calculate the offset for the container's content. The offset is half the difference between the current width (and height) of the container and the effective size of the image with updated level of zoom. In general, you need to have both a horizontal and vertical offset. As in this example, images are assumed to be square so you only need to calculate one offset. Figure 7-10 explains the logic behind the calculation.

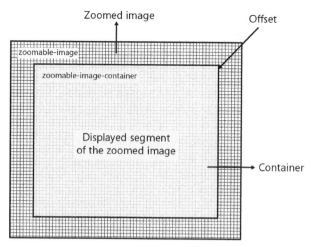

FIGURE 7-10 Mechanics of image zooming via CSS.

Figure 7-11 shows the final result of the exercise.

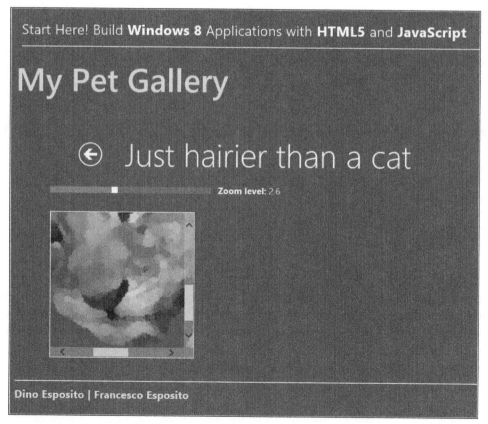

FIGURE 7-11 Zooming the image in and out.

Building a video clip gallery

After having built an image gallery, let's go ahead and try to build a video gallery while using a different control to organize navigation. To be precise, in this new exercise there will be navigation but it will be embedded in a new component—the *SemanticZoom* component. The application will group clips by category and show the available clips once the user has made a selection. Finally, clicking the clip will play the video.

> **Note** The *SemanticZoom* component only provides a fixed form of navigation through some content in a master/detail way. The application programming interface (API) for navigation you discovered in the previous exercise is, instead, a more powerful and general-purpose API for navigating between any number of pages and at any number of nesting levels.

Introducing the *SemanticZoom* component

As you rely on the built-in capabilities of a specific component to switch between master and detail view, there's no need to start from a Navigation App template. Let's create a new Blank App project and name it **Video**. As usual, you might want to add *header.html* and *footer.html* and make edits to *default.css*, so that the look and feel of the application is the same as other examples. In particular, you might want to import into *default.css* the styles for *HEADER*, *FOOTER*, and *BODY* elements that you used for all past examples.

> **Important** Unless otherwise noted, adding *header.html*, *footer.html*, and making related changes to *default.css* will be considered a required preliminary step for any of the upcoming exercises. Note also that you probably won't experience any major inconvenience if you miss it—at worst, you'll run into some graphical inconsistencies!
>
> Another aspect of nearly all Windows Store applications that will be taken for granted in the rest of exercises is the way in which startup code is injected in the application. So far, you added a *then* function call to the *activation* event handler in *default.js*. A neater, but functionally equivalent, way of doing the same thing is the following:
>
> ```
> app.onready = function (args) {
>     VideosApp.init();
> };
> ```
>
> You place this code in the immediate function that the *default.js* file is usually made of. From within the *onready* function, you simply call the *init* function on the application specific object you create for the exercise. A standard pattern of all exercises in the book is having most script gathered in a single JavaScript file with an *init* function to do all the initialization work.

What's semantic zoom, anyway?

In spite of the name, *semantic zoom* has very little to do with zooming—at least according to the common meaning of the term used so far. What the component does is switch between two different views of the same content. One view is the master view; the other is the detail view. The detail view is considered the *zoomed-in* view, namely the most detailed view of the content available. Conversely, the master view is referred to as the *zoomed-out* view, namely the one where elements are grouped in classes for the ease of selection.

Preparing the ground for semantic zoom

You prepare a page for semantic zoom by adding three *DIV* elements. The following is the code you need to enter in the *BODY* element of the *default.html* page.

```
<div id="semantic-zoom-container"
    data-win-control="WinJS.UI.SemanticZoom">
    <!-- The zoomed-in view. -->
    <div id="listview-in"
        data-win-control="WinJS.UI.ListView"></div>

    <!--- The zoomed-out view. -->
    <div id="listview-out"
        data-win-control="WinJS.UI.ListView"></div>
</div>
```

The parent *DIV* is mapped to an instance of the *WinJS.UI.SemanticZoom* component. The two child *DIVs* are mapped to instances of the *WinJS.UI.ListView* components. The great news is that your only concern is giving list views a template and content; switching between views and the user interface for doing that is gently offered by the *SemanticZoom* component.

Defining ad hoc data for semantic zoom

As usual, you add a new JavaScript file to the project to contain most of the logic for the application. In this case, you can name the file *videos.js*. Next, you open the file and add the following code:

```
var VideosApp = VideosApp || {};

var Clip = WinJS.Class.define(function (category, title, id) {
    var that = {};
    that.title = title;
    that.category = category;
    that.videoId = id;
    that.videoUrl = "http://www.youtube.com/embed/" + id + "?html5=1";
    that.posterUrl = "http://img.youtube.com/vi/" + id + "/1.jpg";
    return that;
});
```

The *Clip* object represents the information you'll be working with in the exercise. It represents a YouTube video and it has a category and a title. The *videoId* property represents the unique YouTube identifier of the clip. The *videoUrl* property returns the URL required to view the clip from within a Windows Store application; the *posterUrl* property returns the URL required to get the poster image for the video from YouTube.

The next step consists of creating a bindable collection of data. This step is not really different from the step you accomplished in the previous exercise. Also, add the following code to the *videos.js* file:

```
VideosApp.init = function () {
    var videos = [
        new Clip("Shots", "Top 10 Best Tennis Shots Ever", "WyJM9-7OvZo"),
        new Clip("Fun", "Very funny point", "ybsbzV7fNEo"),
        new Clip("Shots", "Best shot of 2012", "tEAkvegtPyw"),
        new Clip("Shots", "Insane passing shot", "UH5TMp_bH8k"),
        new Clip("Events", "Most important match point", "xHUwmMyRVJI")
    ];

    // Create a WinJS.Binding.List from the array.
    var videosList = new WinJS.Binding.List(videos);
    var videosListGrouped = videosList.createGrouped(
        function (clip) { return clip.category; },              // group by this key
        function (clip) { return { category: clip.category } }  // data for the
        master view data
    );
}
```

So you have a collection of tennis-related video clips and you catalogued them in three main categories: Shots, Fun, and Events. Needless to say, this classification is entirely arbitrary and categories, as well as titles, are entirely up to you.

Grouping data for semantic zoom

In a Windows Store application, you are not allowed to perform data binding on raw JavaScript arrays; you first need to transform arrays in a binding list. You do that through the *WinJS.Binding.List* object. This is just what you did to populate a *FlipView* component in the previous exercise. With a *SemanticZoom* component, an extra step is required.

A binding list object exposes the method *createGrouped* through which you create a groupable binding list. As you can see above, the *createGrouped* method takes two functions as arguments. The first function just identifies the key on which the items will be grouped. The second function returns the JavaScript object that will be used to render each item in the master view. Let's examine the code more closely:

```
var videosListGrouped = videosList.createGrouped(
    function (clip) { return clip.category; },
```

```
        function (clip) { return { category: clip.category } }
);
```

Both functions are called on each item in the bound list. The first function returns the expression to group items on. In this case, you group video clips on category. In other cases, it could have been the initial of contact names or a combination of multiple properties. The second function just returns a literal JavaScript object with the information you intend to display in the master view. It could be the whole *Clip* object; in this case, you may use a simpler object that just includes the category. This means that in the zoomed-out master view, the only information available is the category name.

Binding data for semantic zoom

Binding data to the *SemanticZoom* component and its child *ListView* components requires a few lines of code. You add the following at the end of the *VideosApp.init* function in *videos.js*:

```
var detailView = document.getElementById("listview-in").winControl;
detailView.itemDataSource = videosListGrouped.dataSource;
detailView.groupDataSource = videosListGrouped.groups.dataSource;
detailView.itemTemplate = document.getElementById("zoomed-in-template");
detailView.groupHeaderTemplate = document.getElementById("header-template");

var masterView = document.getElementById("listview-out").winControl;
masterView.itemDataSource = videosListGrouped.groups.dataSource;
masterView.itemTemplate = document.getElementById("zoomed-out-template");
```

Note that you need to bind data twice to the details view. First you provide the plain list of items and then the list of calculated groups. For optimal results, the details view needs an item template and a header template. The master view just needs the list of bound items and an item template.

Before you can have a first look at the work, go back to *default.html* and add a few templates to the markup.

```
<!-- Template for the group headers in the zoomed-in details view -->
<div id="header-template" data-win-control="WinJS.Binding.Template">
    <div class="header-title">
        <h1 data-win-bind="innerText: category"></h1>
    </div>
</div>

<!-- Template for the zoomed-in details view -->
<div id="zoomed-in-template" data-win-control="WinJS.Binding.Template">
    <div class="zoomed-in-item-container">
        <img src="#" data-win-bind="src: posterUrl" />
        <div>
            <h3 data-win-bind="innerText: category"></h3>
            <h6 data-win-bind="innerText: title"></h6>
```

```
            </div>
        </div>
</div>

<!-- Template for the zoomed-out master view -->
<div id="zoomed-out-template" data-win-control="WinJS.Binding.Template">
<div class="zoomed-out-item-container">
        <h1 data-win-bind="innerText: category"></h1>
    </div>
</div>
```

The elements in the markup are richly styled; so some more work on *default.css* is in order, too. Open the file and enter the following CSS styles:

```
.header-title {
    width: 50px;
    height: 50px;
    padding: 8px;
}
.zoomed-in-item-container {
    width: 280px;
    height: 70px;
    padding: 5px;
    overflow: hidden;
    display: -ms-grid;
}
.zoomed-in-item-container img {
    width: 60px;
    height: 60px;
    margin: 5px;
    -ms-grid-column: 1;
}
.zoomed-in-item-container div {
    margin: 5px;
    -ms-grid-column: 2;
}
.zoomed-out-item-container {
    width: 220px;
    height: 130px;
    background-color: #31cfd4;
}
.zoomed-out-item-container h1 {
    padding: 10px;
    line-height: 150px;
    white-space: nowrap;
    color: #fff;
}
```

```
#listview-in {
    width: 650px;
    height: 300px;
    border: solid 2px #111;
}
#semantic-zoom-container {
    width: 600px;
    height: 350px;
    border-top: solid 2px #31cfd4;
    border-bottom: solid 2px #31cfd4;
}
```

Everything is ready for testing the application.

Using gradients for the background

You may have noticed that all colors used so far—especially background colors—are solid colors. Windows 8 makes a strong point of simplicity and solid colors are part of the strategy. However, that doesn't mean you can't use gradients.

A Windows Store application fully supports CSS3, and CSS3 does have a section about gradients. So here's an example of a nice (radial) gradient to make the *listview* background even nicer.

```
#semantic-zoom-container {
    ...
    background: -ms-radial-gradient(center, ellipse cover, #c5deea 0%,#8abbd7
31%,#066dab 100%);
}
```

The syntax is fairly simple and based on the pair color/percentage. In particular, the gradient starts with #c5deea, blends towards #8abbd7, and reaches it around 31 percent of coverage; the gradient ends with color #066dab. If you like linear gradients, you can use the following syntax:

```
background: -ms-linear-gradient(left, #3b679e 0%,#2b88d9 50%,#207cca 51%,#7db9e8
100%);
```

To do a live experiment with gradients, you can pay a visit to *http://www.colorzilla.com*. And once there, you can pick up one of the predefined gradients or create and preview your own ones.

Everything is now ready and the results of the exercise are ready to be unveiled, as shown in Figure 7-12.

FIGURE 7-12 A *SemanticZoom* component showing its master view.

Note that the *SemanticZoom* component defaults to the details, zoomed-in view. To have it display in zoomed-out mode by default, you need an extra attribute in *default.html*:

```
<div id="semantic-zoom-container"
    data-win-control="WinJS.UI.SemanticZoom"
    data-win-options="{initiallyZoomedOut: true}">
```

When the user clicks or taps a category, you get what's in Figure 7-13.

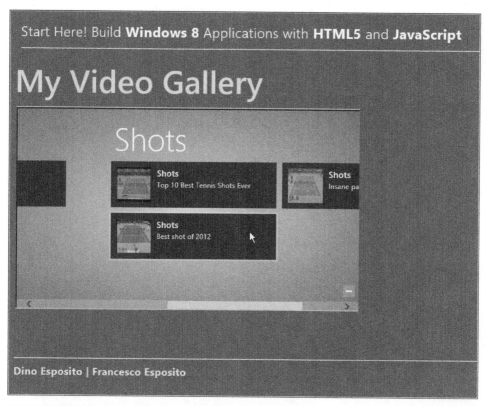

FIGURE 7-13 A *SemanticZoom* component showing its details view.

To return to the zoomed-out view, the user clicks the minus button in the bottom right corner of the screen.

Dealing with video

To end the exercise, you should make users capable of clicking the item that advertises a video clip and actually play it.

Handling selection

The *ListView* component supports clicking displayed items. To get notified of the user's activity, you register an handler for the *iteminvoked* event. Just open the *default.js* file and add the following line to the *VideosApp.init* function.

```
detailView.addEventListener("iteminvoked", VideosApp.select);
```

In addition, you create a brand new function named *VideosApp.select* like so:

```
VideosApp.select = function (eventInfo) {
    eventInfo.detail.itemPromise.then(function (clip) {
```

```
            var player = document.getElementById("player");
            player.src = clip.data.videoUrl;
    });
}
```

The *iteminvoked* event passes a *detail* object to handlers with an *itemIndex* property that simply returns the 0-based index of the clicked item. It should be noted, though, that there's no guarantee that the index really points to the clicked item.

In other words, you may think that, by knowing the index of the clicked item, you're pretty much done and all that remains to do is select the corresponding object from the bound list. Well, depending on the number of categories defined, and the distribution of video clips among categories, the index you get may or may not match the displayed video clip. For example, you may click with the intention of playing video ABC and receive an index of three. However, index three in the bound list may not be video ABC.

The point is that you bind items in a given order, but then items are rearranged based on categories. The index you receive refers to the rearranged order of items; not the original order. For this reason, you need to resort to the *itemPromise* property:

```
eventInfo.detail.itemPromise.then(function (clip) {
    // clip now matches the clicked item
}
```

The *itemPromise* property starts an internal search that uses the index as the key to locate the bound item actually displayed in that position. Once the object has been found, the *ListView* returns the object which can then be processed by your code.

Playing YouTube video clips

In order to play YouTube videos from your page, you need an *IFRAME* element that embeds the clip. So as a first step, you add the following markup to *default.html*:

```
<div id="player-container">
    <iframe id="player" height="100%" width="100%" type="text/html"></iframe>
</div>
```

The *IFRAME* element misses the URL of the video. The URL is provided dynamically as the user clicks a given item in the list view. Usually, the YouTube URL takes the following form:

```
http://www.youtube.com/embed/<id>
```

The *id* placeholder indicates the ID of the video. However, this approach just doesn't work in Windows Store applications. The reason is that, by default in the *IFRAME* body, YouTube inserts a piece of HTML that requires the Flash plug-in to play the video. The Flash plug-in is not available for Windows Store applications.

To fix things for Windows Store applications, you must instruct YouTube to return the video in an HTML5-compatible format. You do that by using a slightly different format for the video URL:

```
http://www.youtube.com/embed/<id>?html5=1
```

In this way, YouTube will insert in the *IFRAME* a piece of HTML that uses the *VIDEO* element of HTLM5 instead of relying on the Flash plug-in. Figure 7-14 provides a screenshot of the final version of the exercise.

Note You should be aware that, currently not all YouTube videos may be played in Windows Store applications. First and foremost, owners of the video may have blocked embedding of the video. Second, currently YouTube doesn't play any video that includes ads or captions through the HTML5 *VIDEO* element. For more information, have a look at *http://www.youtube.com/html5*.

FIGURE 7-14 The final version of the Video Gallery application.

Summary

With this chapter, you completed the overview of the presentation layer of Windows Store applications. You learned how to create and manage specialized views, such as flip views, list views, and master/detail views (known with the fancy name of semantic zoom). You also experienced the navigation system and know what's required to jump to a different page and pass information to that page. In this chapter, we also touched on persistence of state through the application's session state.

In doing so, you also completed a couple of nontrivial exercises and built a couple of interactive galleries for images and videos. In these exercises, you worked on a fixed collection of images and videos; however, you learned the foundation of galleries and interaction. Once you grasp the basics of file and data management, you will be ready for building real-world applications for Windows 8.

The next chapter still revolves around visual aspects of an application. It's not much about new widgets and components, though. It will be about states of an application and related display modes.

Chapter 8

States of a Windows 8 application

A goal without a plan is just a wish.

—*Antoine de Saint Exupery*

A couple of decades ago, the idea of pushing out a window-based operating system where multiple applications could live side by side was quite revolutionary. Before Microsoft Windows (and other similar operating systems) came out, users were used to working with a single application at a time. The active application took control of the machine and its computing resources, and filled up the entire screen with its content.

More recently, the idea of a single application running in the foreground has been revamped by mobile operating systems such as iOS, Windows Phone, and Android. After years of Windows and multiple applications running concurrently in separate windows, the one-application-at-a-time model was kind of a shock for many users.

What about Microsoft Windows 8?

If you run Windows 8 in desktop mode, then it's always the same Windows with multiple and overlapping windows that can be opened at any time. If you run a Windows Store application instead, you find out each application *usually* takes up the full screen and you have no way to interact with other applications without switching to them and having them, in turn, take the full screen. To be precise, a Windows Store application can live in a variety of states—full-screen (both landscape and portrait), filled, and snapped. When not running in any full-screen modes, a Windows Store application splits the available screen with a second application: one application runs *snapped* and the other runs *filled*.

What does that mean to you?

You should ideally provide some degree of adaptation to your application so that the state is preserved and the user interface adjusts to a smaller space. Dealing with filled and snapped views will be the main topic of this chapter.

States of a Windows Store application

Windows Store applications make a point of providing a full-screen and immersive experience to users. On one end, design guidelines recommend that you keep the user interface fairly simple and focused to avoid filling up the screen with too many items. On the other hand, as larger and larger screen resolutions become available, you take the risk of occupying a large PC screen with little content.

Since Windows 8 is an operating system created from the ground up to run on devices of different sizes, the whole theme of adapting the user interface (and subsequently the user experience) to a different screen is topical.

Windows 8 defines a few view states for applications and Windows Store applications receive proper notifications when the view state changes. What happens next is up to the application. Let's find out more about the predefined view states.

Full-screen view states

An application that runs in full-screen mode takes up the entire screen. Unless specified differently during the startup of the application, this is the default view state of any Windows Store application. To be precise, Windows 8 defines two full-screen modes—one for each orientation of the device.

Landscape mode

The landscape mode indicates that the device is being held horizontally and that width is larger than height. The landscape mode can be programmatically detected by looking at the value returned by the *Windows.UI.ViewManagement.ApplicationViewState* object. The following code snippet shows how to detect the landscape mode:

```
// Grab the current view state
var currentState = Windows.UI.ViewManagement.ApplicationView.value;

// Verify if the app is running in full-screen landscape mode
if (currentState === Windows.UI.ViewManagement.ApplicationViewState.
fullScreenLandscape) {
    ...
}
```

The operating system detects rotation of the device and automatically flips the user interface and notifies the application of any change.

Portrait mode

The portrait mode indicates that the available screen height now is larger than the width. This resolution suggests that it could be preferable for the application to flow content vertically because there's both more room to fill and the user may find it easier to scroll down rather than swipe left. The following code snippet shows how to detect the portrait mode:

```
// Grab the current view state
var currentState = Windows.UI.ViewManagement.ApplicationView.value;

// Verify if the app is running in full-screen portrait mode
if (currentState === Windows.UI.ViewManagement.ApplicationViewState.
```

```
fullScreenPortrait) {
    ...
}
```

Also in this case, the operating system detects rotation of the device and automatically orders the application to repaint its user interface.

> **Important** As it turns out, full-screen rotations may require some adjustments to the overall user interface of the application. It is not unusual that some content originally designed to extend horizontally needs be reorganized so that it also looks great on a device held in portrait mode. The operating system doesn't handle this aspect for you. All the operating system does is let the application know about view changes and ordering a repaint.

Snapping applications

The user can turn in the snapped state one of the applications that is currently running in the background. As a user, you pop up the switch list on the left side of the device and right-click the tile of the application of choice. As Figure 8-1 shows, you can decide to snap the application to the left or the right edge.

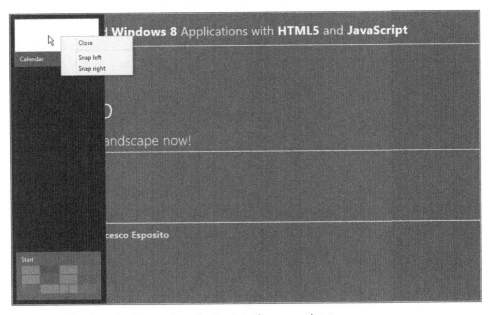

FIGURE 8-1 Turning a background application into the snapped state.

The result of this action is shown in Figure 8-2. When snapping is on, one application is said to be snapped; the other application previously running in full-screen mode is turned into a view state named *filled*.

FIGURE 8-2 The Calendar application is now snapped to the left edge.

The snapped view state

When snapped, an application is resized to a segment of the screen that is only 320 pixels wide and takes the entire height of the screen. As Figure 8-2 shows, the remaining screen is filled up by the application that was running in the foreground when you snapped. With snapping, therefore, users can have two applications in the foreground and can really work with both at the same time.

> **Important** There are a couple of key things to remark on regarding Windows 8 snapping. First, snapping is only available when the horizontal resolution of the screen is at least 1366 pixels. Users who try to snap applications on lower resolutions will simply find the context menu of Figure 8-1 limited to the *Close* option. Second, snapping is only available in landscape mode. If you have an application snapped, and then rotate the device to portrait, you lose the effect. The non-snapped application will regain the full screen in portrait view. However, the setting about snapping is maintained and snapping is automatically restored as soon as the user rotates back to a landscape view.

Also, you should note that users are not allowed to arbitrarily resize the snapped area either. The split bar of Figure 8-2 that separates the snapped and filled applications can't be moved at will. If a user moves the split bar to the right, then she can achieve one of the following effects: the two applications swap their view state or the snapped application gets into full-screen mode, pushing the other to the background. In the former case, the outcome will be that the Calendar app switches to the *filled* state and the other application gets snapped to the right edge.

The filled view state

When snapping is on, the screen is shared horizontally by two applications: the snapped application and the filled application (see Figure 8-3).

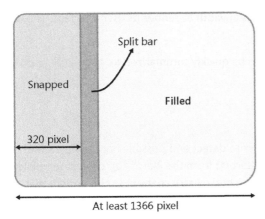

FIGURE 8-3 Fundamental aspects of snapped and filled applications.

Any application can experience both view states during its lifecycle. It's up to the user, not the application, to decide about the display mode. From the application's perspective, support for view states (including snapped and filled view states) is all about being ready to render any content in a screen of different sizes.

The behavior of a Windows Store application is not supposed to change when running in a view state different from full-screen. There's a specific guideline that strongly recommends this. It is *reasonable* to expect that very little changes in the application's behavior and user interface when the application is run in landscape, portrait, or filled mode. At the same time, not all applications can be resized to a sliver of the original screen and still maintain 100 percent of their functionality.

You'll see in a moment how to detect view state changes in a Windows Store application and what it possibly means for your application to support well different resolutions. Before going any further, look at Figure 8-4.

The figure doesn't show a screenshot but it rather contains a diagram that seeks to illustrate the difficulty of (some) applications to adapt to different resolutions.

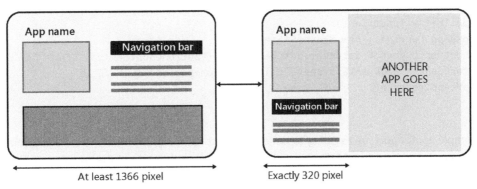

FIGURE 8-4 From full-screen view to snapped view: how to adjust the user interface?

When snapped, an application has only 320 pixels in width to render its user interface. The width is at least three times larger in the majority of cases.

A golden rule of Windows Store applications can be quickly summarized as, "Be ready to do something significant with about 320 x 760 pixels."

Making the application reactive

Let's see now what an application should do in order to detect and possibly handle view state changes. Create a new Windows Store application starting from the Blank App project template; you can name this application **SnapMe**. Next, make all the preliminary changes to the project that you did in all previous examples. This entails, for example, adding a header and footer, some styles to the *default.css* file, and an application-specific script file. Let's call this new script **SnapMeApp.js**.

Introducing new practices for application development

In the previous chapters, you didn't pay much attention to the state of the application. All of the exercises you did, in fact, essentially concerned stateless applications. Nearly any application does have a state that is updated as the user works with the application. The state needs to be saved to a permanent store when the application is suspended. In this way, you can easily restore it when the application is resumed or re-launched thus giving the user a nice feeling of continuity.

With this goal in mind, you add the following code to the newly created *SnapMeApp.js* file:

```
var SnapMeApp = SnapMeApp || {};

var SnapMeState = WinJS.Class.define(function () {
    var that = {};
    that.currentViewState = SnapMeApp.getViewStateForDisplay();
    that.total = 0;
    return that;
});

SnapMeApp.init = function () {
    SnapMeApp.Current = new SnapMeState();
    var buttonCounter = document.getElementById("buttonCounter");
    buttonCounter.addEventListener("click", SnapMeApp.add);
    SnapMeApp.refresh();
}
```

The sample application you're going to build will just contain a button that increments a counter variable when clicked. The *SnapMeState* is a class that describes the state of the application. The property *total* in the class counts the number of clicks. The property *currentState* contains a message referring to the current view state of the application.

In the *SnapMeApp.init* function, you initialize the application's state and register a handler for the *click* event of the button. You also register the *SnapMeApp.init* function to be invoked when the application is ready. You need the following code in *default.js*:

```
app.onready = function (args) {
    SnapMeApp.init();
};
```

This is the markup you need to have in the body of the *default.html* page, placed in between the header and footer pages:

```
<h1>My App</h1>
<h2 id="currentViewState"></h2>
<hr />
<button id="buttonCounter">Counter</button>
<h3 id="total"></h3>
```

Another new concept to practice with is the separation between state, behavior, and the logic that updates the user interface. You add the following code to express the behavior associated with clicking the button. This code goes at the bottom of the *SnapMeApp.js* file:

```
SnapMeApp.add = function () {
    // This is part of the application's behavior
    SnapMeApp.Current.total++;

    // This updates the user interface
    SnapMeApp.refresh();
}
```

Finally, you add the following code for refreshing the user interface:

```
SnapMeApp.refresh = function () {
    // Update the label with the current view state
    var stateElem = document.getElementById("currentViewState");
    stateElem.innerHTML = SnapMeApp.Current.currentViewState;

    // Update the label with the total number of clicks
    var totalElem = document.getElementById("total");
    totalElem.innerHTML = SnapMeApp.Current.total;
}
```

With the *SnapMeApp.refresh* function in place, you don't need to retrieve information from controls before updating the user interface. Likewise, you don't need to refresh the user interface directly from the code that handles events on visual elements. In this way, the entire code is cleaner and easier to develop and improve.

Detecting view state changes

The next step is adding more to the *SnapMe* application to make it capable of detecting view state change and reacting accordingly. For now, you will only record the new view state and display it to the user via the *currentViewState* label.

Any Windows Store application written using JavaScript and HTML receives notification of view state changes via the *onresize* event on the *window* object. The event is fired whenever the window that hosts the application is resized. In Windows 8, this can only happen when the device is rotated and the orientation changes or one application is snapped or unsnapped. To receive the *onresize* event, you need to register a handler. The best place to do so is the *SnapMeApp.init* function. Here's the final version of the function's code:

```
SnapMeApp.init = function () {
    window.onresize = addEventListener('resize', SnapMeApp.onResize, false);

    SnapMeApp.Current = new SnapMeState();
    var buttonCounter = document.getElementById("buttonCounter");
    buttonCounter.addEventListener("click", SnapMeApp.add);

    SnapMeApp.refresh();
}
```

Subsequently, you also need to add a new *SnapMeApp.onResize* function at the bottom of the *SnapMeApp.js* file.

```
SnapMeApp.onResize = function (e) {
    // Detect the current view state and saves it as a string
    SnapMeApp.Current.currentViewState = SnapMeApp.getViewStateForDisplay();

    // Refresh the user interface
    SnapMeApp.refresh();
}
```

As mentioned, the current view state is returned as an integer by a system provided global object: the *Windows.UI.ViewManagement.ApplicationViewState* enumeration. The enumeration counts four possible values—one for each of the possible view states. Four readymade constants make it easy for developers to make checks against a particular view state. The constants are as follows:

```
Windows.UI.ViewManagement.ApplicationViewState.snapped
Windows.UI.ViewManagement.ApplicationViewState.filled
Windows.UI.ViewManagement.ApplicationViewState.fullScreenLandscape
Windows.UI.ViewManagement.ApplicationViewState.fullScreenPortrait
```

The following code transforms the code that indicates a view state into a displayable text. The following code also belongs to the *SnapMeApp.js* file.

```
SnapMeApp.getViewStateForDisplay = function () {
    var viewState = Windows.UI.ViewManagement.ApplicationView.value;
    switch (viewState) {
        case Windows.UI.ViewManagement.ApplicationViewState.snapped:
            return "I'm snapped now!";
        case Windows.UI.ViewManagement.ApplicationViewState.filled:
            return "I'm filled now!";
        case Windows.UI.ViewManagement.ApplicationViewState.fullScreenLandscape:
            return "I'm full screen landscape now!";
        case Windows.UI.ViewManagement.ApplicationViewState.fullScreenPortrait:
            return "I'm full screen portrait now!";
    }
}
```

You're now ready to compile the sample application. Figure 8-5 shows what you get: the application is initially launched in full-screen landscape mode. Note that on a device held in portrait mode when the application is launched, you would get a different view state value—full-screen portrait.

FIGURE 8-5 The SnapMe application in landscape mode.

It is interesting to note that Microsoft Visual Studio has a simulator with built-in functions to experiment with orientation. Figure 8-6 shows how to change the orientation in the simulator to test if the portrait mode is detected correctly by the SnapMe application.

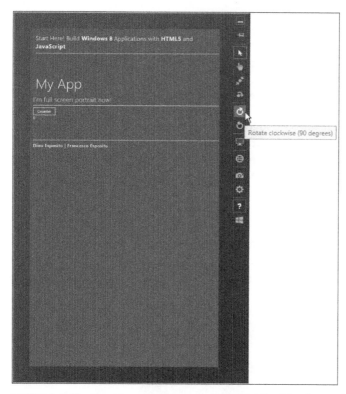

FIGURE 8-6 The SnapMe application run within the Visual Studio simulator.

Finally, Figure 8-7 shows the user interface of the sample application when snapped to the left edge of the screen.

FIGURE 8-7 The SnapMe application just snapped.

Whenever the user clicks the button, the *total* property of the application's state object is updated and displayed through the user interface. What happens to the state when the application is snapped, unsnapped, or the orientation changes?

Orientation and view change events do not affect the application's state if the application is in the foreground—whether full-screen, snapped, or filled. If the application is in the background, it doesn't receive any of these events.

Adapting the application's content

So far, you haven't really experienced the intricacies of having an application that has to support multiple resolutions. To bang against the problem, make the following changes to the *default.html* file:

```
<div style="width: 500px; background-color: red;">
    <h1>My App</h1>
    <h2 style="text-align: right" id="currentViewState"></h2>
    <hr />
    <button id="buttonCounter">Counter</button>
    <h3 id="total"></h3>
</div>
```

You just styled the main page in a slightly different manner. Now the entire user interface of the page (expect header and footer) is wrapped in a square 500 pixels wide and painted red so that it is more visible. In addition, the message about the current view state is now aligned to the right edge of the user interface container. The width chosen for the containing box (500 pixels) is not coincidental: any value significantly larger than 320 would work as well. Keep in mind that 320 pixels is the width of the snapped area.

The application doesn't experience any particular issues when run in filled, landscape, and portrait mode. Note, though, that this is more of the exception than the rule. Filled, landscape, and portrait modes still take the application to run in different resolutions and, more importantly, different aspect ratios. However, when you snap the SnapMe application to the edge, you see what's in Figure 8-8.

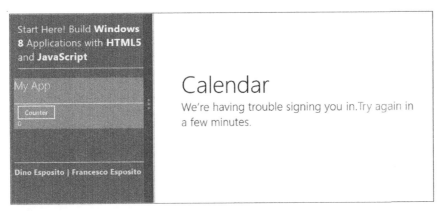

FIGURE 8-8 Some content is cut off in the snapped view.

The label with the text *"I'm snapped now!"* is not visible anymore. This is because the window is forced to a fixed width and the text—right-aligned after the last changes—doesn't fit anymore in the available space.

This example raises a few rendering problems that you can fully address only by giving your application an adaptive layout.

Towards an adaptive layout

When it comes to snapped and filled views, the bottom line is that users can snap any applications. Your application can adapt to the snapped view, but it can't prevent snapping from happening. If the application is not designed with snapping in mind, then its area is forcedly resized and this might cause some content to be cropped off, as in Figure 8-8.

General principles of snapped and filled views

Generally speaking, all Windows Store applications should abide by a few guidelines for snapped and filled views. There might be scenarios and situations in which this is not entirely possible. However, every effort should be put forth to work out a layout that seamlessly adapts to any size. Here are the principles at the foundation of the snapped view in Windows 8.

Be aware of view changes

Any Windows Store application should always register a handler for the resize event of the host window. This ensures that any application can properly react to any view changes that are reckoned significant. In the previous exercise, you just checked this principle off.

Parity of features across states

Ideally, you should have just *one* application that provides some uniform behavior across the possible view states. Whenever possible, the application should expose 100 percent of its functionality regardless of the view state—whether snapped, filled, landscape, or portrait.

In practice, though, this principle isn't the law and needs some elastic interpretation. What if your application needs to display a large input form? What if the application displays large data items like videos or photos? Both videos and photos can be shrunk to some extent, but the resulting quality may or may not be ideal for the purposes of the application.

Unsnap with care

If parity of features is not something you can guarantee, then you should consider unsnapping the application programmatically when the user selects one of the critical functions. As an example, consider a to-do list application.

To comfortably create a new task, you probably want to use a larger section of the screen. At the same time, you can probably comfortably list tasks in the 320 pixels of the snapped view. So when the user pushes some "Add new task" button, you programmatically unsnap the application. To practice with the *unsnap* functionality, add the following code to the *SnapMeApp.add* function in the *SnapMeAdd.js* file.

```
SnapMeApp.add = function () {
    SnapMeApp.Current.total++;
    var viewState = Windows.UI.ViewManagement.ApplicationViewState;
    if (SnapMeApp.Current.total >== 10 &&
        viewState === Windows.UI.ViewManagement.ApplicationViewState.snapped) {
        Windows.UI.ViewManagement.ApplicationView.tryUnsnap();
    }
    SnapMeApp.refresh();
}
```

In the example, when the counter reaches a threshold value of 10, the application will automatically unsnap if it is currently snapped. If you call the *tryUnsnap* function from within a non-snapped application, then the call results in a no-operation.

Use a proportional design

A proportional design refers to the idea that any content you display should be rendered using sizes and measurements proportional to the width of the container element. Using a proportional layout (also often referred to as *liquid* or *fluid* layout) automatically makes the application's content potentially capable of adapting to any size.

In the context of a proportional layout, you won't give, say, a *DIV* element a fixed width—as we've done in the code behind Figure 8-8. In general, though, there's no guarantee that any applications can be given a fluid layout that renders well in a 320-pixel width.

In Windows Store applications, developers tend to employ a user interface that works by listing and flowing elements. The underlying framework encourages this by the means of ad hoc components such as *ListView* and *SemanticZoom*—components that you practiced with in the previous chapter. Any content displayed through any of these components has a great chance to render nicely in a snapped view.

Let's learn a bit more about fluid layouts.

Fluid layouts

The linchpin of fluid layouts is the ability of HTML elements (such as, images, containers, text) to maintain their position and size relative to each other and the screen. In addition to proper resizing and font scaling, another major issue of fluid layouts is how to manage excess space so that elements can be allocated proportionately in the available area.

In Windows 8, you find excellent support for an approach that is becoming a ratified standard. This approach is based on the concept of *flexible boxes*. You can read more about the background of flexible boxes here: *http://bit.ly/SUM20b*.

Flexible boxes

In Windows Store applications, you create a flexible box by giving a *DIV* element a particular set of CSS styles. For a practical hands-on session, open the *default.css* file of the SnapMe project and add the following text:

```css
.flexible-container  {
    display: -ms-flexbox;
    -ms-flex-direction: row;
    -ms-flex-align: start;
    -ms-flex-wrap: wrap;
    color: white;
    font-size: 2em;
    text-align: center;
    height: 400px;
    overflow: auto;
    margin-top: 10px;
}
#block1 {
    background: #43e000;
    padding: 10px;
    border: solid 2px #fff;
}
#block2 {
    background: #166aff;
    padding: 20px;
    border: solid 2px #fff;
}
#block3 {
    background: #43e000;
    padding: 20px;
    border: solid 2px #fff;
}
#block4 {
    background: #ababab;
    padding: 25px;
    border: solid 2px #fff;
}
#block5 {
    background: #ff6a00;
    padding: 10px;
    border: solid 2px #fff;
}
```

Now go back to *default.html* and add the following markup that includes the elements to be styled with the preceding style sheet classes:

```
<div id="flexBox" class="flexible-container">
    <div id="block1">Europe</div>
    <div id="block2">North America</div>
    <div id="block3">Australia</div>
    <div id="block4">Asia and Far East</div>
    <div id="block5">South America</div>
</div>
```

You have now a container—the *DIV* element named *flexBox*—that is capable of flowing its content—the five child elements named *block*N—within any available space. The major benefit is that no content will be cropped. In addition, child blocks will wrap and be aligned as specified by the *-ms-flex-XXX* attributes of the *flexible-container* CSS class. The key style, however, is the *-ms-flexbox* value assigned to the *display* attribute of the *flexible-container* CSS class: this is the attribute that makes the content of a *DIV* element flow vertically or horizontally and according to other parameters. Table 8-1 provides a quick summary of the options you have to further customize the rendering of child elements in a flexible box.

TABLE 8-1 Styles supported by a flexible box

Style	Description
-ms-flex-direction	Indicates the orientation of all child elements within the flexible box. Possible values are: *row, column, row-reverse, and column-reverse.* The default value is *row*. A value of *row* indicates that child elements flow horizontally to fill up space. Elements are listed in the order they are declared in the source code. A value of *column*, instead, makes elements flow vertically. The *reverse* qualifier is used if you want to invert the order of elements and proceed from the last to the first.
-ms-flex-align	Indicates the alignment of child elements within the flexible box. The alignment is meant to be vertical if the direction *(ms-flex-direction* style) is horizontal and horizontal if the direction is vertical. Possible values are: *start, end, center*, and *stretch* (default). A value of *start* aligns elements to the top (or left). A value of *end* aligns to the bottom (or right). A value of *center* just centers elements, whereas a value of *stretch* gives all elements the maximum width/height available.
-ms-flex-pack	Indicates how excess space is distributed between child elements in the flexible box. Possible values are: *start, end, center*, and *justify* (default). A value of *start* leaves any space at the end of the row/column. A value of *end* leaves any space at the beginning of the row/column. A value of *center* just centers elements, whereas a value of *justify* splits the excess space between child elements.
-ms-flex-wrap	Indicates whether child elements wrap onto multiple lines or columns based on the space available in the object. Possible values are: *none (default), wrap*, and *wrap-reverse*. A value of *none* indicates that each child element goes on a separate row/column. A value of *wrap*, instead, forces the flexible box to accommodate child elements sequentially in the order of declaration. A value of *wrap-reverse*, instead, flows elements in the reverse order.

At this point, try compiling and running the application. You should get the output of Figure 8-9 when the application is filled.

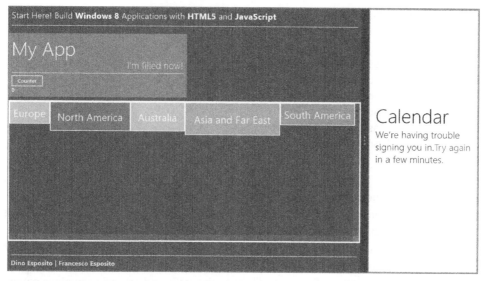

FIGURE 8-9 The SnapMe application in filled mode.

As you can see, all blocks within the flexible container are listed horizontally and fit nicely into the available space. If you display the application in full-screen landscape mode, the container will extend for the entire width and excess space is allotted at the end of the row. This is due to the *-ms-flex-align* setting of *start*.

Figure 8-10, instead, provides a view of the application when snapped to the left edge. The available space is now too small to fit multiple blocks on the same row. The result is that elements flow vertically. Should you have an element too large to fit the 320 pixel size, then you have two options: accept the excess content to be cropped or make the flexible container scrollable. You can do that by adding the following style to the flexible container.

```
.flexible-container {
    overflow: scroll;
    ...
}
```

Note that this setting was already included in the code you added to the *default.css* file earlier in the exercise.

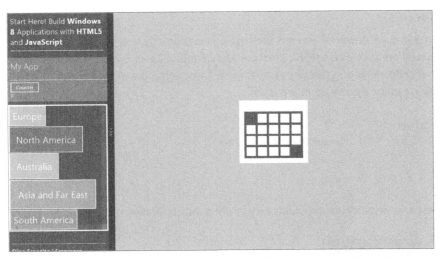

FIGURE 8-10 The SnapMe application in snapped mode.

Finally, Figure 8-11 provides a glimpse of the flexible container in full-screen portrait mode.

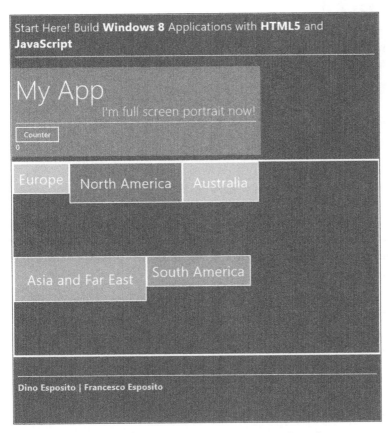

FIGURE 8-11 The SnapMe application in full-screen portrait mode.

CSS media queries

A flexible container is quite powerful and it is the core CSS technology that components specific to Windows 8 are based on, such as *GridView, ListView,* and *SemanticZoom.* Suppose now you increase the font size for all child elements. You can easily do that by opening the *default.css* file and making the following change in the *flexible-container* class.

```
.flexible-container {
    font-size: 3em;    // former value was 2em
    ...
}
```

You may not experience particular problems except when the application is snapped (see Figure 8-12).

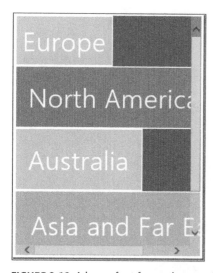

FIGURE 8-12 A larger font forces the use of scrollbars in snapped mode.

The use of scrollbars is necessary to make excess content visible. Is there a way to automatically adjust some CSS styles when the application goes in snapped mode? You bet; this is precisely the purpose of CSS media queries. You briefly touched on CSS media queries in Chapter 3, "Making sense of CSS."

A CSS media query is a query expressed on some run-time conditions that instruct the browser to pick up a particular CSS file. You can define a media query using a *LINK* element (as discussed in Chapter 3) or by directly embedding it in the CSS file. This is the standard approach followed by Windows Store applications.

Every time a new project is created, the *default.css* file contains the following CSS code:

```
@media screen and (-ms-view-state: fullscreen-landscape) {
}
@media screen and (-ms-view-state: filled) {
```

```
}
@media screen and (-ms-view-state: snapped) {
}
@media screen and (-ms-view-state: fullscreen-portrait) {
}
```

These are just predefined media queries for the four view states of a Windows Store application. All you need to do is add CSS settings that you want to be applied to each particular view state. For example, to shrink the font size only when the application is snapped, you enter the following code to *default.css*:

```
@media screen and (-ms-view-state: snapped) {
    .flexible-container {
        font-size: 2em;
    }
}
```

You basically overwrite any existing styles with the values that apply in the specific scenario. You don't need to completely rewrite the style; you just indicate what's different.

CSS media queries vs. resize events

In the course of this chapter, you have learned two techniques to deal with view changes—detecting resize events and CSS media queries. What's the difference and when should each be used?

CSS media queries are managed by the host browser and are limited to applying a different CSS style sheet to the application. If all you need is to change font sizes, adjust some fixed widths or heights you may still have, or fix margins and padding, then using CSS media queries is just fine and effective. Moreover, media queries also allow you to hide elements and move them around.

There might be situations, instead, where you can't just fix the application's layout with the sole use of CSS. A common example is when you use a *ListView* component to list items. In a view mode that is large enough, it is convenient opting for a multicolumn layout. When the application is snapped, instead, it is advisable that you switch to a single column layout. Because the *ListView* is a Windows 8 component, you need some JavaScript code to switch its layout accordingly. This can't be done from within a CSS file; an event handler is then the only possible approach. By using events, you can also programmatically replace all (or in part) the layout of the application by selecting a different layout for each significant view state. (You'll have an exercise that addresses this in just a moment.)

> **Important** The bottom line is that CSS media queries should be your first option; and you should turn to events if CSS media queries are not enough. Having said that, though, it's really hard to find a non-toy application that can manage view states without resorting (at some point) to events.

Adjusting the video application

In Chapter 7, "Navigating through multimedia content," you created a video application. A *listview* allowed users to select a YouTube video which was then played through an *IFRAME* element. The application was written while blissfully ignoring view states; and the behavior of the application with respect to view states is poor, as Figure 8-13 shows.

FIGURE 8-13 The Video application of Chapter 7 cuts off video when filled or snapped.

When filled, the application cuts off a significant part of its user interface—the video player. You can easily figure out that in portrait and snapped mode, where the width of the screen is smaller, things can only go worse. Some changes are in order to make the Video application integrate well with the surrounding environment.

The user interface is made of two main elements—the *listview* to pick up a video and the player. The first thing you might to do is put both in a flexible container. Second, you might want to get rid of most of the fixed-size values introduced in the last chapter. Basically, you only need to indicate an explicit width or height in the following cases:

- Define the height of the *listview* where the user selects the video to play.

- Define the width of the *listview* items so that they show up nicely in snapped mode.

- Define the expected size of the video player.

So open the *default.css* file; skip classes defined for body, header, footer, and title; and then wipe out everything else. Next, add the following:

```
.flexible-container {
    display:-ms-flexbox;
    border: solid 1px #fff;
    -ms-flex-pack: center;
    -ms-flex-wrap: wrap;
}
```

```css
/* Template for headers in the zoomed-in ListView */
.header-title {
    padding: 8px;
}

/* Template for items in the zoomed-in ListView */
.zoomed-in-item-container {
    overflow: hidden;
    display: -ms-grid;
}
.zoomed-in-item-container img {
    -ms-grid-column: 1;
}
.zoomed-in-item-container div {
    -ms-grid-column: 2;
}

/* Template for items in the zoomed-out ListView */
.zoomed-out-item-container {
    background-color: #00f;
    padding: 8px;
    text-align: center;
    width: 320px;
}
.zoomed-out-item-container h1 {
    color: #fff;
    font-size: 3em;
}

/* CSS for the zoomed-in/out ListView(s) */
#listview-in {
}
#listview-out {
}

/* Overall container */
#semantic-zoom-container {
    height: 240px;
    width: 100%;
    border-top: solid 2px #31cfd4;
    border-bottom: solid 2px #31cfd4;
    background: -ms-radial-gradient(center, ellipse cover, #c5deea 0%,#8abbd7
31%,#066dab 100%);
}

/* Video player */
#player-container {
```

```
    height: 338px;
    width: 450px;
    border: solid 1px #111;
    background: -ms-linear-gradient(left, #111 0%,#444 50%,#444 51%,#111 100%);
}
```

As you can see, the *listview* is set to 240 pixels of height and items are 320 pixels wide, which it is good to have just one item show up per row in snapped mode. Now open up *default.html* and fix the markup as follows. Remove the entire *TABLE* element you find next to the *H1* element with the page title. Replace it with the following markup:

```
<div class="flexible-container">
    <div id="semantic-zoom-container"
        data-win-control="WinJS.UI.SemanticZoom"
        data-win-options="{initiallyZoomedOut: true}">

        <!-- The zoomed-in view. -->
        <div id="listview-in"
            data-win-options ="{layout: {type: WinJS.UI.GridLayout}}"
            data-win-control="WinJS.UI.ListView"></div>

        <!--- The zoomed-out view. -->
        <div id="listview-out"
            data-win-options ="{layout: {type: WinJS.UI.GridLayout}}"
            data-win-control="WinJS.UI.ListView"></div>
    </div>
    <div id="player-container">
        <iframe id="player" height="100%" width="100%" type="text/html"></iframe>
    </div>
</div>
```

Finally, open up *Videos.js* and add the following line to the *VideosApp.init* function:

```
// Register handler for resize events
window.onresize = addEventListener('resize', VideosApp.onResize, false);
```

The extra line will register a handler for the resize event. By handling this event, you can switch the layout of both *listviews* of the semantic zoom component to the list layout when the application is snapped. Here's the code for the *VideosApp.onResize* function:

```
VideosApp.onResize = function (e) {
    var detailView = document.getElementById("listview-in").winControl;
    var masterView = document.getElementById("listview-out").winControl;
    var viewState = Windows.UI.ViewManagement.ApplicationView.value;

    switch (viewState) {
```

```
            case Windows.UI.ViewManagement.ApplicationViewState.snapped:
                detailView.layout = new WinJS.UI.ListLayout();
                masterView.layout = new WinJS.UI.ListLayout();
                break;
            case Windows.UI.ViewManagement.ApplicationViewState.filled:
            case Windows.UI.ViewManagement.ApplicationViewState.fullScreenLandscape:
            case Windows.UI.ViewManagement.ApplicationViewState.fullScreenPortrait:
                detailView.layout = new WinJS.UI.GridLayout();
                masterView.layout = new WinJS.UI.GridLayout();
                break;
        }
}
```

The grid layout gives components a multicolumn layout where items are displayed vertically up
until the bottom is reached and they then wrap to the next column. In snapped mode, when the
horizontal space is limited, you are better off choosing a list layout where a single column is created.
Figure 8-14 shows the new look-and-feel of the Video application. In this way, the Video application is
fully usable regardless of the view state.

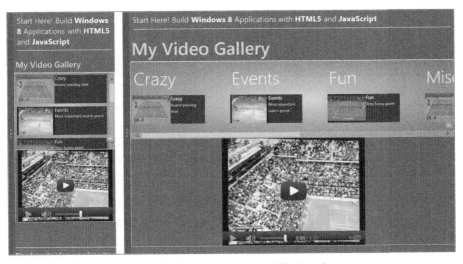

FIGURE 8-14 The new Video application in snapped and filled modes.

Early on, you set the width of the video player to over 400 pixels. As you can see in Figure 8-14,
when the application is snapped the player is still entirely visible. This is the effect of one more
changes: adding a media query for the snapped state.

```
@media screen and (-ms-view-state: snapped) {
    #player-container {
        height: 225px;
        width: 300px;
    }
}
```

The media query selects a smaller size for the player when the application is snapped to a screen edge.

 Note In this chapter, you practiced only with applications made of a single page. However, it should be noted that considerations on view states apply to any page you may have in the application.

Summary

Windows Store applications can be viewed in four different modes—full-screen, landscape, and portrait, as well as filled or snapped. In the latter cases, the application is sharing the screen with a second application. This means that you should be thinking of the layout of your application for at least four different scenarios and aiming to make your application fully functional even within a container as small as 320 x 760 pixels. At the same time, Windows 8 applications will also likely be consumed on very large screens.

Therefore, it is key for developers to opt at the beginning for a layout that is easily extensible. If a single flexible layout is not possible, then you should plan for having multiple different layouts and programmatically switch between them as resize events are detected.

Snapped applications are a very interesting case, as it happens when the application is forced to a sliver of the screen that is only 320 pixels wide. Guidelines of good Windows Store programming say that you should aim at reaching parity for features across view states. However, this is more a vector that points you to the right direction than a mandatory requirement. Users reasonably expect to be able to snap any applications; but not all applications can reasonably be fully functional with only 320 pixels of horizontal resolution. If this is the case, however, you should be ready to offer an alternate layout and unsnap programmatically as users hit a function that requires the full screen.

In this chapter, you learned about snapped and filled applications, and experimented with the code and styles that make it easy to create Windows Store applications that behave as good citizens of the Windows 8 world.

Chapter 9

Integrating with the Windows 8 environment

The heart has its reasons which reason knows nothing of.

—Blaise Pascal

Operating systems owe their acceptance and circulation mostly to successful applications. There are many ways to measure the success of an application. From the viewpoint of users, though, a successful application is often simply an application that allows the user to perform a common task in a seamless and comfortable way.

Consider a basic application that needs to save some text to a disk file. The primary goal of the application is getting and then saving the text. However, to save the text users probably need to choose a file name and a location on disk. These are ancillary tasks; necessary for the sake of the application but beyond the primary goal of the application. As a developer, you should allocate time to code these tasks too.

How would you code these accessory tasks, such as picking a file from disk? Without rules, each application could come up with its own user interface. This is nefarious for users, who potentially face a myriad of different interfaces; but it is also nefarious for developers, who have to write extra code each and every time.

In this chapter, you will learn about *contracts* and practice with them. Contracts are specific services for common tasks that applications can consume and expose for other applications to consume. The ultimate goal of contracts is having more and more applications doing the same things in the same way.

Contracts and common tasks

Microsoft Windows 8 is an operating system that imposes several constraints on applications. In particular, applications are isolated from each other. How can applications communicate with one another under these conditions? Contracts are the answer.

A contract defines a system-wide protocol for applications developed by different companies to communicate and exchange data. A contract refers to a particular common task, such as sharing data, searching for data, picking files, defining settings, and more. Applications that need that particular behavior can rely on existing implementations of that contract instead of coding their own. At the same time, applications may expose themselves to a given contract so that other applications can consume it.

Aspects of Windows 8 contracts

There are three aspects of a contract that deserve a bit more attention: how to discover available services, how to consume services, and how to expose services.

The Charms bar

In Windows 8, the Charms bar is a system's toolbar that users can access at any time, regardless of the application that is currently active. The Charms bar slides in from the right edge of the screen as soon as you point the mouse to the top/right or bottom/right corner of the screen. You can also display the bar by pressing Windows+C on your keyboard. Finally, on touch-enabled devices, you invoke the bar by swiping from the side. The Charms bar is shown in Figure 9-1.

FIGURE 9-1 The Charms bar in action.

The Charms bar counts five elements: Search, Share, Settings, Start, and Devices. The first three are the most interesting from the perspective of contracts. In fact, Search, Share and Settings are three of the basic contracts that most Windows Store applications should at least seriously consider.

An application that wants to share some of its content with other applications (and in turn with other users) implements the *Share* contract. Users of the Windows 8 operating system know that there's a standard way for them to share any content the current application may have—the Share button on the Charms bar. By implementing the *Share* contract, an application can push its selected content to any of the applications enlisted in the Share section of the Charms bar.

Likewise, an application that allows users to search for some content (such as, a cooking application that supports searching for a particular recipe) doesn't need to incorporate an ad hoc user interface for the search bar. Users know that the standard way for them to search for content is through the Charms bar. So an application that supports the *Search* contract can have its content searched every time the user uses the Search panel in the Charms bar.

Finally, the Settings button brings up the settings page of the current application. By implementing the *Settings* contract, the application can bring its own menu and set of options in the Settings panel in much the same way Microsoft Internet Explorer does in the screenshot of Figure 9-2.

FIGURE 9-2 The Settings panel of Internet Explorer.

Search, Share, and Settings are just the principal contracts available in Windows 8. A few other contracts are available, as you'll see in the rest of the chapter.

Consuming and publishing services

There are two ways for a Windows Store application to deal with contracts—to consume a service and to publish a service. In terms of coding, the first scenario is far easier to code since it just entails using a readymade set of Windows 8 components. The second scenario is only a bit harder to code since it requires that the application complies by the rules set in the definition of the contract.

A *to-do* list application may implement the *Share* contract as a source to enable users to share some of their tasks with friends. The user will invoke the Charms bar and pick up, say, the Mail application from the Share panel. The Mail application will then receive the content as exposed by the TodoList application and uses that to prepare an email message.

At the same time, your application may act as the receiver of information that another application may decide to share. Suppose you have an application that posts to the user's Facebook account. By making the application implement the *Share* contract as a target, you enable users of other applications to send their shared content to yours. So for example users of the TodoList application can now post their task directly to their Facebook account.

What makes contracts particularly attractive is that Windows Store applications may in the end result from the composition of functionality picked from different applications. Each application is then simpler and quicker to write.

Contracts and extensions

In this chapter, you'll go through a few exercises that involve the most commonly used contracts. The purpose of this section, instead, is to give you a quick overview of the available contracts so that you know where to look when you need to implement or consume a particular service.

Supported contracts

Table 9-1 lists and describes the contracts that Windows Store applications may support. As you can see, some of the contracts so far referenced under a single name (such as, *Share*) are actually available for coding in two or more flavors (such as, *Share source* and *Share target*).

TABLE 9-1 Contracts available for Windows Store applications

Contract	Description
Share source	The application implements this contract to share some of its content with any registered applications that support the *Share target* contract. Target applications appear in the Share menu of the Charms bar. For example, the default Weather application in Windows 8 is enabled to share forecasts.
Share target	The application implements this contract to be listed in the Charms bar as an application which can receive any data the current application can share. For example, the default Mail application acts as a Share target.
File open/Save picker	The application implements this contract to expose its own view of files and relevant folders. This contract entails providing a custom user interface for the user to pick a file or folder.

Contract	Description
Settings	The application implements this contract to let users access customizable application settings that affect the way in which users interact with the application. Windows 8 requires that applications expose settings in a standard way that passes through the implementation of the *Settings* contract.
Search	The application implements this contract to let user search within any content application-specific content that may be available.
Play to	The application implements this contract to enable users to easily stream audio, video, or images from their computer to any connected devices in their home network (such as, a large TV screen).
Cache updater	The application implements this contract if it is providing customized access to files and folders (via the *File picker provider* contract) and needs to notify applications of detected changes to listed files and folders.

As you can see, not all of the supported contracts make sense for just any Windows Store application. For example, *Share* and *Settings* contracts are much more common than the *Play to* contract or the *Cache updater*. Yet, the Windows 8 framework does provide a large offering of customizable aspects that is not even limited to contracts.

Extensions

While contracts are about agreements set between applications, *extensions* relate to agreements set between an application and the Windows operating system. By registering an extension, the application intends to extend or customize one or more standard Windows features such as, for example, the way in which files with a given extension (such as, TXT files) are managed within the operating system. Table 9-2 lists extensions available in Windows 8.

TABLE 9-2 Extensions available for Windows Store applications

Extension	Description
Account picture provider	The application provides this extension to be listed in the Account Picture Settings control panel as an application which can provide a picture for the user account.
AutoPlay provider	The application provides this extension to be listed as an AutoPlay choice for the one or more *AutoPlay* events. Windows fires the *AutoPlay* event whenever the user connects a device to the computer.
Background task provider	The application provides this extension if it needs to do some work in the background when the application is suspended. Background tasks are intended to be small work items that require no interaction with the user.
Camera settings provider	The application provides this extension if it can provide a custom user interface for selecting camera options and choosing effects when a camera is used to capture a photo or video.
Contact provider	The application provides this extension to be included in the list of applications that Windows displays whenever the user needs to pick a contact.
File activation provider	The application provides this extension if it intends to register as the handler of files with a given extension.
Print settings provider	The application provides this extension if it can provide a custom user interface for selecting printer options.

Implementing contracts and extensions requires writing code following strict rules and making some changes to the application's manifest file. The purpose of the second requirement is informing Windows about the system-wide changes that the application may introduce.

Consuming the *File picker* contract

Nearly any application needs to save data to the user's disk. When it comes to this, nearly any application needs to be able to create and open files in folders. Sometimes the application can use files and folders with fixed names and disk locations; sometimes, instead, it is preferable that the user has the final word on the name of a given file and the location of the containing folder.

How would you let a user to choose a file name and a disk location?

This is precisely the purpose of the *File picker* contract. If you are familiar with earlier versions of Windows, the concept behind file pickers should be nothing new: the *File picker* contract is just the programming artifact necessary to implement a common dialog box, such as the one in Figure 9-3.

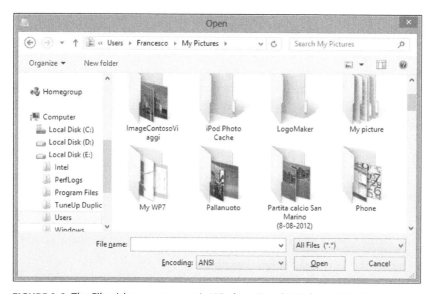

FIGURE 9-3 The File picker counterpart in Windows 7 and Windows 8 Desktop.

Let's extend the TodoList application you developed in Chapter 6 to consume file pickers and let users choose a file and location where to save the task. You won't be dealing yet with the physical details of how to create a file. You limit picking a file in this chapter and complete the exercise with file and folder creation in the next chapter.

Choosing a file to save data

You start the exercise by making a copy of the TodoList project from Chapter 6, "The user interface of Windows Store applications," in a new folder of your choice. Before you go any further with contracts, it is advisable that you make some little changes to the existing code to improve the application.

Preliminary changes to the TodoList application

First thing, you define an HTML layout for the summary fly out displayed to the user before attempting to save. Open the *default.html* file and replace the content of the *DIV* element with the ID of *flyoutSummary*. Here's the new content:

```
<div data-win-control="WinJS.UI.Flyout" id="flyoutSummary">
    <div class="tableLabel">DESCRIPTION:</div>
    <div class="tableValue"><span data-win-bind="innerText: description" /></div>
    <div style="clear:both" />
    <div class="tableLabel">DUE DATE:</div>
    <div class="tableValue">
      <span data-win-bind="innerText: dueDate TodoList.dateForDisplay"></div>
    <div style="clear:both" />
    <div class="tableLabel">PRIORITY:</div>
    <div class="tableValue"><span data-win-bind="innerText: priority" /></div>
    <div style="clear:both" />
    <div class="tableLabel">STATUS:</div>
    <div class="tableValue"><span data-win-bind="innerText: status" /></div>
    <div style="clear:both" />
    <div class="tableLabel">COMPLETED:</div>
    <div class="tableValue"><span data-win-bind="innerText: percCompleted" /></div>
    <div style="clear:both" />
    <br /><hr />
    <button onclick="TodoList.pickFileAndSaveTask()">It's OK. Please save!</button>
</div>
```

As you can see, the markup now contains a button for the user to click to trigger the save process. The markup being used also contains a couple of new CSS styles that must be added to the *todolist. css* files you have in the project.

```
.tableLabel {
    float: left;
    width: 100px;
    text-align: right;
    font-weight: 600;
}
.tableValue {
    float: left;
    font-weight: 400;
    margin-left: 10px;
}
```

Finally, you open *todolist.js* and modify the content of the *displaySummary* function as shown below:

```
TodoList.displaySummary = function (task) {
    // Prepare the content for the flyout
    var bindableElement = document.getElementById("flyoutSummary");
    WinJS.Binding.processAll(bindableElement, task);

    // Display the flyout
    var anchor = document.getElementById("buttonAddTask");
    var flyoutSummary = document.getElementById("flyoutSummary").winControl;
    flyoutSummary.show(anchor);
}
```

You learned the basics of Windows 8 data binding back in Chapters 5 and 6. In this chapter, you face a new requirement: formatting the content of data for display purposes. The task you're creating through the TodoList application has a due date; in the summary, you might want to show the date as well as the rest of the content. You want, however, to display the date in a common format. The default format you get, instead, is the ISO format of dates which is not really easy to read for humans. You need a converter that preprocesses the date just before display. In the markup for the *flyout* you entered earlier, you find code like below:

```
<span data-win-bind="innerText: dueDate TodoList.dateForDisplay">
```

The *SPAN* element is being bound to the *dueDate* property of the *Task* object; but the real content is massaged by the *TodoList.dateForDisplay* function. This function must be added to the *todolist.js* file.

```
// Converter to date display in the flyout
TodoList.dateForDisplay = WinJS.Binding.converter(function (value) {
    return value.toLocaleDateString();
});
```

Finally, you add the code that serves as the placeholder for file picking functionality. This code is invoked when the user clicks on the button now displayed in the flyout to start the save process. Add this code at the bottom of the *todolist.js* file.

```
TodoList.pickFileAndSaveTask = function () {
    // Get the task object to save
    var currentTask = TodoList.getTaskFromUI();

    // Placeholder for more interesting things
    TodoList.alert("Ready to pick a file and save...");
}
```

Figure 9-4 shows the new look and feel of the summary displayed to the user when the task is ready for storing.

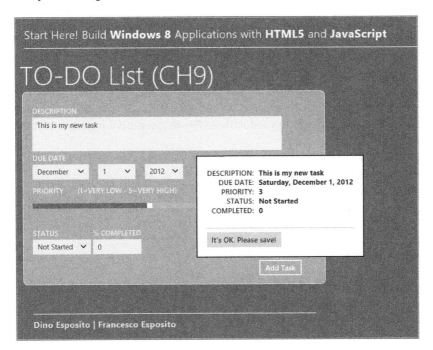

FIGURE 9-4 The summary flyout as modified in this chapter.

Unsnap before you pick

Once the user clicks the button in Figure 9-4, the application should let her pick up a file where the task will be saved. This entails consuming the *File picker* contract as it is implemented by the operating system. Windows 8 provides its own version of the dialog box shown in Figure 9-3. The Windows Store counterpart of the familiar file Open/Save dialog box is just a component that exposes the *File picker* contract.

At this stage, you don't need yet to get acquainted with the nitty-gritty details of contracts, as the details of the *File picker* contract are buried in the folds of a few new high-level components and functions. These components and functions are the only ones you need to get familiar with.

A key rule you need to cope with is that a Windows Store application is not allowed to invoke a file picker if it is in a snapped state. Because of this, you should add the following code at the very beginning of the *TodoList.pickFileAndSaveTask* function in the *todolist.js* file.

```
var currentState = Windows.UI.ViewManagement.ApplicationView.value;
if (currentState === Windows.UI.ViewManagement.ApplicationViewState.snapped &&
    !Windows.UI.ViewManagement.ApplicationView.tryUnsnap()) {
    // Fail silently if you can't unsnap the app
    return;
}
```

If the application is not in a snapped state, then you are ready to invoke the system's picker for saving a file.

Dealing with the default File save picker

Windows 8 provides two distinct components whether you need to pick the file to save or read some content. You use the *Windows.Storage.Pickers.FileOpenPicker* object if your goal is picking an existing file for reading its content. You use the *Windows.Storage.Pickers.FileSavePicker* object, instead, if you intend to create a new file or override an existing one. To save the task, you opt for the second option. This is the code you need to have in the *TodoList.pickFileAndSaveTask* function within the *todolist.js* file.

```
TodoList.pickFileAndSaveTask = function () {
    // Code to check if in snapped state
    ...

    // Get the task object to save
    var currentTask = TodoList.getTaskFromUI();

    // Create the picker object and set options
    var savePicker = new Windows.Storage.Pickers.FileSavePicker();
    savePicker.commitButtonText = "Create task";
    savePicker.suggestedStartLocation = Windows.Storage.Pickers.PickerLocationId.
computerFolder;
    savePicker.suggestedFileName = currentTask.description;
    savePicker.fileTypeChoices.insert("TodoList Task", [".todo"]);

    // More code will go here
    ...
}
```

This code is not sufficient yet to display the user interface for picking up files. It lacks the specific instruction that pops up the standard user interface. Let's spend a few moments understanding the role of the properties involved in the code above.

Preferred settings

You should notice that the *SuggestedStartLocation* property is set to an expression that indicates the *Computer* folder as the starting location of the search. As the property name seeks to indicate, that is not necessarily going to be the real start location for the file picker. In an attempt to give users a continuous feel, the file picker tracks the last folder visited and starts from there. Should the folder be unavailable (such as, the folder has been deleted) or unreachable (such as, you are disconnected from the network), then the picker will take the suggestion. The suggestion is also taken if there's no current record on track about the last folder visited.

Note also that developers are not entitled to suggest programmatically any start folder not listed in the *PickerLocationId* enumeration. By design, only the predefined system folders can be presented to the user. The *PickerLocationId* enumeration includes the folders listed in Table 9-3.

TABLE 9-3 Predefined system folders

Location	Description
computerFolder	The folder that provides access to all disks and connected devices.
desktop	The Windows desktop.
documentsLibrary	The user's Documents folder.
downloads	The folder where software is downloaded by default.
homeGroup	The folder that provides access to all computers in the home group.
musicLibrary	The Music library folder.
picturesLibrary	The Pictures library folder.
videosLibrary	The Videos library folder.

Similarly, you can suggest the name for the file to be saved. You do that through the *Suggested-FileName* property. In the example above, you set the suggested file name to the description of the task being created:

```
savePicker.suggestedFileName = currentTask.description;
```

Another parameter you can customize is the list of extensions recommended for the file being created. In this case, you provide the *.todo* custom extension:

```
savePicker.fileTypeChoices.insert("TodoList Task", [".todo"]);
```

The *commitButtonText* property sets the caption of the button the user will need to click to save content.

Getting the name of the file to create

To display the user interface through which the user will be able to select a file to save, you need to add the following code to the body of the *TodoList.pickFileAndSaveTask* function.

```
// Invoke the file picker
savePicker.pickSaveFileAsync().then(function (file) {
    if (file) {
        TodoList.alert(file.name);
    }
});
```

The method *pickSaveFileAsync* displays the user interface and returns only once the user has dismissed the dialog or has selected a file. The method runs asynchronously; this means that you need to use the *then* method to specify any behavior you want to run after the file has been selected.

The File save picker returns a *file* parameter that refers to the name of the file being created. If the file argument is *null*, then the user has dismissed the picker; otherwise, the user has successfully selected a file. The next step of this exercise consists of displaying some properties of the file. In the next chapter, you'll learn how to create and read files. Figure 9-5 shows the user interface of the file picker about to create a new file in an empty folder.

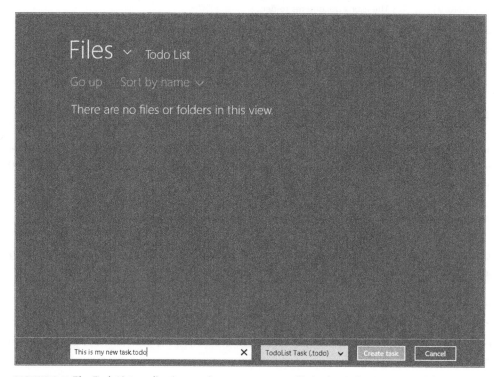

FIGURE 9-5 The TodoList application ready to create a new file in the *Todo List* custom folder.

The object you receive from the file picker is a *StorageFile* object. To get its name, you can invoke the *name* property. You can also invoke the *displayName* property if you want to get rid of the associated extension. Figure 9-6 shows a message box with the name of the created file.

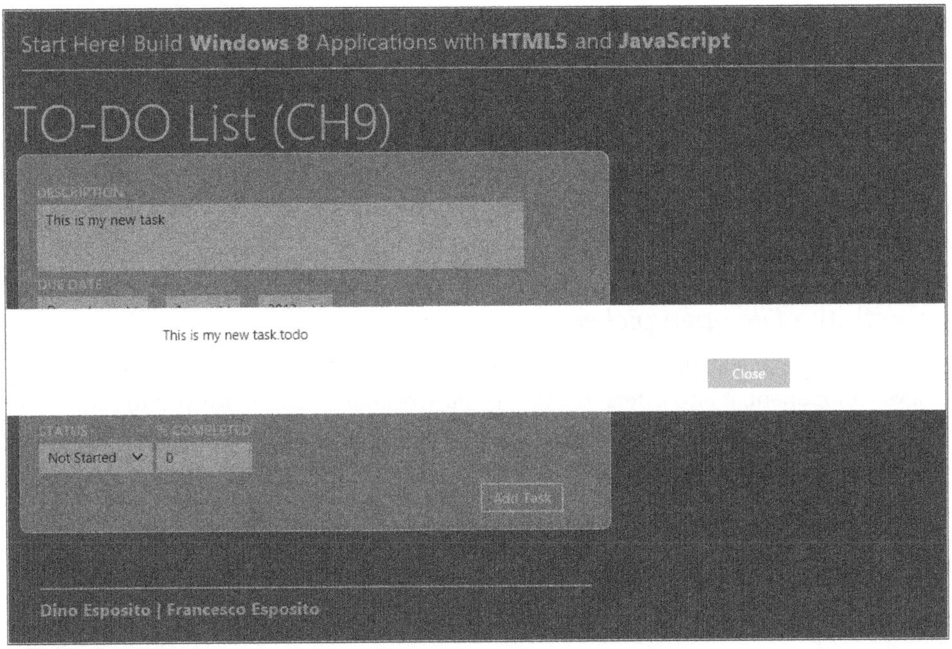

FIGURE 9-6 Getting the name of the selected file.

You don't need to take any special care to get the name of a file or its file type. Three properties are available: *name, displayName,* and *fileType*. If you need to read some additional file properties (such as, size or date), then you need a call to *getBasicPropertiesAsync*, as shown below:

```
savePicker.pickSaveFileAsync().then(function (file) {
    if (file) {
        file.getBasicPropertiesAsync().then(function (basicProperties) {
            TodoList.alert(file.name + "(" + basicProperties.size + " bytes)");
        });
    }
});
```

File properties are split in three groups: built-in, basic, and extended. Built-in properties are name and file type, and they are retrieved along with the file content. Basic properties include *size* and *dateModified*; basic properties must be retrieved via a call to *getBasicPropertiesAsync*. Extra properties must be accessed via a preliminary call to *retrievePropertiesAsync*. Here's an example:

```
file
  .properties
  .retrievePropertiesAsync([fileOwnerProperty, dateAccessedProperty])
  .done(function (extraProperties) {
      TodoList.alert(extraProperties[dateAccessedProperty]);
  }
```

Typical properties you retrieve in this way are *fileOwner* and *dateAccessed*.

Choosing a file to load data

Once you have some files saved to disk, at some point you need to read them back. Before you can read their content, however, you need to pick them up from storage. For this purpose, you need a *File open picker* component. As mentioned, any application can serve as a File open picker as long as it implements the *File open picker* contract. Most of the time, however, you will be dealing with the system default *File open picker* rather than offering your own picker to other applications. Here's how you deal with the default File open picker.

Dealing with the *File open picker*

The File open picker is an instance of the *FileOpenPicker* component. Much like the companion *FileSavePicker* component, it also offers a *suggestedStartLocation* property for you to suggest a preferred location where the user should start searching for a file. The following code shows how you set up a file picker to select an image file:

```
var openPicker = new Windows.Storage.Pickers.FileOpenPicker();
openPicker.suggestedStartLocation = Windows.Storage.Pickers.PickerLocationId.
picturesLibrary;
openPicker.fileTypeFilter.replaceAll([".png", ".jpg", ".jpeg"]);
```

The *replaceAll* function indicates the files you are interested in viewing in the list to select. The list of accepted file extensions is passed in as an array. You can also set a view mode and specify that you want file items to be represented with thumbnails.

```
openPicker.viewMode = Windows.Storage.Pickers.PickerViewMode.thumbnail;
```

Finally, you use the *pickSingleFileAsync* function to display the picker's user interface and show the user the name of the selected file:

```
openPicker.pickSingleFileAsync().then(function (file) {
    if (file) {
        TodoList.alert("You picked: " + file.name);
    }
});
```

Figure 9-7 shows the user interface of the *File open picker* component. It displays the content of the *Pictures* library on the current computer. As the user clicks the *Pictures* link to see more locations to search for files, a drop-down menu unfolds. The menu contains the default locations of a Windows 8 machine plus all registered custom file pickers.

By default, you find a custom picker for Photos, one for taking pictures right from the webcam. Finally, you find the *SkyDrive* component that allows you to pick up a file from the cloud. All of these are ad hoc file pickers that implement the aforementioned *File open picker* contract.

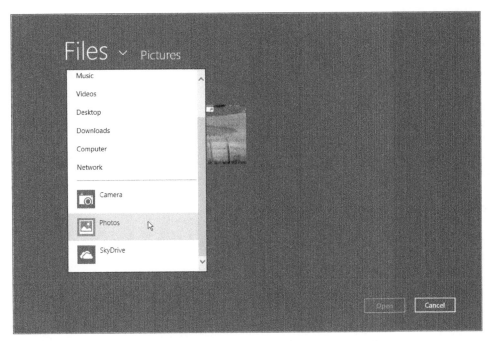

FIGURE 9-7 The *File open picker* component in action.

Multiple selections

The previous example only allows users to select a single file. To enable multiple selections, you just change the function that triggers the user interface. Here's how:

```
openPicker.pickMultipleFilesAsync().then(function (files) {
    if (files.size > 0) {
        var buffer = "You picked:\n";
        for (var i = 0; i < files.size; i++) {
            buffer = outputString + files[i].name + "\n";
        }
        TodoList.alert(buffer);
    } else {
        // The user dismissed the picker without selecting any files.
    }
});
```

The *pickMultipleFilesAsync* function passes to the next callback—the code you pass to function *then*—the list of files that the user may have selected. You can gain access to all files by running a loop over the list.

Note that the application has read/write access to any files referenced by the file open/save pickers.

Selecting a folder

Another common scenario is when your application just needs users to select a folder; not a file. Windows 8 has a handy object for the purpose—the *FolderPicker* object. You use this object in much the same way you use other pickers.

```
// Create the picker object and set options
var folderPicker = new Windows.Storage.Pickers.FolderPicker();
folderPicker.fileTypeFilter.replaceAll(["*"]);
folderPicker.suggestedStartLocation = Windows.Storage.Pickers.PickerLocationId.
desktop;
```

To display the user interface, you need the following code:

```
folderPicker.pickSingleFolderAsync().then(function (folder) {
    if (folder) {
        TodoList.alert(folder.name);
    }
});
```

Note that the application gains read/write access not just on the selected folder but also on all subfolders.

The *Share* contract

If you've used Windows, you should know about the Windows clipboard. It's a system feature that allows users to copy data from one application (typically with Ctrl+C) and paste that into another (typically with Ctrl+V). The clipboard does support a variety of formats—data can be copied as plain text, rich text, and bitmap, but also application-specific formats are supported.

The clipboard is essentially a user-oriented feature, but it was backed by a programming interface in all versions of Windows. Windows Store applications have no access to the clipboard, but that doesn't mean that distinct applications can't communicate and exchange data. Instead of the clipboard, a user will just use the *Share* menu from the Charms bar.

Publishing an application's data

In this exercise, you'll learn how to make some application-specific data potentially available to any other applications registered to receive shared data. The exercise consists of extending the TodoList application to make it act as a Share source application.

Choosing the data format

To be a share source provider, your application doesn't need to be written in a special way. It only needs to use a set of ad hoc components, such as the *DataPackage* and the *DataTransferManager* objects. The former defines the package with the data to share; the latter passes the package on to requesting applications.

When it comes to sharing data, the primary aspect to consider is the format of the data, whether plain text, HTML, or perhaps bitmaps. Ideally, the more formats you support, the more your application can share. In the end, though, the best choice is just supporting the formats that make the most sense for the specific application. These formats are usually just one or two. Table 9-4 lists the supported data formats.

TABLE 9-4 Supported formats for shared data

Data format	Method	Description
Plain text	*setText*	Shared data consists of a plain string of text.
URI	*setUri*	Shared data consists of a link to a URL that receivers may render as a clickable item.
HTML	*setHtmlFormat*	Shared data consists of HTML markup including styles, script, and images.
Rich text format	*setRtf*	Shared data consists of text formatted as RTF (such as, data you get from Microsoft Word).
Bitmap	*setBitmap*	Shared data consists of an in-memory image.
Files	*setStorageItems*	Shared data consists of files.

The data package

The column Method in Table 9-4 just refers to the methods available on the *DataPackage* object that allow sharing data in a particular format. Creating a valid data package is the primary responsibility of the Share Source application. A *DataPackage* object can contain data in one or more of the formats listed in Table 9-4. It is up to the requesting application to pick up data in the format that makes the most sense.

For example, the default Windows 8 Mail application operates as a Share target. It can accept data in a variety of formats and embeds data into the body of the email. If an application passes data as plain text as well as HTML, the HTML format is picked up as the preferred format. You'll experiment with this behavior in a moment.

Adding share source capabilities to TodoList

As the first step on the way to sharing data with other applications, you should register a handler within the application for the *datarequested* event. You do this as soon as possible in the application lifecycle.

Handling requests for data

You open the *todolist.js* file and add the following code at the bottom of the *TodoList.init* method:

```
// Initialization of Share source contract
var clipboard = Windows.ApplicationModel.DataTransfer.DataTransferManager.
getForCurrentView();
clipboard.addEventListener("datarequested", function (e) {
    // Get the information to share
    var currentTask = TodoList.getTaskFromUI();

    // Share information as plain text
    TodoList.shareDataAsPlainText(e, currentTask);

    // Share information as HTML
    TodoList.shareDataAsHtml(e, currentTask);
});
```

The *clipboard* variable references the data transfer manager object active for the current window. Data transfer manager is the system component responsible for transferring data in and out of your application. You use the *addEventListener* method to register a handler for the *datarequested* event. This event is fired whenever the user brings up the Share panel and there's at least one application ready to receive data.

Note Windows 8 doesn't disable the Share button on the Charms bar if the current application doesn't support the *Share source* contract. So the user can always try to share content from within any application. However, if the *DataTransferManager* object detects that the current application doesn't expose a handler for the *datarequested* event, a message is shown like in Figure 9-8.

In the handler for the *datarequested* event, you collect the data to share, format the data in the way you like and package data up in a *DataPackage* object. In the code snippet above, the data to share is represented by the task being created. Task information is shared as plain text and HTML. The order in which data is added to the package (plain text is added first in the previous code snippet) is unimportant. The format shared actually depends on the settings of the receiver application.

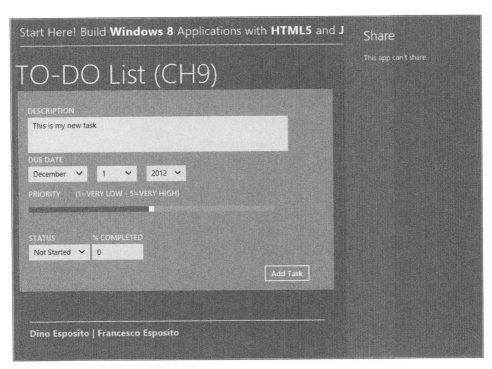

FIGURE 9-8 The user interface displayed when the user attempts to share content from an application that doesn't support the *Share source* contract.

Sharing data as plain text

Now you add the following new function to the bottom of the *todolist.js* file. The new function is responsible for sharing the task information with other applications.

```
TodoList.shareDataAsPlainText = function (e, task) {
    var request = e.request;

    // Add data to the package
    request.data.properties.title = "TO DO";
    request.data.properties.description = task.description;
    request.data.setText(task.description + " due by "
+ task.dueDate.toLocaleDateString());
}
```

The data package to fill up is given by the *request.data* object. The *DataPackage* component has a couple of generic properties, such as *title* and *description*. You might want to set them as a way to describe the data you're going to provide. Consider that both the Share panel and target applications may be using these properties. So setting them to a meaningful value is always a good thing. In this case, you set the *title* property to a static text such as "TO DO" and the *description* property to the actual description of the task.

Finally, you prepare the actual string of text to share and copy it to the package using the *setText* method. Figure 9-9 shows the effect of the change: the TodoList application can now pass data to the Mail application through the Share panel of the Charms bar.

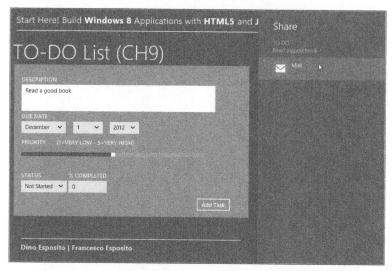

FIGURE 9-9 The TodoList application ready to share task information.

Once the user has clicked one of the listed applications (only the Mail is listed as a receiver in the screenshot), the control passes to the selected application. The application inspects the data package, ensures it contains data it can handle, extracts data in the most convenient format, and then uses it. Figure 9-10 shows what the Mail application can do with the passed data: it prepares a new email and automatically sets to the body of the email to the shared text.

FIGURE 9-10 The Mail application is consuming data from TodoList.

Sharing data as HTML

Sharing data as HTML is only a bit more complicated. The most intriguing part is how you format the HTML. You can create the HTML string programmatically by concatenating text and HTML elements or you can write the HTML directly in the HTML page and read it from there. If you do so, the benefit is that your code is cleaner and the HTML structure can be understood more easily and modified quickly. In addition, you can use any visual editor to edit it.

You open *default.html* and add the following markup at the bottom of the file just before the closing tag of the *BODY* element:

```
<div id="shareHtml" style="display:none;">
    <img style="float:left;" src="ms-appx:///images/todolist-icon.png" alt="" />
    <div style="padding:3px;background:#999;color:#fff">DESCRIPTION:</div>
    <div><span data-win-bind="innerText: description" /></div>
    <div style="padding:3px;background:#999;color:#fff">DUE DATE:</div>
    <div><span data-win-bind="innerText: dueDate TodoList.dateForDisplay" /></div>
    <div style="padding:3px;background:#999;color:#fff">PRIORITY:</div>
    <div><span data-win-bind="innerText: priority" /></div>
    <div style="padding:3px;background:#999;color:#fff">STATUS:</div>
    <div><span data-win-bind="innerText: status" /></div>
    <div style="padding:3px;background:#999;color:#fff">COMPLETED:</div>
    <div><span data-win-bind="innerText: percCompleted" /></div>
</div>
```

This is the layout of the HTML the application will be sharing. The HTML layout is populated with task data via data binding—this is the same approach we used earlier for the task summary. Note also that you don't want this piece of HTML to show up in the page. For this reason, it is essential that you explicitly set the *display* CSS attribute on the root element to *none*. This ensures the HTML block will stay invisible.

Now add the following function to the bottom of the *todolist.js* file:

```
TodoList.shareDataAsHtml = function (e, task) {
    var request = e.request;
    request.data.properties.title = "TO DO";
    request.data.properties.description = task.description;

    // Load the HTML layout and run data binding
    var elem = document.getElementById("shareHtml");
    WinJS.Binding.processAll(elem, task);
    var rawHtml = elem.innerHTML;

    // Make the raw HTML compliant with Windows 8 requirements
    var html = Windows.ApplicationModel.DataTransfer.HtmlFormatHelper.
createHtmlFormat(rawHtml);
    request.data.setHtmlFormat(html);
```

```
    // This extra work is necessary ONLY if the HTML references an image.

    // This is the URL of the image as in the HTML block.
You transform it in a URI object
    // and store it as an in-memory stream in the DataPackage resources.
    var localImage = "ms-appx:///images/todolist-icon.png";
    var url = new Windows.Foundation.Uri(localImage);
    var streamRef = Windows.Storage.Streams.RandomAccessStreamReference.
createFromUri(url);
    request.data.resourceMap[localImage] = streamRef;
}
```

You retrieve the HTML block as a string by reading the content of the *innerHTML* property of the *DIV* element. The raw HTML must be formatted to comply with Windows 8 requirements. This is accomplished by the *createHtmlFormat* helper method. Finally, you call *setHtmlFormat* to package the HTML description of the task.

If the HTML references one or more images, then some extra work is required. In particular, images must be referenced using an ad hoc protocol—the *ms-appx* protocol. This protocol identifies images as a native part of the application. In other words, if you want to include an image that belongs to the resources of the application, then you must use the *ms-appx* protocol. If you intend to reference images from remote URLs, then using the HTTP protocol is fine. In the example above, *todolist-icon. png* is an image file stored in the *images* folder of the application's project.

Figure 9-11 shows the content of the email used to share the task.

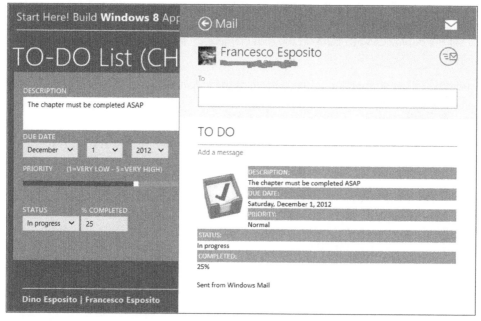

FIGURE 9-11 Sharing a task as HTML.

Conditional sharing

There might be situations in which an application that shares data is unable to do so. A common example is when the user is required to select some data in order for the data to be shared. For example, in the TodoList application it might be wise to require that data is shared only if a non-empty description has been provided.

You deal with conditional sharing in the handler of the *datarequested* event. Here's how to modify the code you previously added to the *TodoList.init* method to enable the *Share source* contract:

```
TodoList.clipboard.addEventListener("datarequested", function (e) {
    var currentTask = TodoList.getTaskFromUI();

    if (currentTask.description.length === 0) {
        e.request.failWithDisplayText("Indicate a description of the task.");
        return;
    }

    TodoList.shareDataAsHtml(e, currentTask);
    TodoList.shareDataAsPlainText(e, currentTask);
});
```

The *failWithDisplayText* method causes the share action to fail. The optional text is displayed to the user. If you don't provide any help text, then the user will receive a generic message stating that the application is not currently able to share anything.

Programmatic sharing

Using the Charms bar is not the only way to trigger the Share panel. Each application can offer its own user interface for the user to start the sharing process. For example, you can add a new button to *default.html* that sits side by side with the existing Add Task button.

```
<button id="buttonShare">Share</button>
```

In *TodoList.init*, you also add a click handler for the button:

```
document.getElementById("buttonShare").addEventListener("click", TodoList.
shareClick);
```

Finally, here's the code for the new function *TodoList.shareClick* which does the trick of programmatically displaying the Share panel out of the Charms bar.

```
TodoList.shareClick = function () {
    Windows.ApplicationModel.DataTransfer.DataTransferManager.showShareUI();
}
```

Note In order to be listed as share target (that is, as the Mail application you dealt with in this exercise), an application needs to implement the *Share target* contract. You implement this contract by adding a special item to the project from the Add New Item dialog of Microsoft Visual Studio. Adding a new share target item will bring three new files to your project and some changes to the project manifest. You'll get new CSS, HTML, and JavaScript files that provide style, markup, and code respectively for a new page. Changes in the manifest inform Windows 8 that your application intends to participate in the *Share* contract. When the user selects your application to receive some shared content, the new page is displayed and its logic allows you to receive and process data. A Share Target application is not expected to display the full-blown user interface. It is, instead, expected to display the minimum user interface for the execution of a particular task on the received content. An example of a Share target application can be found in the Windows SDK.

Providing a Settings page

The Settings panel in the Charms bar is meant to be the place where users always look for quick access to the settings that an application may have. A Windows Store application can provide a collection of additional pages to be listed in the Settings panel for the user to change options that affect the behavior of the application, as well as get to the Help or About pages. In this exercise, you'll create a Settings page for the TodoList application.

Populating the Settings charm

When the user clicks the Settings panel in the Charms bar, the application receives an *onsettings* event. Therefore, providing a handler for this event is the very first step to accomplish.

Creating the settings flyout

The Settings panel is essentially a flyout component that gets configured with a list of application commands. An application command is a HTML page and a title string. You open *default.html* and add the following code before the call to *app.start*.

```
app.onsettings = function (e) {
    e.detail.applicationcommands = {
        "about": {
            href: "/pages/about.html",
            title: "About"
        },
        "privacy": {
            href: "/pages/privacy.html",
            title: "Privacy"
        },
```

```
            "settings": {
                href: "/pages/settings.html",
                title: "Settings"
            }
        }
        WinJS.UI.SettingsFlyout.populateSettings(e);
    };
```

The mandatory next step is creating three new HTML pages. You create all of them in the *pages* project folder and name them as above: *about.html, privacy.html*, and *settings.html*. You do this using the Add New Item function of the context menu of the project window in Visual Studio. For now, skip over the required content and just keep the default markup that Visual Studio adds to any newly created HTML page.

As you can see in Figure 9-12, the Settings panel lists three additional items, one for each of the registered commands. If you click any of them, though, nothing happens. This is the time to make some changes to the HTML of the various pages.

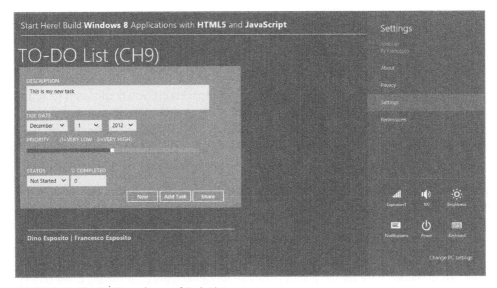

FIGURE 9-12 The Settings charm of TodoList.

Creating a read-only page

With the notable exception of the page used to configure the application, most of the pages you have listed here are read-only pages. They just provide users with information such as release notes, an end-user agreement, help, or perhaps information about the author. All these pages can have a common layout on top of different content. Let's address, for example, the About page.

You open the *about.html* page and assign the following markup to the *BODY* tag:

```
<div id="aboutContainer"
     data-win-control="WinJS.UI.SettingsFlyout"
     data-win-options="{settingsCommandId:'about'}">
    <div class="win-ui-dark win-header">
        <button type="button"
                onclick="WinJS.UI.SettingsFlyout.show()"
                class="win-backbutton"></button>
        <div class="win-label">About TodoList</div>
    </div>
    <div class="win-content">
        <div class="win-settings-section">
            <!-- Your content goes here -->
            <h1>v1.0.0.0.1</h1>
        </div>
    </div>
</div>
```

It is important that the page contains a root *DIV* bound to the *SettingsFlyout* component. The ID of the *DIV* is unimportant but it should be unique within the application. Also the command ID you assign through the *data-win-options* attribute should be unique.

To give the page a look and feel consistent with other applications, you might want to add a child *DIV* element styled with the *win-header* CSS class. Also using the *win-ui-dark* class is a matter of graphical preference. You can choose between *win-ui-dark* and *win-ui-light*. Finally, you need a button to navigate back to the application. For this reason, you add a *BUTTON* element, as in the listing above. Finally, the *DIV* styled with the *win-label* class determines the caption of the page.

Any page-specific content goes into the *DIV* styled as *win-content*. You are completely free to structure and style this content as you like. It is purely a matter of style; it doesn't affect the behavior of the application.

Figure 9-13 shows the look and feel of the About page.

All the steps described here for the About page can be safely replicated for any other page you want to list in the Settings charm that doesn't require interaction with the user.

 Note As a user, you can dismiss the Settings panel by clicking or tapping outside the area or just clicking or tapping the Back button.

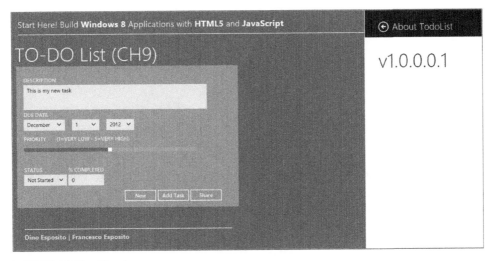

FIGURE 9-13 The About page.

Creating a functional Settings page

The layout of the Settings page—namely the page the user displays to change options and configure the application to work differently—is the same as read-only pages. However, creating a Settings page is much more challenging since it requires that you save settings somewhere and use them throughout the application. This will take you to make some relevant changes to the code used so far.

Defining an application-wide settings object

If your application is expected to support customizable settings, then you should have an object that defines all possible options. You open *todolist.js* and add the following code:

```
var TodoListSettings = WinJS.Class.define(function () {
    var localSettings = Windows.Storage.ApplicationData.current.localSettings;
    var that = {};
    that.defaultPriority = TodoList.Priority.Normal;
    that.load = function () {
        _loadFromSettings();
    };
    that.save = function () {
        _saveToSettings();
    };

    function _loadFromSettings() {
        var priority = localSettings.values["defaultPriority"];
        if (priority) {
            that.defaultPriority = priority;
        }
    };
```

```
    function _saveToSettings() {
        localSettings.values["defaultPriority"] = that.defaultPriority;
    };

    return that;
});

TodoList.settings = new TodoListSettings();
```

 Important The exact position of this code is not particularly important, so long as it is preceded by the definition of the *TodoList.Priority* object. It is suggested that you add this code at top of the file right after the definition of the *TodoList* object and make it follow only the definition of the *TodoList.Priority* object.

The *TodoListSettings* object is an object with one property—the *defaultPriority* property. This is because in the current example you are going to have only one customizable option—the default priority level of any newly created task. So far, you had it default to Normal; now you want to make this value configurable on a per user basis.

However, the *TodoListSettings* object is not limited to defining the *defaultPriority* property; it also features a couple of load/save methods. The idea is that the *TodoListSettings* object makes itself responsible for loading and saving its content to a persistent store without requiring more than a plain call to the *load* or *save* method. The details of how settings are persisted or retrieved are not known outside the boundaries of the object.

In addition, an instance of the *TodoListSettings* object is created during the initialization of the application and is made available through the *TodoList.settings* object. The bottom line is that in this way, the application loads its settings from a persistent store at startup and these settings are globally available for the entire lifecycle.

Persisting application settings

Windows 8 provides applications with a system dictionary where data can be saved in pairs—a unique ID and a corresponding value. Values can only be primitive types, such as strings and integers. The system object that provides access to this data store is *Windows.Storage.ApplicationData.current. localSettings*. The object exposes a *values* property that is the actual dictionary where data is stored.

For example, the default priority level set for the application is stored in an entry whose ID matches the property name.

```
var priority = localSettings.values["defaultPriority"];
```

Note that this is only a recommended practice; you can name the dictionary entry in any arbitrary way. To save values permanently, you use code as below:

```
localSettings.values["defaultPriority"] = someValue;
```

To complete the initialization of the application, you need to place a call that actually loads settings upon application startup.

```
TodoList.settings.load();
```

In *todolist.js*, you also add the previous line of code at the end of the *TodoList.init* method. Now that settings have been integrated in the application, you need to use them where it makes the most sense. This drives some further changes in *todolist.js*.

In particular, you edit the *Task* object so that it defaults the priority property to the value read-out of the settings:

```
var Task = WinJS.Class.define(function () {
    var that = {};
    that.description = "This is my new task";
    that.dueDate = TodoList.firstOfNextMonth();
    that.priority = TodoList.Priority.Normal;
    ...
    if (TodoList.settings.defaultPriority != "undefined")
        that.priority = TodoList.settings.defaultPriority;
    return that;
});
```

Another change regards the *TodoList.performInitialBinding* method. At this point, you might want it to initialize the user interface based on the *Task* object it receives; not on the *Task* object it creates internally:

```
TodoList.performInitialBinding = function (task) {
    // var task = new Task();      // This line must be removed

    // Rest of the code here
    ...
}
```

Finally, you introduce a new function like this:

```
TodoList.displayTask = function (task) {
    TodoList.performInitialBinding(task);
}
```

A call to the new *TodoList.displayTask* function is placed now at the very bottom of the *TodoList.init* method. At the same time, you remove any call to *TodoList.performInitialBinding* you may have in the *TodoList.init* method. Here's the new layout of the *TodoList.init* method:

```
TodoList.init = function () {
    // Register handler for resize events
    window.onresize = addEventListener('resize', TodoList.onResize, false);

    // Register handler for buttons
    document.getElementById("buttonAddTask").addEventListener("click", TodoList.
addTaskClick);
    document.getElementById("buttonShare").addEventListener("click", TodoList.
shareClick);

    // Initialization of Share source contract
    var view = Windows.ApplicationModel.DataTransfer.DataTransferManager.
getForCurrentView();
    view.addEventListener("datarequested", function (e) {
        var currentTask = TodoList.getTaskFromUI();
        if (currentTask.description.length === 0) {
            e.request.failWithDisplayText("Indicate a description of the task.");
            return;
        }
        TodoList.shareDataAsHtml(e, currentTask);
        TodoList.shareDataAsPlainText(e, currentTask);
    });

    // Load settings and initialize the view
    TodoList.settings.load();
    TodoList.displayTask(new Task());
}
```

With these changes, every time the application starts up the default value of the priority parameter is read from application settings and used to initialize the user interface.

Note In particular, the changes you made here to *performInitialBinding* and the introduction of the *displayTask* function will make it much easier to add new functions to the application in the upcoming chapters.

Creating the Settings page

At this point, you're ready to turn your attention to the *settings.html* page. You give the page the same layout as other pages. You add the following markup to the *BODY* element.

```
<div id="settingsContainer"
    data-win-control="WinJS.UI.SettingsFlyout"
    data-win-options="{settingsCommandId:'settings', width:'narrow'}">

    <div class="win-ui-dark win-header">
        <button type="button" onclick="WinJS.UI.SettingsFlyout.show()"
                class="win-backbutton"></button>
        <div class="win-label">TodoList Settings</div>
    </div>
    <div class="win-content">
        <div class="win-settings-section">
            <h3>DEFAULT PRIORITY <br />(1=VERY LOW - 5=VERY HIGH)</h3>
            <input id="taskPriority_settings" type="range" min="1" max="5"
                data-win-bind="value: defaultPriority;" />
        </div>
    </div>
</div>
```

Figure 9-14 shows the graphical aspect of the Settings page.

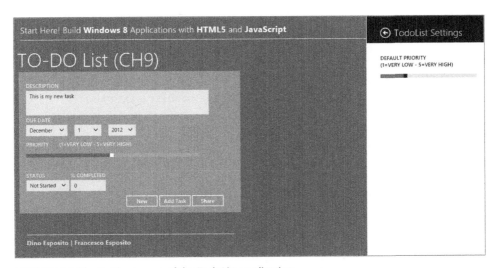

FIGURE 9-14 The Settings page of the TodoList application.

The final step is initializing the Settings page with the current settings and saving any new value that the user may select in the page back to the application settings. For this to happen, you need to hook up a couple of events in the settings flyout. You add a new JavaScript file to the project and name it **settings.js**. Also, you reference this file as well as *todolist.js* from *settings.html*, as shown below:

```
<script src="/js/todolist.js"></script>
<script src="/js/settings.js"></script>
```

In the *settings.js* file, you add the following code:

```
(function () {
    "use strict";
    var page = WinJS.UI.Pages.define("/pages/settings.html", {
        ready: function (element, options) {
            document.getElementById("settingsContainer")
                    .winControl
                    .addEventListener("beforeshow", beforeShow);
            document.getElementById("settingsContainer")
                    .winControl
                    .addEventListener("afterhide", afterHide);
        }
    });

    function beforeShow() {
        loadSettings();
    };

    function afterHide() {
        saveSettings();
    };

    function loadSettings() {
        var bindableElement = document.getElementById("settingsContainer");
        WinJS.Binding.processAll(bindableElement, TodoList.settings);
    };

    function saveSettings() {
        var priorityElem = document.getElementById("taskPriority_settings");
        var currentPriority = priorityElem.value;
        TodoList.settings.defaultPriority = currentPriority;
        TodoList.settings.save();
    };
})();
```

The code registers handlers for the *beforeshow* and *afterhide* events of the flyout behind the Settings page. In this way, you can run your code just before the Settings panel is displayed and just after it is hidden.

Needless to say, you initialize the controls in the Settings panel with current settings in the handler of the *beforeshow* event and save changes back to the application settings in the handler of the *afterhide* event.

Important It is key to note that thanks to the effort made earlier in the exercise—isolating access to the application settings in a single object—you can now read and save settings quickly and easily without knowing many details of the infrastructure.

The net effect of these changes is that you can now open the Settings page, modify the default priority value, and have it honored anytime a new task is created.

 Note If you successfully proceeded through the steps of the exercise, you might have an outstanding question at this point. Why on earth did you tell me to handle before/ after events on a window instead of just placing a Save button in the Settings page? The guidelines for Windows Store applications warmly recommend you avoid save buttons on the Settings page and, subsequently, handling before/after events is the only choice left.

Summary

In this fairly long chapter, you learned how to better integrate a Windows Store application with the surrounding environment. Technically speaking, integration is achieved via contracts and extensions. Contracts and extensions are also the main tool for developers to customize and extend basic Windows functionalities.

Implementing contracts and writing extensions is beyond the scope of this beginner's book; examples can be found in the Windows SDK, as well as in more advanced books on the subject of Windows 8 programming. Using contracts as services, instead, is much easier and only requires learning about a few objects. In this chapter, you touched on files and storage. That is just the topic of the next chapter.

Chapter 10

Adding persistent data to applications

It matters if you just don't give up.

—*Stephen Hawking*

No applications that are expected to be more than just a basic exercise can operate without persistent data. As users work with the application, they produce information by entering fresh data or processing known values. This information will not be lost with the shutdown of the application. This information is vital and must be persisted somewhere to be reloaded on the next session or on demand.

To make data persistent, software uses files; sometimes applications make use of very special files known as *databases*. A database is ultimately a large collection of files owned and managed by a specific and distinct application. Interacting with a database is more expensive in terms of system resources since it involves ad hoc protocols for an app-to-app communication.

In this chapter, you won't use any database, but you will go through a number of exercises that involve files. In particular, you'll be extending the TodoList application to make it able to save tasks to files and reload them on demand. In doing so, you will also learn a lot about the application programming interface (API) available to Windows Store applications to deal with persistent data.

Persisting application objects

The first exercise of this chapter consists of taking the version of the TodoList application you worked on in the last chapter one step further. You will enable the application to pick a file and save some of the details of the task to it.

Making *Task* objects persistent

You make a copy of the TodoList project as you left it at the end of Chapter 9, "Integrating with the Windows 8 environment"; name this new project **TodoList-Persistence**. To avoid confusion, you might also want to open *default.html* and edit the title of the application. In the *BODY* element of the page, replace the *H1* element as shown below:

```
<h1>TO-DO List (CH10)</h1>
```

The application currently lets you pick a file name from a folder on the local disk and returns you an object that represents the file you'd like to have. This file, however, doesn't exist yet; so the next step is creating a real file and storing some real data to it. For this to happen, you must be familiar with the Input/Output (I/O) objects of Windows 8.

The add-task use case

In Chapter 9, you learned how to invoke the *File Save Picker* component to pick up a file name from a disk folder. Figure 10-1 briefly recalls the steps of the *add-task* workflow.

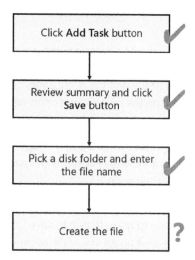

FIGURE 10-1 The add-task workflow.

First the user clicks the Add Task button; next she is presented a summary of the current task, and if everything is OK then she proceeds to save the task to disk. The application pops up a file picker and she selects a folder and enters a file name. In Chapter 9, you had the following code in the *TodoList.invokeSavePicker* method within the *todolist.js* file:

```
savePicker.pickSaveFileAsync().then(function (file) {
    if (file) {
        TodoList.alert(file.name);
    }
});
```

It is now about time you replace the basic message box with the code that actually creates the file.

Saving data to a file

In Microsoft Windows 8, the *File Save Picker* component seeks to be more helpful than one might expect. It doesn't simply return you an object that describes the file you intend to create; it returns you a true file object. In other words, the object you get from the picker refers to a file that has already been created for you. The file is empty, but it exists already. Subsequently, all you have to do is write some text to it.

You open the *todolist.js* file and add the following code to the *TodoList.invokeSavePicker* method to deal with the File Save Picker:

```
savePicker.pickSaveFileAsync().then(function (file) {
    if (file) {
        // The file ALREADY exists; the file picker CREATED it with 0 bytes
        Windows.Storage.FileIO
            .writeTextAsync(file, "Some data")
            .done(function () {
                    TodoList.alert("Data successfully saved");
                },
                function (error) {
                    TodoList.alert("Unable to save data. Sorry about that!");
                }
            );
    }
});
```

Admittedly, the syntax of the I/O objects in Windows 8 is a bit convoluted, but not really scary. The basic object for I/O manipulations is *Windows.Storage.FileIO*. This object exposes a method called *writeTextAsync*; it takes a file object and some text and simply writes the text to the file. In the example above, you are saving the text "Some data" to the picked file.

In Windows Store applications, most system operations are performed in an asynchronous way. This means that the instruction that follows the asynchronous call executes immediately without waiting for the other instruction to complete. While asynchronous calls ensure the highest responsiveness of the application's user interface, they make underlying code harder to read and write.

In particular, to express a sequential semantic where two or more actions occur one after the completion of the previous, you need to resort to a "fluent" syntax, as shown below:

```
Windows.Storage.FileIO
            .writeTextAsync( ... )
            .done( ok, error )
```

It reads like you write some content to a given file and when this has been done you take different routes, whether the operation completed successfully or with some errors. You'll be using this pattern quite often in Windows Store applications.

Figure 10-2 shows the state of the folder now that a file has been created.

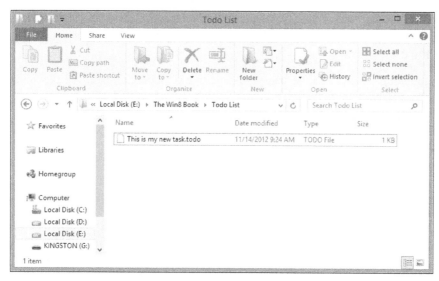

FIGURE 10-2 The newly created file viewed through Windows Explorer.

Creating your own files

The next time you go through the Add Task workflow from within TodoList and select the same file, you'll get the following message from the file picker, as shown in Figure 10-3.

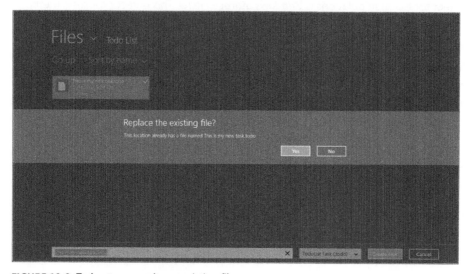

FIGURE 10-3 Trying to overwrite an existing file.

This means that the file picker is trying to create a file but it finds out that a file with the same name already exists. The picker then asks advice. Let's have a look at the API required to create a new file programmatically. The following example provides an alternate route to pick a file. Instead of using a File Save Picker, you pick a folder and then create a file programmatically:

```
TodoList.invokeFolderPicker = function (task) {
    var folderPicker = new Windows.Storage.Pickers.FolderPicker();
    folderPicker.fileTypeFilter.replaceAll(["*"]);
    folderPicker.SuggestedStartLocation = Windows.Storage.Pickers.PickerLocationId.
desktop;

    // Invoke the folder picker
    var fileOptions = Windows.Storage.CreationCollisionOption;
    var io = Windows.Storage.FileIO;
    folderPicker
        .pickSingleFolderAsync()
        .done(
            function (folder) {
                if (folder) {
                    folder.createFileAsync("sample.todo", fileOptions.replaceExisting)
                        .done(function (file) {
                            io.writeTextAsync(file, "Some more data.")
                                .then(function () { io.appendTextAsync(file, " By me."); })
                                .done(function () { TodoList.alert("All done!")})
                        },
                        function (error) {
                            TodoList.alert("Unable to create file. Sorry about that!");
                        });
                }
            });
}
```

Once you get a folder object, you can call the *createFileAsync* method, which takes the file name and some options. In particular, the *Windows.Storage.CreationCollisionOption* enumeration includes values to silently replace the file if it exists (*replaceExisting*) or fail if a name collision is detected (*failIfExists*).

In the *done* method which runs once the file has been created, you put the code to write text. Again the *done* method can be used to trigger any subsequent code, such as displaying an all-done message to the user.

Appending text versus just writing text

When you use the *writeTextAsync* method, Windows 8 just opens the file, writes any content, and then closes it. If you call *writeTextAsync* twice, then the content is overwritten; the second call completely wipes out the existing content.

If you want to just append text to an existing file, you have to use the *appendTextAsync* method. The method has the same syntax as the *writeTextAsync* method. In the previous code snippet, you see an example of the two methods used sequentially.

Because of the asynchronous API, however, you might want to keep sequential tasks to a minimum to prevent your code from reaching an unmanageable level of nesting. As far as file writing is concerned, you might always want to focus on writing any content to files in a single step.

Deleting files

Another common operation that an application may perform is deleting files it had previously created or, more in general, any files that, for some reason, it needs to delete. As noted a moment ago, file deletion is an operation that requires a file object to be performed. Here's an example where you assume to have the file object available:

```
file.deleteAsync()
    .done(function () { TodoList.alert("File deleted" },
        function () { TodoList.alert("Unable to delete the file" });
```

Choosing a serialization format

Now that you have grabbed the basics of file manipulation in Windows 8, let's return to the TodoList application. You integrated file saving in the code, but you didn't actually save any task yet. The code discussed earlier, in fact, created a file with a given name that was limited to store sample text in it. The next step is therefore choosing a format to store real data to a file. The process of streamlining real data to a file is commonly referred to as *serialization*.

Adding a data serialization component

Some changes are required to the *TodoList.invokeSavePicker* method to make it save the current *Task* object. First, you change the line that calls into *writeTextAsync* so that instead of writing down a constant sample text, it now writes the string returned by a new wrapper function:

```
Windows.Storage.FileIO
    .writeTextAsync(file, TodoList.serializeTask(task))
```

In addition, you write the skeleton of the *TodoList.serializeTask* function and add it to *todolist.js*:

```
// Task Serializer
TodoList.serializeTask = function (task) {
    // Just save the description of the task
    return task.description;
}
```

In this way, the file saves only the description of the task but loses all other information. How would you save the entire data set of a *Task* object?

A quick answer to the question simply says that the serialization format is entirely up to you. You should just be aware that the *TodoList.serializeTask* function will return a string that is saved as is to the file. From the perspective of the function, whatever string works well.

The *Task* object is made of several pieces of information: description, due date, priority, and so forth. You might want to save them all. One option could be concatenating each piece of information using a particular character (such as, the pipe character |) as the separator. Here's an example:

```
TodoList.serializeTask = function (task) {
    return task.description + "|" +
        task.dueDate + "|" +
        task.priority + "|" +
        task.status + "|" +
        task.percCompleted;
}
```

The resulting string may look like the one shown below:

```
This is my new task|Sat Dec 1 12:00:00 UTC+0100 2012|3|Not Started|0
```

There's nothing wrong with this format, except that it requires an ad hoc piece of code to be read and parsed back to a *Task* object. The process of transforming a string of text to an object is referred to as *deserialization*.

Generally, the problem here is that by choosing a custom serialization format you make yourself responsible for writing both the serializer and the deserializer. In addition, every format requires a distinct ad hoc pair of serializer and deserializer.

In JavaScript, a better option does exist; it entails using a special notation known as the JSON format. The acronym JSON stands for JavaScript Object Notation.

The JSON format

JSON is a text format easy to handle and read for both humans and software. Basically, JSON defines a set of conventions through which any object can have its data serialized to a standard format. A JSON string is made of a collection of name/value pairs each of which identifies a property name and its value. A special convention also exists for rendering arrays. The following text shows the JSON version of a *Task* object filled with default values:

```
{
    "description":"This is my new task",
    "dueDate":"2012-12-01T11:00:00.000Z",
    "priority":"3",
    "status":"Not Started",
    "percCompleted":"0"
}
```

The great news is that JavaScript and Windows 8 provide native tools to create a JSON string from a JavaScript object and to obtain a JavaScript object from a JSON string. In addition, the generality of the JSON format makes it suitable to treat just about any object. This means that you need only one pair of serializer and deserializer in your code, regardless of the number of objects you intend to persist and also regardless of their structure.

Serializing the *Task* object to JSON

To use JSON in the TodoList application, all you need to do is use the following code for the *TodoList.serializeTask* function:

```
TodoList.serializeTask = function (task) {
    return JSON.stringify(task);
}
```

JSON.stringify is a JavaScript native function that turns any JavaScript object into a JSON compatible string. Figure 10-4 shows the JSON content of a *Task* object being read with a plain text editor, such as Notepad.

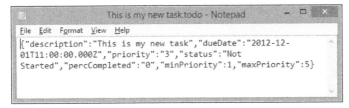

FIGURE 10-4 The JSON content of a *.todo* file created by TodoList.

The next challenge is now making TodoList capable of loading and editing existing JSON-formatted tasks.

Creating *Task* objects from files

On the way to reading back the content of saved *Task* objects, you make a couple of changes to the user interface of the TodoList application. You add a button to create a blank new task and a button to open an existing task from the specified file.

Making changes to the user interface

You open the *default.html* page and add the following markup to the *DIV* element that contains the other two buttons to add and share a task.

```
<button id="buttonNewTask">New</button>
<button id="buttonOpenTask">Open</button>
```

Next, in the *todolist.js* file, you locate the *TodoList.init* method and add the following code to register handlers for the click event of the two new buttons.

```
document.getElementById("buttonNewTask").addEventListener("click", TodoList.
newTaskClick);
document.getElementById("buttonOpenTask").addEventListener("click", TodoList.
openTaskClick);
```

Here's the body of the handlers to add to the same JavaScript file:

```
TodoList.newTaskClick = function () {
    TodoList.displayTask(new Task());
}

TodoList.openTaskClick = function () {
    TodoList.pickFileAndOpenTask();
}
```

The click handler for the New button is fairly straightforward: it just creates a blank new *Task* object and displays through the helper method *displayTask*. The click handler for the Open button is a bit more elaborate since it is connected to a File Open Picker that locates and selects the file to open.

Locating the file to open

The code for the *TodoList.pickFileAndOpenTask* method is similar to the code you used earlier for the File Save Picker. This time you configure the picker object to select files with a *.todo* extension. This function must be added to the *todolist.js* file as well:

```
TodoList.pickFileAndOpenTask = function () {
    var currentState = Windows.UI.ViewManagement.ApplicationView.value;
    if (currentState === Windows.UI.ViewManagement.ApplicationViewState.snapped &&
        !Windows.UI.ViewManagement.ApplicationView.tryUnsnap()) {
        // Fail silently if we can't unsnap
        return;
    }

    TodoList.invokeOpenPicker();
}
```

The code first ensures that the application is not in a snapped state and then invokes another helper function that deals with the File Open Picker. Note that file pickers can only be used in filled or full screen and can't be invoked from snapped applications and from flyouts, including settings flyouts. Here's the code for the helper function *TodoList.invokeOpenPicker*:

```
TodoList.invokeOpenPicker = function () {
    var openPicker = new Windows.Storage.Pickers.FileOpenPicker();
    openPicker.suggestedStartLocation = Windows.Storage.Pickers.PickerLocationId.
computerFolder;
    openPicker.fileTypeFilter.replaceAll([".todo"]);
    openPicker.pickSingleFileAsync().then(function (file) {
        if (file) {
            // Do something with the selected .todo file
        }
    });
}
```

Once the user has picked up a *.todo* file, the code should read the entire content and try to build a *Task* object out of it. As mentioned, the *.todo* file is a file that contains JSON-formatted text resulting from the previous serialization of a *Task* object.

Reading file content

To read the content of the selected file you use the *readTextAsync* method on the *Windows.Storage.FileIO* object. The method returns the entire content of the file as a string of text. The *Windows.Storage.FileIO* object, however, also provides two more methods. One is *readLinesAsync,* which reads the entire content and returns it as an array of lines of text. Using *readLinesAsync* or *readTextAsync* depends on what you plan to do with the read text. For the purpose of deserializing some JSON content, this method is the perfect fit since you are not going to split the text in lines anyway.

The other method available on the *Windows.Storage.FileIO* object is *readBufferAsync.* This method returns a buffer object, namely an array of bytes. This might be a good fit if you are working with binary files such as images. For text-based applications, you may safely ignore this method.

Here's the code to add to the *TodoList.invokeOpenPicker* method to grab the JSON string stored in the selected file.

```
openPicker.pickSingleFileAsync().then(function (file) {
    if (file) {
        var io = Windows.Storage.FileIO;
        io.readTextAsync(file)
            .done(function (json) {
                    // JSON deserialization takes place here
                }
});
```

The final step is deserializing the JSON string into a newly created *Task* object.

Deserializing *Task* objects

To serialize a *Task* object to a string you used the *JSON.stringify* method. A reverse method also exists to revive a JSON string back to a JavaScript object. This method is *JSON.parse.* Here's the code you need to add to the *TodoList.invokeOpenPicker* method:

```
// Build a Task object
var task = JSON.parse(json);

// Display the Task object
TodoList.displayTask(task);
```

Unfortunately, during execution this code raises an exception. The exception is due to a failure in the building of the date of the *Task* object. As weird as it may sound, what *JSON.stringify* serializes, its counterpart *JSON.parse* can't properly deserialize.

To be precise, this conflict shows up only if the serialized object has *Date* properties. If dates are not involved, then everything goes smoothly. The problem can be tracked back to the JSON specification that does not officially include the *Date* type. The major issue here is not that *JSON.parse* can't handle a date string. More subtly, the issue is that it deserializes it as a plain string. So you won't experience any troubles when you deserialize, but only when (and if) you ever happen to work on deserialized data. In other words, the exception you may run into may come from places in your code that are not directly related to the deserialization operation.

What can you do?

The fix is actually quick and easy, but it needs be applied on a per-call basis.

```
// jsonDate is the string you get for a date from JSON.parse.
// To get a date object, you just pass this string to the constructor of the Date object.
var date = new Date(jsonDate);
```

You need to apply the fix when your applications deserialize from JSON and dates are involved. Here's the final version of the code you need to have in the *TodoList.invokeOpenPicker* method:

```
openPicker.pickSingleFileAsync().then(function (file) {
    if (file) {
        var io = Windows.Storage.FileIO;
        io.readTextAsync(file)
                .done(function (json) {
                        var task = TodoList.deserializeTask(json);
                        TodoList.displayTask(task);
                    },
                    function () { TodoList.alert("Unable to read the file") });
    }
});
```

You first deserialize the JSON string to a *Task* object and then you fix any *Date* properties. To keep code cleaner, you might want to move the deserialization code to a specialized method in *todolist.js*:

```
TodoList.deserializeTask = function (json) {
    var task = JSON.parse(json);
    task.dueDate = new Date(task.dueDate);
    return task;
}
```

Figure 10-5 shows the process of selecting a task and Figure 10-6 shows the selected task displayed in the application's user interface.

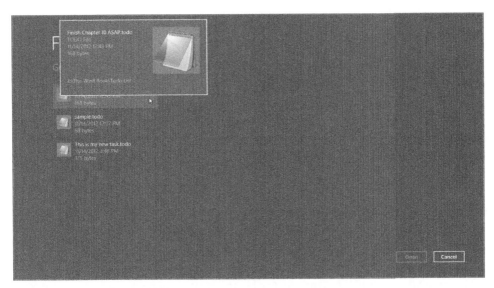

FIGURE 10-5 Selecting a task file.

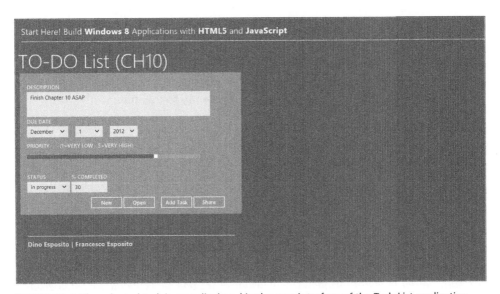

FIGURE 10-6 The selected task is now displayed in the user interface of the TodoList application.

Using the application's private storage

So far, you have created and managed files by accessing the local disk of the machine directly. As you may have noticed, a Windows Store application is not always allowed full access to the disk; but still a section of the disk is freely accessible in reading and writing. In the rest of chapter, you will practice with another form of storage that involves a section of the disk that is private to each application and totally invisible to others.

Storage options in Windows 8

Windows Store applications have three options as far as storage is concerned. In Chapter 9, you practiced with *LocalSettings*; earlier in this chapter you also practiced with files in the local disk. These are two of the three storage options for a Windows Store application. The third option consists in a section of the local disk that is reserved to the application. Let's briefly compare the three options to identify proper use-cases for each.

Saving to the *localSettings* storage

The *localSettings* storage is a data container specific to the application that takes the form of a dictionary. You access it programmatically, as shown below:

```
var applicationData = Windows.Storage.ApplicationData.current;
var localSettings = applicationData.localSettings;
```

You read and write data to the container using the classic dictionary approach. Each entry is uniquely identified by a key and references a value. The key is a string of up to 255 characters in length; the value can be any valid Windows 8 type (including arrays and collections of custom types) not larger than 8 KB. You used the *localSettings* already in Chapter 9 to store the default settings of the TodoList application. Here's how you write and read an entry to the store:

```
// Write to the store
localSettings.values["sampleKey"] = "Some data";

// Read from the store
var value = localSettings.values["sampleKey"];
```

The *localSettings* dictionary provides a fairly rich programming interface with methods to remove an item, check for existence, and also some query commands. You can find out more looking at the MSDN documentation for the *ApplicationDataContainerSettings* class at the following URL: *http://msdn.microsoft.com/en-us/library/windows/apps/windows.storage.applicationdatacontainersettings*.

The *localSettings* store is not limited to storing only user preferences and also can be used to store live data of the application. However, the dictionary layout and limitations in the size of individual entries make it a good choice for small pieces of data that can be retrieved and stored as a key/value pair. As long as you can retrieve the data you want with a direct call, this store can serve you well. In addition, using this API doesn't require you to deal with the intricacies of asynchronous programming and basic I/O operations, such as creating, opening, and locating files.

> **Important** If you use the *roamingSettings* dictionary instead of *localSettings,* then all of your stored data will be automatically synchronized by Windows 8 across all devices and computers running the application under the same Windows account. This means that you can set a preference on, say, a Microsoft Surface device and retrieve that setting when you use the same application on a PC equipped with Windows 8. The API for reading and writing data to the *roamingSettings* dictionary is identical to the API required for *localSettings.* The only barrier to using *roamingSettings* by default is whether the stored data does really make sense if used on a different device. Usually, this is not an issue with settings that represent user preferences on the configuration of an application.

Saving to the local disk

As you've seen so far, Windows Store applications can gain a partial access to the local disk. You can programmatically access the *Documents* or *Pictures* folder and read and create files there. You can use file pickers to gain access to any file in nearly any folder. However, you can't programmatically point your code to the root folder of a drive and start creating files and subfolders there. To fully use the local disk, you need to rely on file pickers.

It is important to note that while programmatic access to known folders such as *Documents* and *Pictures* is permitted, it is still subject to user's approval. More precisely, a Windows Store application that needs to manipulate a known folder must pre-emptively declare its intention so that the user installing the application can be notified by the operating system. You do this by opening the manifest file of the project in Microsoft Visual Studio and selecting the Capabilities tab (see Figure 10-7).

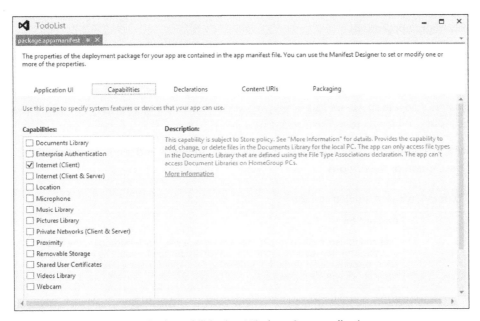

FIGURE 10-7 Declaring required capabilities in a Windows Store application.

With the few exceptions represented by library folders (*Documents, Pictures, Music*), using the local disk from within a Windows Store application is restricted to using file pickers to locate files. Once you hold a reference to a file or folder, though, you can freely operate on them. The local disk option is effective for those applications which intend to create and consume data that remain on the disk for other applications to consume. If the data your application manipulates doesn't make sense outside the application, then a direct use of the local disk is not probably the handiest option.

Note Files created in a local disk folder won't be deleted when the user uninstalls the application. This aspect may be a pro or a con for an application depending on its intended use.

Important As you may see in Figure 10-7, a Windows Store application must also declare as a special capability its ability to manipulate files on a removable storage device such as an external hard disk or a USB pen drive. In addition, an application that intends to support removable storage must declare in the Declarations tab of the manifest the types of file it intends to work on. This is done to prevent an application's access to only any files the user may have on an external device.

Saving to the isolated storage

Sometimes the application and its data form a monolith that users want to keep or get rid of as a whole. This pattern is kind of new for developers used to writing classic desktop applications; it should be instead familiar to developers with some background in the development of mobile and Microsoft Silverlight applications.

Windows Store applications can also have their own private space where they can create files and folders. This space is physically located on the local disk, but its content can't be accessed from outside the application, either programmatically or through file pickers. Any files and folders created in the application's private space are lost when the user uninstalls the application. The application's private space is often referred to as the *isolated storage*.

There are three different types of isolated storage: *local, roaming,* and *temporary.* Table 10-1 provides a description of the options.

TABLE 10-1 Different types of isolated storage

Storage	Description
local	Files and folders created within the *local* storage will only be stored on the local machine and stay there until the user uninstalls the application. The application is solely responsible for updating or deleting files. These files are inaccessible for other applications and file pickers.

Storage	Description
roaming	Files and folders created within the *roaming* storage are subject to the same rules as the *local* store, except that they are synchronized between all Windows 8 machines running your application under the same Windows account.
temporary	Files and folders created within the *temporary* storage are subject to the same rules as the *local* store, except that they will be deleted periodically by Windows.

The API for manipulating files (that is, creating, writing, and reading content) in the local disk or the isolated storage is the same. All that changes is the root object to which you apply your I/O actions.

Note If none of the options listed here for storing data are satisfying, then you probably want to consider using a true database. A database allows you to store data in tables where a table is a collection of related data organized in columns. For example, the *Task* object you used so far can easily be rendered as a row in a database table. The positive aspect of using a database is mostly in the query capabilities it has; in this case, a database will offer unparalleled capabilities of searching for tasks based on their priority, due date, or perhaps completion. If these aspects are key for you, then embedding a database in your Windows Store application is probably a wise choice. Having said that, which database can you run on a Windows 8 device? The best choice is probably using SQLite. You can install the SQLite runtime for Windows Store applications directly from the *Tools | Extensions and Updates* menu of Visual Studio. Once there, you select the Online | Visual Studio Gallery tab, and then query for SQLite. Details on the setup process and a quick introduction to using SQLite in Windows 8 can be found here: *http://bit.ly/MuzL1e*.

Creating tasks in the isolated storage

The final exercise of this chapter consists of creating a new version of the TodoList application that saves tasks to the isolated storage using the configuration that allows for tasks to roam across multiple Windows 8 devices. This means that your users will be able to create a task on a Windows 8 PC and retrieve the same task when they use the application from a Microsoft Surface device.

Reworking the user interface of TodoList

To preserve the current version of TodoList that uses file pickers and creates tasks all over the disk, let's fork the project and create a fresh new copy of it. You can copy the folder and name it differently—for example, **Todolist-Local**. To avoid confusion, you also change the title bar in *default.html* by replacing the *H1* element with the following markup:

```
<h1>TO-DO List (CH10-Local)</h1>
```

The main trait of this new version is that you are not going to use file pickers anymore. Subsequently, you don't need an Open button anymore; at the same time, you need a view where all current tasks are listed to be picked for further editing. In *default.html*, you add the following markup right below the *H1* element.

```
<div id="list-of-tasks">
    <button id="buttonNewTask">New</button>
    <div id="task-listview"
            data-win-options ="{layout: {type: WinJS.UI.Listayout}}"
            data-win-control="WinJS.UI.ListView">
    </div>
</div>
<div id="task-listitem" data-win-control="WinJS.Binding.Template">
    <div class="listitem"><span data-win-bind="innerText: description"></span></div>
</div>
```

You also locate the last *DIV* in the page with a form-section class and remove the *BUTTON* elements with the New and Open title. To be precise, the New button has been moved into the newly added *DIV*.

In addition, you might want to wrap the visual controls used to create the task in a new *DIV* element named *editor-container*, as shown below:

```
<div id="task-editor" class="form-container">
    <div id="editor-container">
        <div id="buttonCancel-container"><button id="buttonCancel">Cancel</button></div>
        <!-- The existing task editor goes here -->
    </div>
</div>
```

The reason for this additional container is that it will let you hide and show the editor while maintaining the outermost container with its graphical settings. On top of the additional *DIV*, you also place another *DIV* that contains a Cancel button.

To complete the reworking of the user interface, you also add a bit to the *default.css* file to give new elements some non-default graphical aspects.

```
#list-of-tasks {
    float: left;
    width: 300px;
    height: 480px;
    color: #eee;
    padding: 5px;
    background-color: #1593dc;
    margin-top: 20px;
    margin-left: 20px;
}
#list-of-tasks button {
```

```
        margin: 5px;
}
#task-listview {
    background-color: #daf5f7;
    height: 440px;
}
.listitem {
    color: #eee;
    padding: 4px;
    background-color: #00f;
    width: 280px;
}
#task-editor {
    float: left;
    margin-top: 48px;
}
#buttonCancel-container {
    text-align: right;
}
#editor-container {
    display: none;
}
```

Figure 10-8 shows the new user interface that you created.

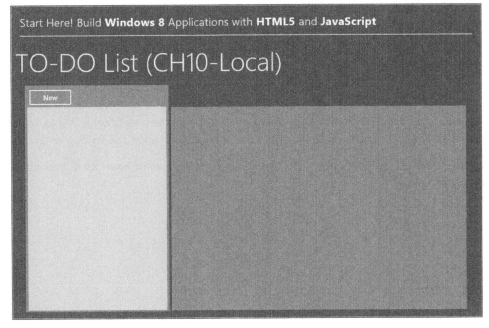

FIGURE 10-8 The new user interface of TodoList.

Well, not exactly! To really get the outcome of Figure 10-8, you also need to add some script to *todolist.js*.

The idea of the new application is that the user picks a task from the left-side list and edits it in the rightmost panel. If the user wants to create a new task, she clicks the New button on the top of the list view. This means that there's no need any more to create and display an empty task at the start of the application. For the moment, all changes are limited to *TodoList.init*.

You begin by ensuring that the following line exists at the beginning of the method. It is reasonable to expect that this line is already in place, because all you did with respect to the older version of the application was move the New button to a different position in the page.

```
document.getElementById("buttonNewTask").addEventListener("click", TodoList.
newTaskClick);
```

At the bottom of the *TodoList.init* method, you also comment out (or just remove) the following line:

```
// TodoList.displayTask(new Task());
```

The *TodoList.displayTask* still remains a key asset of your script; it will just be called from other places. The method needs some changes too:

```
TodoList.displayTask = function (task) {
    TodoList.performInitialBinding(task);

    // Ensure the editor is visible
    var editor = document.getElementById("editor-container");
    editor.style.display = "block";
}
```

In particular, the *displayTask* method now needs to ensure that the task editor is visible, since the changes in the CSS file you made earlier just keep the editor hidden upon the application's start.

When the user clicks the New button, she should get back the familiar interface of the TodoList application, as shown in Figure 10-9.

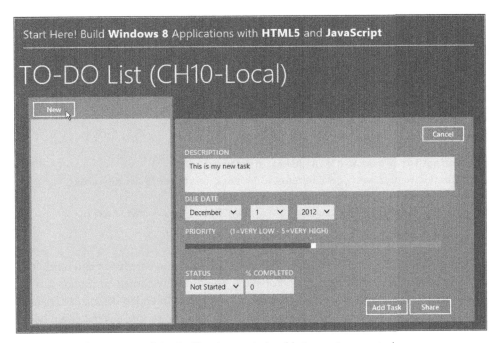

FIGURE 10-9 The user now clicks the New button to be able to create a new task.

The *Cancel* button will simply close up the editor. You need to register and create a handler for the button. You register the button in the usual way shown here:

```
document.getElementById("buttonCancel").addEventListener("click", TodoList.
cancelTaskClick);
```

Here's the required implementation:

```
TodoList.cancelTaskClick = function () {
    var editor = document.getElementById("editor-container");
    editor.style.display = "none";
}
```

So much for the graphical changes; you're now ready for the more engaging task of populating the list view with any *Task* files found in the local storage.

Retrieving current tasks

Ideally, you want to populate the list view with all available tasks when the application starts up. For this to happen, you add the following call as the final instruction in the *TodoList.init* method:

```
TodoList.populateTaskList();
```

Next, you give this function at least a fake body:

```
TodoList.populateTaskList = function () {
    var tasks = [
            { description: "Task #1" },
            { description: "Task #2" },
            { description: "Task #3" }
    ];

    var bindingList = new WinJS.Binding.List(tasks);
    var listview = document.getElementById("task-listview").winControl;
    listview.itemDataSource = bindingList.dataSource;
    listview.itemTemplate = document.getElementById("task-listitem");
}
```

The method takes a static array of objects with the property name *description* and binds it to the *ListView* you previously added to the *default.html* page. The property named *description* is key here since it is the property referenced by the list item template. In the amended *default.html* page, you should have markup such as what is shown below—which is used to render any data item bound to the *ListView*:

```
<div id="task-listitem" data-win-control="WinJS.Binding.Template">
    <div class="listitem"><span data-win-bind="innerText: description"></span></div>
</div>
```

Figure 10-10 provides the current state-of-the-art TodoList application.

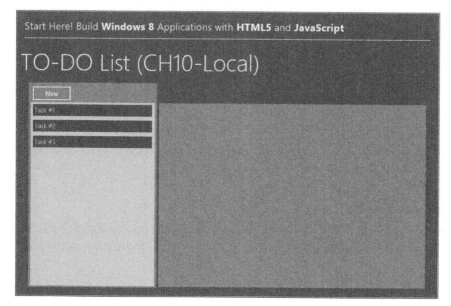

FIGURE 10-10 A list view populated with fake tasks.

The next step is changing the code of *populateTaskList* to make it create a list of *Task* objects from the files found in the application's local folder. You reference the application's local folder with the following code:

```
var localFolder = Windows.Storage.ApplicationData.current.localFolder;
```

If you want to make your application's data available for roaming, you simply reference a different folder:

```
var localFolder = Windows.Storage.ApplicationData.current.roamingFolder;
```

Any further code that you'll be writing doesn't need updates whether you want it to save to the machine's local or roaming folder.

To get the list of files in a folder, you use the *getFilesAsync* method. The method passes its *then* callback the list of files found in the folder. Note that if the folder contains subfolders, both subfolders and their content are not included in the output of the *getFilesAsync* method. To get both files and folders in the folder, you use *getItemsAsync* instead.

```
var localFolder = Windows.Storage.ApplicationData.current.roamingFolder;
localFolder.getFilesAsync()
        .then(function (files) {
            var io = Windows.Storage.FileIO;
            files.forEach(function (file) {
                // Do something with the file
            });
        });
});
```

What should you do with any retrieved file? Assuming the file contains a JSON string, you read its content and then deserialize it to a *Task* object. Next, you add the newly created object to an array. Finally, the array will be transformed in a binding list and displayed through the *ListView* component. Here's the full implementation of the *TodoList.populateTaskList* method:

```
var tasks = new Array();
var localFolder = Windows.Storage.ApplicationData.current.roamingFolder;
localFolder.getFilesAsync()
    .then(function (files) {
        var io = Windows.Storage.FileIO;
        files.forEach(function (file) {
            io.readTextAsync(file)
            .then(function (json) {
                var task = TodoList.deserializeTask(json);
                tasks.push(task);
            })
            .then(function () {
```

```
                    var bindingList = new WinJS.Binding.List(tasks);
                    var listview = document.getElementById("task-listview").winControl;
                    listview.itemDataSource = bindingList.dataSource;
                    listview.itemTemplate = document.getElementById("task-listitem");
                });
            });
        })
```

As you may notice, the need for using asynchronous methods requires an extra effort to keep code readable and properly formatted. Also, keep in mind that *any* operation on folder content must be wrapped in a *then* callback.

As a final touch, you might want to add a bit of code here to sort tasks by date. That entails adding a couple of lines of code to the *bindingList* object. Here's the code you need in the final *then* block where the binding takes place:

```
var bindingList = new WinJS.Binding.List(tasks);

// Now sort the content of the list before binding to the listview
bindingList = bindingList.createSorted(function (first, second) {
    return first.dueDate > second.dueDate;
});
```

You also might want to use a slightly more sophisticated template for the *ListView* items. Instead of simply showing the name of the file (or the description of the task), you might also want to display the due date so that the sorting makes more sense to the user. Here's a modified template for the *ListView* items:

```
<div id="task-listitem" data-win-control="WinJS.Binding.Template">
    <div class="listitem">
        <span data-win-bind="innerText: dueDate TodoList.dateForDisplay"></span>
        <br />
        <span data-win-bind="innerText: description"></span>
    </div>
</div>
```

At this point, you're all set as far as listing tasks are concerned, as you can see in Figure 10-11. You now need to adjust the code that saves tasks to the local (or roaming) folder.

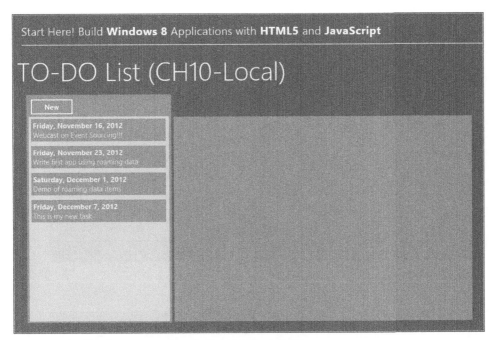

FIGURE 10-11 Creating a new task and refreshing the task list.

Saving tasks to the roaming folder

When the user clicks to add or update the task, the current version of the code invokes the *TodoList. pickFileAndSaveTask* method. This method in turn uses the file picker to find the file and saves content to it. You can keep the same method name and just rewrite its body, as shown below:

```
var task = TodoList.getTaskFromUI();

var localFolder = Windows.Storage.ApplicationData.current.roamingFolder;
var name = task.description;
var io = Windows.Storage.FileIO;
var fileOptions = Windows.Storage.CreationCollisionOption;
localFolder.createFileAsync(name, fileOptions.replaceExisting)
          .done(function (file) {
                    io.writeTextAsync(file, TodoList.serializeTask(task))
                    .done(function () {
                        TodoList.alert("All done!");
                        TodoList.populateTaskList();
                        TodoList.cancelTaskClick();  // clears the UI after saving
                    })
              },
              function (error) {
                  TodoList.alert("Unable to create file. Sorry about that!");
              });
```

The name of the file is the description of the task; the folder where the file is created or saved is the roaming folder of the application. Note that files will be silently overwritten if the names match. This means that you can't have two tasks with the same description.

Note that once the task has been saved, the user receives a confirmation message and the list of tasks is automatically refreshed to include the newly created (or updated) task (see Figure 10-12).

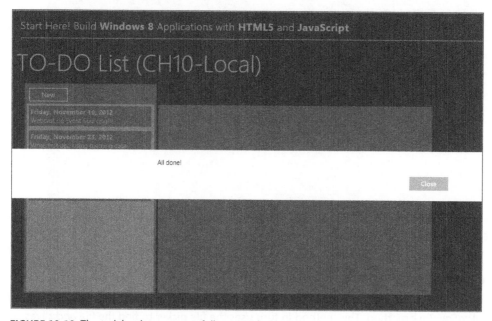

FIGURE 10-12 The task has been successfully created.

Once the task is created successfully, the list view is refreshed and the newly created item is hidden from view. The next step is selecting an existing item and editing it further.

Selecting tasks for editing

In Chapter 7, "Navigating through multimedia content," you saw how to deal with the selection of an item in a *ListView* component. It's the same here to select a task from the list and have it fully displayed in the editor. You add an *iteminvoked* handler to the *ListView*. In *todolist.js*, add a new method, as shown below:

```
TodoList.setupTaskList = function () {
    var listview = document.getElementById("task-listview").winControl;
    listview.itemTemplate = document.getElementById("task-listitem");
    listview.addEventListener("iteminvoked", TodoList.taskSelected);
}
```

This method takes a few of the lines you already had in *TodoList.populateTaskList*. In particular, it takes out the configuration work (such as, template and event binding) that only needs be done once. You call *TodoList.setupTaskList* from within *TodoList.init* just before calling *TodoList.populateTaskList*.

```
TodoList.setupTaskList();
TodoList.populateTaskList();
```

Of course, you remove the two lines moved to *TodoList.setupTaskList* from *TodoList.populateTaskList*.

Finally, you take care of the code that runs when the user selects a task from the list. You add the following method to *todolist.js*:

```
TodoList.taskSelected = function (eventInfo) {
    eventInfo.detail.itemPromise.then(function (item) {
        TodoList.displayTask(item.data);
    });
}
```

You ask (asynchronously) for the selected item and, when you get it, you extract the contained *data*—the *Task* object—and pass it to the familiar *TodoList.displayTask* method, as shown in Figure 10-13.

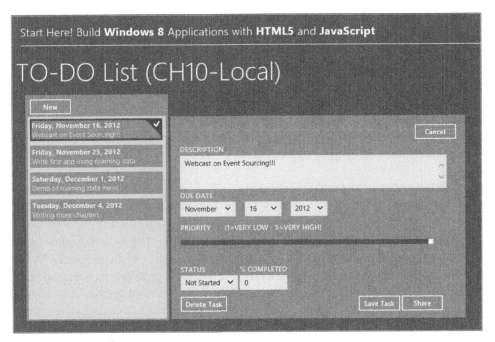

FIGURE 10-13 Selecting a task for editing.

One extra step you might also want to take consists of removing the selection on the *ListView* when the current task is closed. Users close a task by clicking the Cancel button. Here's the new version of the *cancelTaskClick* method:

```
TodoList.cancelTaskClick = function () {
    // Hide the editor
    var editor = document.getElementById("editor-container");
    editor.style.display = "none";

    // Remove any selection on the list view
    var listview = document.getElementById("task-listview").winControl;
    listview.selection.clear();
}
```

The last feature left for the exercise is deleting an existing task.

Deleting tasks

In Figure 10-13, you see a new button—the Delete Task button. When you use the local or roaming folder, users have no way to dismiss in all or in part the entire data set they created. They can only uninstall the application to get rid of the data. It is then wise that the application provides some UI elements that will help users remove any undesired pieces of data. Here's the markup for the Delete Task button:

```
<div style="float:left">
    <button id="buttonDeleteTask">Delete Task</button>
</div>
```

You place the button close to the other buttons (Add Task and Share), but the *style* attribute that is used aligns the element to the left edge of the container. You also need to register a handler for the *click* event by adding the following line to *TodoList.init*:

```
document.getElementById("buttonDeleteTask")
        .addEventListener("click", TodoList.deleteTaskClick);
```

Next, you move to the implementation of *TodoList.deleteTaskClick*. The implementation of the method is split into two parts—first, you ask for confirmation and second, you proceed with the deletion of the file behind the currently opened task. The following code sets up a message box with a couple of buttons. The button that confirms the operation ends up invoking the *TodoList.deleteTask* method that you'll be writing in a moment. The button that denies the operation just exits from the current operation.

```
TodoList.deleteTaskClick = function () {
    var message = "Are you sure you want to delete the task?";
    var msg = new Windows.UI.Popups.MessageDialog(message);
```

```
    msg.commands.append
(new Windows.UI.Popups.UICommand("Yes, proceed!", TodoList.deleteTask));
    msg.commands.append
(new Windows.UI.Popups.UICommand("No, I'm not sure...", function() {}));
    msg.defaultCommandIndex = 1;
    msg.showAsync();
}
```

The *defaultCommandIndex* property sets the 0-based index of the button to be selected by default. In this case, the No button is selected, as seen in Figure 10-14.

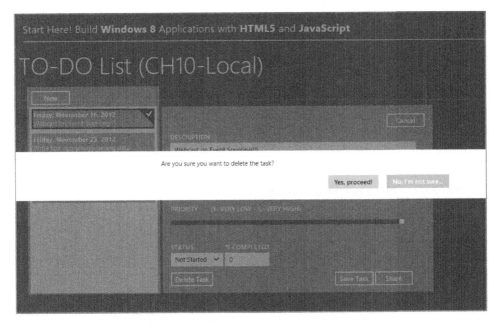

FIGURE 10-14 Deleting a task.

Here's the code that actually deletes the file:

```
TodoList.deleteTask = function () {
    // Get the task
    var task = TodoList.getTaskFromUI();

    // Locates the file and deletes it
    var name = task.description;
    var localFolder = Windows.Storage.ApplicationData.current.roamingFolder;
    localFolder.getFileAsync(name)
        .then(function (file) {
            file.deleteAsync().then(function () {
                TodoList.cancelTaskClick();
                TodoList.populateTaskList();
```

```
        });
    });
}
```

You first get the object that references the task currently displayed in the editor, and then you get the name of the corresponding file—in this case, the file name matches the description of the task. Finally, you locate the file in the roaming folder. This is done by using the *getFileAsync* method, which returns a reference to a single file, if it exists. To delete the file, you use the *deleteAsync* method. When done, you clear up the editor and refresh the list view to remove the deleted task.

Summary

Using files is a necessity for any serious application. Windows Store applications are no exception. In this chapter, you have learned the basics of file operations and the various storage options that are available to applications. Of particular interest for Windows Store applications are the roaming folder and roaming settings. By storing data in the roaming folder, and/or user settings in the roaming settings dictionary, you enable the operating system to synchronize that data across the cloud so that any other copy of the application running on other devices (under the same Windows account) can use it.

If this story hasn't caught you enough yet, think of some fairly impressive commercials of the iOS system you may have seen some time ago. In the commercial, a user on a train is reading a given page of an e-book with an iPad. Then she gets back home and sits comfortably in front of a Mac computer. She runs the same application and, magically, she is served the last page read. You can achieve the same kind of magic in your Windows Store application by using the roaming folder and roaming settings.

Another piece that you need to add to the Windows Store puzzle is getting remote data that is accessible over the Internet. This is the topic of the next chapter.

Chapter 11

Working with remote data

The least of things with a meaning is worth more in life than the greatest of things without it.

— *Carl Jung*

With very few exceptions, all mobile applications fall into one of the following categories: applications that just can't work without an Internet connection and applications that are only partially functional unless an Internet connection is present. You can't truly call yourself a good Microsoft Windows 8 developer until you have learned how to work with remote data across the Internet.

In this chapter, you will practice with data downloaded from a remote location using the HTTP protocol. First, you will learn how to make an HTTP call to download data. Next, you will face the more challenging task of interpreting the downloaded data so that you can make use of it in your Windows application.

The first exercise will show you how to retrieve and display the news feed from a public site. You'll download a Really Simple Syndication (RSS) feed and adjust the data so that it displays within a list view component. The second exercise will show you how to download JSON data from a different site—the Flickr photo service—and arrange it in a dynamically built layout.

Working with RSS data

Many websites share their content via marked-up text available for download from a public and documented URL, with the data usually formatted as an RSS feed. An RSS feed is essentially XML text that follows a fixed schema. RSS is commonly used to publish frequently updated content, such as blog posts, news headlines, and links to items in multimedia galleries in a standard format. A typical RSS feed contains a summary of the data available on the origin site plus some additional information, such as the publication date, the name of the author, and a link to the effective content.

Getting remote data

You start by creating a new Windows 8 project using the Blank App template. Next, you create a new *Pages* folder and add files such as *header.html* and *footer.html* from the previous chapters; edit the *default.html* and *default.css* files accordingly. (This work is required only to ensure that all applications have a consistent look and feel.) More importantly, open *default.js* and add the following bootstrapping code:

```
app.onready = function (args) {
    rssReaderApp.init();
};
```

The *init* function will be invoked when the application is fully loaded and ready to respond to the user's commands. However, the *init* function doesn't exist yet. To create it, add a new JavaScript file to the project under the *Js* folder and name it **rssReaderApp.js**. Here's the initial content for the new file:

```
var rssReaderApp = rssReaderApp || {};
rssReaderApp.init = function () {
    // To be done
}
```

At this point you should have a working—but empty—application. Let's spice it up a bit.

Getting familiar with XHR

In Windows 8, you use the *WinJS.xhr* object to perform access to remote HTTP endpoints. This object gives you the ability to request an external URL and return whatever content the remote web server provides. The *WinJS.xhr* object supports a variety of parameters, as you'll see in a moment; however, most of the time you need only pass the plain HTTP address you want to reach to make it work. Modify the *rssReaderApp.init* function, as shown below:

```
// This is the URL that provides RSS content
rssReaderApp.Feed = "http://news.google.com/news?pz=1&output=rss";

rssReaderApp.init = function () {
    WinJS.xhr({ url: rssReaderApp.Feed }).then(function (rss) {
        // Do something with the data
    });
```

First, you save the URL you want to access as a public member of the *rssReaderApp* global object. It is your responsibility to choose a URL that returns RSS data. If you are unfamiliar with RSS content, you should recognize it on most websites from the popular icon shown in Figure 11-1.

FIGURE 11-1 The popular icon that identifies links to URLs that return RSS data.

After you have determined the URL to invoke, you pass it along to the *WinJS.xhr* object. As usual with operations that can be potentially lengthy, you need to write the code in asynchronous form.

```
WinJS.xhr({ url: rssReaderApp.Feed }).then( ... );
```

You pass an object to *WinJS.xhr* with the *url* property set to the URL to invoke. That's all that's required; you don't need anything else for the call to take place. In the *then* method, place the code that you want to run after a response has been obtained from the URL—in this case, after the RSS data has been received. (The code in the *then* method will process the data and prepare it for display in this case.)

A moment ago, you read that the URL is the only prerequisite for *WinJS.xhr* to be called. Remember, though, that setting the URL correctly is no guarantee of success. A call may fail for a number of reasons, and you must be able to detect failures. In addition, you should ensure that the Windows 8 environment allows you to venture beyond the local machine and access the World Wide Web. Finally, you should make sure that the request you are sending out is well formed for the server that is going to receive it. Let's explore the options that you have to further configure the request.

Configuring the *WinJS.xhr* object

Table 11-1 enumerates the parameters you can optionally associate with a call to *WinJS.xhr*. These allow you to do things such as set the request type (for example, *GET* or *POST*), specify user credentials for remote authentication, set HTTP headers, and so forth.

TABLE 11-1 Options for calling the *WinJS.xhr* object

Parameter	Description
url	This is a required parameter that indicates the URL to invoke. The URL can be absolute or relative. The HTTPS protocol is supported as well.
type	Indicates the HTTP method to be used to open the connection with the specified URL. Valid values for this parameter are *GET, POST, PUT, DELETE*, or *HEAD*. The parameter is not case-sensitive. If not specified, the *type* parameter defaults to *GET*.
user password	You can use these parameters to specify credentials that are validated at the destination before servicing the request. If the *user* parameter is empty or missing, and the site requires authentication, then the user will be shown a logon window. If the *user* parameter is missing or empty, the *password* parameter is ignored.

Parameter	Description
headers	You can set this parameter to a JavaScript object whose property names indicate valid HTTP header names. The property values are then set as header values in the HTTP request.
data	The parameter refers to a JavaScript object that contains data to be passed to the server usually via a *POST* request.
responseType	Indicates the type of the expected response from a *GET* request. Feasible values are text (the default), *json*, *blob* for binary content, and *document* for an XML object.

The *WinJS.xhr* object returns a JavaScript *Promise* object so that the developer can easily arrange any subsequent steps following the asynchronous HTTP operation. When it comes to JavaScript promises and asynchronous operations, you've used both *then* and *done* functions in previous chapters, but it's useful to briefly revisit the difference between the two.

Windows 8 JavaScript (WinJS) library asynchronous operations always return a *Promise* object. As the name may suggest, the object represents the promise of getting some usable data at some point in the (near) future. So as a developer, you are allowed to specify those next steps using functions such as *Promise.done* and *Promise.then*. Both functions indicate a future action to perform as soon as the promised data becomes available. But what's the difference?

Promise.done and *Promise.then* are exactly the same except that *Promise.done* breaks the chain by returning *undefined* instead of a *Promise* object. In other words, you could write code such as:

```
WinJS.xhr(url).then(doThis).then(doThat).done(doAlsoThis);
```

But you can't write code like this:

```
WinJS.xhr(url).done(doThis).then(doThat);
```

In other words, when you use the *done* function, you must be at the end of a chain of instructions.

Handling errors during HTTP requests

An HTTP request may fail for a number of reasons. For example, you may lose your connection before the request completes, or the request may be refused by the server because it is malformed or because you didn't provide valid credentials. Finally, the request may hang indefinitely and time out. How do you deal with all these situations? This is just where the advanced capabilities of JavaScript *Promise* objects come into play.

Both the *done* and *then* functions have the following prototype:

```
WinJS.xhr({ url: ... }).then(
        function completed(request) {
            // The request completed successfully.
        },
        function error(error) {
            // The request failed for some reasons.
```

```
    }
});
```

So far, you have passed only one function to the *then* function of the promise. The *then* function invokes the first passed function when the request completes successfully. The completed function receives the response from the server as its single argument.

As you can see from the prototype, however, you can also pass a second function to the promise. That second function is the error handler for the request. The error handler function will be invoked automatically by the system if the request fails for some reason. The error function receives an *error* object, which has properties such as *status*, *statusText,* and *message*. Note that depending on which error occurred, some of these properties may not be set. You might want to use a generic message such as the one below and depicted in Figure 11-2.

```
WinJS.xhr({ url: rssReaderApp.Feed }).then(
    function (response) {
        rssReaderApp.parseFeed(response);
    },
    function (error) {
        rssReaderApp.alert("A download error occurred.");
    }
);
```

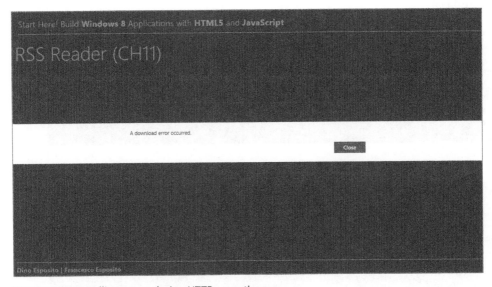

FIGURE 11-2 Handling errors during HTTP operations.

Giving requests a timeout

A request to a remote server may take a while to complete. The time-to-response depends on a number of factors, including bandwidth, and traffic on the target site. If completing the operation in a fixed amount of time is critical for your application, you might want to associate a timeout with your *WinJS.xhr* request. When you do that, if the request is still pending after the specified amount of time elapses, the request is automatically canceled and raises an error that propagates back to the calling application. Here's the code you need to set up a timeout:

```
WinJS.Promise.timeout(3000,
    WinJS.xhr({ url: ... }).then(
        function (response) {
            // Process response
        },
        function (error) {
            rssReaderApp.alert(error.message);
        })
);
```

Basically, all you do is wrap your *WinJS.xhr* call within a call to *WinJS.Promise.timeout*. The first parameter sets the expected timeout (in milliseconds); the second parameter is your call to *WinJS.xhr*. Note that if the request fails because it times out, then the error object you receive has the *message* property set to a generic message you can display directly to users, in this case, just "Canceled" (see Figure 11-3).

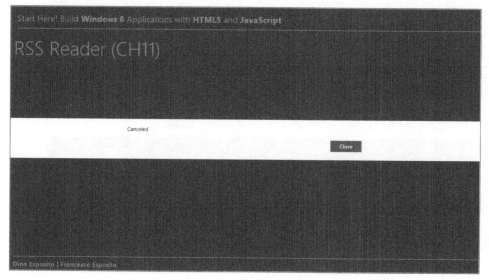

FIGURE 11-3 A timed-out request.

A look at the application's manifest

All Windows Store application projects include a manifest file. So far, you haven't needed to deal with the manifest. However, when your app needs special capabilities, such as the ability to make HTTP requests over the Internet, the manifest becomes important. So let's take a look at it.

Locate the file *package.appxmanifest* in your project's folder and open it. Next, select the Capabilities tab. If you do that for the sample *RssReader* project you have been working on in this chapter, you should see the screen shown in Figure 11-4.

Each capability listed represents an action that your application may be able to perform when running on a Windows 8 system. The key point here is that for all unchecked capabilities, the Windows 8 runtime will restrict your application from invoking any application programming interface (API) that relates to those capabilities. As you can see in Figure 11-4, you must check the Internet Client capability for the *WinJS.xhr* object to function properly.

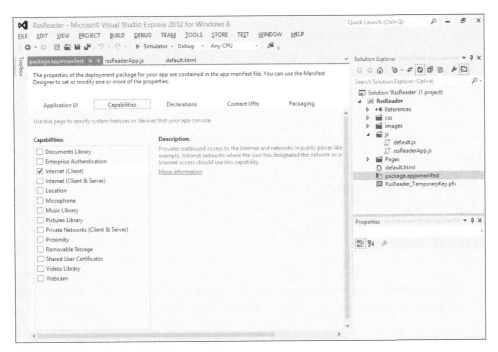

FIGURE 11-4 The manifest file of the sample project.

Now, try disabling the Internet Client capability and running the *RssReader* sample application. The application compiles and deploys successfully to the device. However, it doesn't produce any visible effect—no error messages, no crashes, and no failure. What's going on? Quite simply, the Windows 8 runtime system blocked any call that required an explicitly declared capability.

Important The lesson you should learn from this is that if at some point you code a feature and it just doesn't work, without any apparent reason, check to make sure that you have declared the appropriate capability for each Windows 8 API your feature requires. Note also that in Microsoft Visual Studio 2012, the Internet Client capability—the minimum capability required to make *WinJS.xhr* work—is the only capability turned on by default.

Parsing and displaying downloaded data

At this point, you know everything you need to place a successful call to a remote HTTP endpoint and grab some data. The next step is to do something significant with that data. In this exercise, you will call into the Google News service to download the latest news as an RSS feed. Next, you will parse the returned string into a list of items and use them to populate a list view.

Extending the RSS Reader application

Before you turn your attention to parsing RSS data, some changes to the user interface of the application are in order. To make those changes, first open *default.html* and enter the following markup:

```html
<h1>RSS Reader (CH11)</h1>
    <div id="newslist" data-win-control="WinJS.UI.ListView">
    </div>
<div id="splitView">
  <div id="titleDetail"></div>
  <div id="pubDateDetail"></div>
  <div id="categoryDetail"></div>
  <div id="descriptionDetail"></div>
</div>
```

The *DIV* element named *newslist* is the *ListView* component that will contain all the downloaded news. The *DIV* element named *splitView* is where you'll provide a preview of a selected news item.

Another important piece of markup to add is the HTML template for the news. Before you can write this template, however, you must have a clear idea of what you're getting from the HTTP endpoint and how you intend to transform that content into usable data.

Parsing the RSS content

Open the *rssReaderApp.js* file, select the *rssReaderApp.init* function, and edit it as shown below:

```javascript
WinJS.xhr({ url: rssReaderApp.Feed }).then(
    function (response) {
        rssReaderApp.parseFeed(response);
    },
```

```
    function (error) {
        rssReaderApp.alert("A download error occurred.");
    }
);
```

The *rssReaderApp.parseFeed* function will receive whatever content the remote URL returns and will attempt to transform it into a format usable by the application. It should be clear that if something goes wrong with the download operation, then the control passes to the error function. This means that if the *rssReaderApp.parseFeed* function gets invoked, it actually has some data to work with.

The primary responsibility for the *rssReaderApp.parseFeed* function is to ensure that the data it received is in a format it can handle. Because you are downloading RSS data, and because RSS is an XML format, this is a good starting point for the *parseFeed* function.

```
rssReaderApp.parseFeed = function (response) {
    if (response.responseXML == null) {
        rssReaderApp.alert("Invalid data");
        return;
    }

    // More action here ...
}
```

The response received from the server is encapsulated in the object passed to the function. If received data can be rendered as an XML document object model, then the *responseXML* property will not contain *null*, and control will pass to the code you will write next to query for the various RSS elements.

```
An RSS feed follows the schema shown below:
<rss ...>
   <channel ...>
      <item>
         <title> ... </title>
         <link> ... </link>
         <guid> ... </guid >
         <description> ... </description >
         <category> ... </category>
      </item>

      ...
   </channel>
</rss>
```

In your parser, the first thing you want to do is select all the *item* elements and then loop through them to extract specific information, such as the title, description, a link to the source, and perhaps a category. The following code selects all the *item* elements from the entire XML document.

```
var items = response.responseXML.querySelectorAll("rss > channel > item");
```

The query syntax is nearly identical to the CSS query syntax you discovered in Chapter 3, "Making sense of CSS": it means "get me all the elements named *item* that are children of the *rss* and *channel* elements." Next, you create a *for-each* loop and work on each item individually. As an example, the following code shows how to retrieve the title of the first published news item.

```
var title = items[0].querySelector("title").textContent;
```

The final problem to solve, as far as parsing is concerned, is determining where you will store parsed data. Ideally, you might want to gather information in an easy-to-manage array that you can then bind to the list view. Here's the final version of the code for the parser:

```
rssReaderApp.parseFeed = function (response) {
    if (response.responseXML == null) {
        rssReaderApp.alert("Invalid data");
        return;
    }
    var items = response.responseXML.querySelectorAll("rss > channel > item");
    for (var n = 0; n < items.length; n++) {
        var newsElement = {};
        newsElement.title = items[n].querySelector("title").textContent;
        newsElement.link = items[n].querySelector("link").textContent;
        newsElement.guid = items[n].querySelector("guid").textContent;
        newsElement.pubDate = items[n].querySelector("pubDate").textContent;
        newsElement.description = items[n].querySelector("description").textContent;

        // Check category
        var category = "[No category]";
        if (items[n].querySelector("category") != null)
            category = items[n].querySelector("category").textContent;
        newsElement.category = category;

        RssReader.Items.push(newsElement);
    }
}
```

There are a couple of things to note. First, if you're working with one specific RSS feed then you can adapt your code to the expected format. If you instead plan to write a rather generic RSS Reader that users can configure to get data from a variety of different sources, then you should pay attention to each and every piece of data you try to access. For example, you'll find the *category* node in the Google

News feed, but many other RSS feeds omit the *category* node. To avoid runtime exceptions, you should check to make sure that the *category* node exists before attempting to read it programmatically. To stay on the safe side, you might also want to extend such a check to any node you attempt to read generically from an RSS feed. You never know what you will really get from web servers!

The second thing to notice in the preceding code is the *RssReader.Items* collection, which stores all the parsed news items. In the exercises you completed in past chapters, you always managed data binding programmatically. In other words, you always wrote some script code to bind a collection of data to a Windows 8 *ListView* object, or to any other bindable user interface components.

But in this exercise you'll do something different. You can also create data bindings declaratively, at design time. This is where the *RssReader* object comes into play. You define this object at the top of the *rssReaderApp.js* file, as shown below:

```
WinJS.Namespace.define("RssReader", { Items: new WinJS.Binding.List() });
```

The *RssReader* object is given a property named *Items* initialized to an empty binding list. During the loop, the parser just adds news items to the *RSSReader* object's *Items* collection. Subsequently, the *RssReader.Items* object will become the data source for the *ListView* you created in the user interface.

> **Note** You can code data binding either programmatically or declaratively; it's fully functional either way. The choice between programmatic and declarative data binding is primarily a matter of personal preference.

Mapping an RSS feed item to the user interface

Now you're ready to map the news content to the HTML template which will render items within the *ListView*. Here's a sample HTML template:

```
<div id="newsItemTemplate"
data-win-control="WinJS.Binding.Template" style="display: none;">
    <div class="listItem">
        <div id="titleDiv" data-win-bind="innerText: title"></div>
        <div id="categoryDiv" data-win-bind="innerText: category"></div>
        <div id="pubDateDiv" data-win-bind="innerText: pubDate"></div>
    </div>
</div>
```

As you can see, the template grabs data from *title*, *category,* and *pubDate* properties of the bound news object. You're almost done. The final step consists of binding the *ListView* itself to its data source. You do this declaratively in the *default.html* file through the *data-win-options* attribute.

```
<div id="newslist"
    data-win-control="WinJS.UI.ListView"
```

```
                data-win-options="{ itemDataSource: RssReader.Items.dataSource,
                                    itemTemplate: newsItemTemplate,
                                    layout: {type: WinJS.UI.ListLayout} }">
</div>
```

At this point, if you compile and run the sample project you should see something similar to
Figure 11-5.

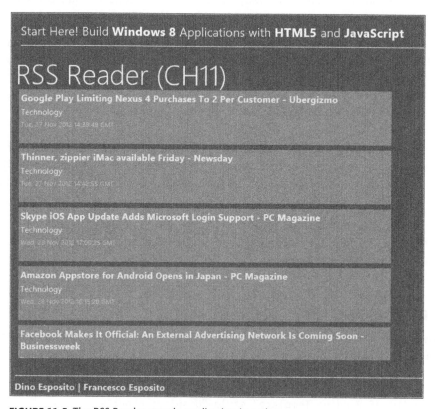

FIGURE 11-5 The RSS Reader sample application in action.

Drilling down into data

In previous chapters, you saw how to make any item displayed within a *ListView* clickable, which can
result in more data being presented to the user, in a "drill-down" process. As shown in Figure 11-5, so
far only the title, publication date, and category are displayed to the user. But what if you want to give
users a preview of the news content, or let them navigate to the actual source of the content? Sure,
you could add more UI elements and bind them within the list view, but that would take extra screen
space. Instead, you can let users drill down when they want more information. To do that, you need
to make the *ListView* items clickable, and then you need to find a way to show at least the *description*
field of the downloaded news.

Making any displayed news item clickable

The first step in taking control of a user-click of a displayed news item will look familiar if you have completed all the exercises in previous chapters. Edit the options for the *ListView* to configure direct selection on tap behavior and enable single selection:

```
<div id="newslist"
     data-win-control="WinJS.UI.ListView"
     data-win-options="{ itemDataSource: RssReader.Items.dataSource,
                         itemTemplate: newsItemTemplate,
                         layout: {type: WinJS.UI.ListLayout},
                         selectionMode: 'single',
                         tapBehavior: 'directSelect' }">
</div>
```

Next, in the *rssReaderApp.js* file, register a handler for the *itemInvoked* event of the *ListView* object.

```
rssReaderApp.init = function () {
    var listview = document.getElementById("newslist");
    listview.addEventListener("iteminvoked", rssReaderApp.preview);

    // Rest of the code here
    ...
}
```

Finally, you get to write the code that displays the news description.

Displaying raw HTML

Depending on the RSS feed you have retrieved, you may receive plain text or rich HTML as the news description. You might decide to sanitize the content, removing and/or escaping any HTML tags you encounter in the text. To do so, you pass the description to a function that returns a clean string. Alternatively, you might decide that you want to display rich HTML, especially when the platform—like the Windows 8 platform—gives you full access to the rendering capabilities of a web browser. The primary reason for making a decision between the two approaches is how much you trust the RSS provider and the overall level of security of the platform. If you were, for example, writing a website that retrieves data from a source provided by a user, you should be warned in advance: don't display raw HTML! In contrast, if you're getting data from a single and well-known RSS provider in the context of a Windows 8 application, showing potentially unsafe HTML is definitely doable. Here's the code to preview the selected news:

```
rssReaderApp.preview = function (e) {
    var index = e.detail.itemIndex;
    var currentArticle = RssReader.Items.getAt(index);
    var amended = currentArticle.description;
    amended = amended.replace("src=" + '"//', "src=" + '"http://');
```

```
document.getElementById("titleDetail").innerHTML = currentArticle.title;
document.getElementById("pubDateDetail").innerHTML = currentArticle.pubDate;
document.getElementById("categoryDetail").innerHTML = currentArticle.category;
document.getElementById("descriptionDetail").innerHTML = amended;
}
```

You first get the index of the selected item and retrieve the news it refers to. At this point you set the *innerHTML* property of the HTML element that is expected to contain the description of the news, as well as some other context information such as publication date and category. When you provide the news item preview you set the elements of the *splitView DIV* you created earlier in the exercise.

The description of the news you get from the Google News feed usually contains *IMG* tags. For some reason the URL to these images is missing the *http://* prefix, which causes Windows 8 to be unable to render the image. A simple string replace operation does the trick, as you can see in the preceding code. Figure 11-6 shows the final result.

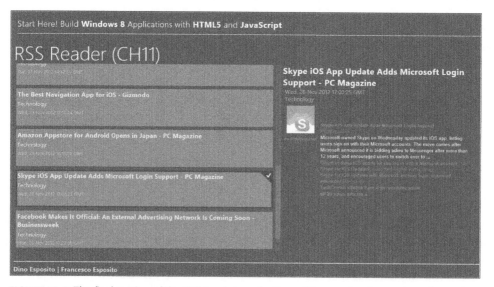

FIGURE 11-6 The final version of the RSS Reader application, with a preview for a selected news item.

Working with JSON data

Another common scenario for Windows Store applications involves downloading data from services that expose JavaScript Object Notation (JSON) data rather than RSS. Usually, web services make their content available in a variety of formats, the most common of which are XML (and RSS in particular) and JSON. You already worked with the WinJS API for JSON in a previous chapter. In Chapter 10, "Adding persistent data to applications," you saved application data to JSON and read it back later. In that example, you were entirely responsible for the full data cycle—serialization, persistence, and deserialization.

However, when you get your JSON data from a remote source, you can only control the deserialization portion of the full data cycle. Unfortunately, this doesn't mean that you need to do only half the work. Although commonly used and close to a *de facto standard* state, JSON is not an exact science. As you'll see in this exercise, there's always the risk that you will get invalid JSON. When that's the case, you're responsible for fixing it.

Laying out a Flickr viewer

In this exercise, you'll build an application that retrieves and displays public photos from the popular website Flickr. Links to photos, and related information such as author and description are downloaded as a JSON string and then rendered using a *ListView* component.

Setting up the Flickr Viewer app

Create a new Blank App project and name it **FlickrPhotoViewer**. After adding the usual new *Pages* folder with *header.html* and *footer.html* files (as you did in previous exercises), open up the *default.js* file and add the usual handler for the *onready* event. Using that method, you can control the application's initialization, as shown below:

```
app.onready = function (args) {
    flickrApp.init();
};
```

The next step is to add a new JavaScript file to the project named *flickrApp.js*. Initially, the file will contain only the following:

```
var flickrApp = flickrApp || {};
flickrApp.init = function () {
    // More to go here
}
```

Now turn your attention to the user interface of the application and open *default.html*. Make sure it contains the following markup:

```
<!DOCTYPE html>
<html>
<head>
    <meta charset="utf-8" />
    <title>Flickr Photo Viewer</title>

    <!-- WinJS references -->
    <link href="//Microsoft.WinJS.1.0/css/ui-dark.css" rel="stylesheet" />
    <script src="//Microsoft.WinJS.1.0/js/base.js"></script>
    <script src="//Microsoft.WinJS.1.0/js/ui.js"></script>
```

```
    <!-- Flickr Photo Viewer references -->
    <link href="/css/default.css" rel="stylesheet" />
    <script src="/js/default.js"></script>
    <script src="/js/flickrApp.js"></script>
</head>

<body>
    <div data-win-control="WinJS.UI.HtmlControl"
        data-win-options="{uri:'/pages/header.html'}"></div>

    <h1>Flickr Viewer (CH11)</h1>
    <br />
    <input type="text" placeholder="Subject" id="subject" value="" />
    <button id="buttonSearch">Search</button>

    <div id="picturesList" data-win-control="WinJS.UI.ListView">
    </div>
    <div data-win-control="WinJS.UI.HtmlControl"
    data-win-options="{uri:'/pages/footer.html'}"></div>
</body>
</html>
```

In addition to the usual markup, the page contains a Windows 8 *ListView* bound to a *DIV* element named *picturesList*. An input text box and a button have been added to let users of your application type in keywords to select corresponding pictures.

The Search button needs a click handler; add it in the *flickrApp.init* method, as shown below:

```
flickrApp.init = function () {
    document.getElementById("buttonSearch")
            .addEventListener("click", flickrApp.searchClick);
}
```

The click handler will be responsible for placing the HTTP call to the Flickr web service and processing the JSON data it receives in response.

Looking at the Flickr public feed

In this example, you will access the public photo feed of Flickr, which requires neither authentication, nor any Flickr-specific application ID. All you need to know here is the URL to call. As in the first exercise of this chapter, you save it to a member on the global *flickrApp* object:

```
flickrApp.Source = "http://api.flickr.com/services/feeds/photos_public.gne" +
                   "?tagmode=any&format=json&nojsoncallback=1&tags='{0}'";
```

Table 11-2 provides a brief explanation of the URL parameters.

TABLE 11-2 Query string parameters for the Flickr public web service

Parameter	Description
tagmode	This parameter can take the value *all* or *any*; and indicates whether any selected photos must match all or just any of the specified tags.
format	Set this parameter to *json* if you want to get a JSON response. You can also specify that the call should return RSS or a variety of other formats as listed here: *http://www.flickr.com/services/ feeds/docs/photos_public*.
nojsoncallback	In a Windows Store application, this parameter is *required* and must be set to *1*. You don't need this parameter if you're calling the Flickr API from within a JavaScript web application. It is a setting that relates to how the host environment actually places the call to the remote site.
tags	You can set this parameter to a comma-separated list of keywords to match appropriate photos.

As you may have noticed, the *flickrApp.Source* property is set to a string that contains a placeholder—the *{0}* item. In .NET programming, this type of notation is used to format strings dynamically. The idea is that when the user clicks the Search button, the handler will read the typed tags and insert them in the URL string, replacing the placeholder.

The *{0}* notation is common in .NET Windows programming, but it isn't in JavaScript. So you need to create a helper function that does the replacement. This is interesting because it shows you a powerful JavaScript technique—manipulating object prototypes.

Preparing the Flickr URL

It is advisable that you create yet another JavaScript file; call it **helpers.js**. Add a reference to that file in your *default.html* file and make sure that the *helpers.js* reference precedes the *flickrApp.js* reference. Here's the initial content for *helpers.js*:

```
////////////////////////////////////////////////////////
// Applies the .NET {n} convention to format strings
//
String.prototype.format = function () {
    var theString = this,
        count = arguments.length;

    while (count--) {
        theString = theString.replace(
            new RegExp('\\{' + count + '\\}', 'gm'), arguments[count]);
    };

    return theString;
};
```

The code adds the *format* function to the *prototype* of the JavaScript's native *String* object. By doing this, any string manipulated under the scope of the *helpers.js* file will expose an additional *format* method. After you reference *helpers.js*, you can write the following code:

```
flickrApp.searchClick = function () {
    var tags = document.getElementById("subject").value;
    flickrApp.download(tags);
}
flickrApp.download = function (tags) {
    // Add tags to the Flickr URL
    var url = flickrApp.Source.format(tags);

    // Get photos
    WinJS.xhr({ url: url }).then(function (json) {
        // Parse the JSON feed here
    });
}
```

In the click handler of the Search button, you get any text typed into the input field and pass it down to the newly created *download* function. Internally, this function composes and invokes the Flickr URL via *WinJS.xhr*. Note that if you pass an empty tag list, you will still get some photos in response; that's why it is not strictly required that you check the *tags* variable for *null* or *empty*.

Getting the JSON data

You use the *WinJS.xhr* function to download the JSON string that describes selected photos. Using the *WinJS.xhr* function is the same as in the previous exercise. You define two functions: one that executes when the download completes successfully and one when the request fails, and pass them to the *then* method on the promise object returned by *WinJS.xhr*.

```
WinJS.xhr({ url: url }).then(
    function (response) {
        flickrApp.parseFeed(response.responseText);
    },
    function (response) {
        var message = "Error downloading photos.";
        if (response.message != null)
            message += response.message;
        flickrApp.alert(message);
    }
);
```

The *then* method passes to its functions an object that represents the response retrieved from the remote source. To get the plain text contained in the body of a JSON response, query the *responseText* property.

The heart of the Flickr application is inside the body of the *flickrApp.parseFeed* method. Here's its implementation:

```javascript
flickrApp.parseFeed = function (json) {
    var pictures = JSON.parse(json);
    for (var i = 0; i < pictures.items.length; i++) {
        var pictureElement = {};
        pictureElement.photoUrl = pictures.items[i].media.m;

        // Bind to the listview
        ...
    }
}
```

The JSON string you receive has the following form:

```json
{
    "title": "Recent Uploads tagged tennis",
    "link": "http://www.flickr.com/photos/tags/tennis/",
    "description": "",
    "modified": "2012-11-30T07:56:42Z",
    "generator": "http://www.flickr.com/",
    "items": [
        {
            "title": "...",
            "link": "http://www.flickr.com/photos/craftydogma/8232121888/",
            "media": {
                "m": http://farm9.staticflickr.com/8350/8232121888_9f762d7e5e_m.jpg
            },
            "date_taken": "2012-05-05T19:04:48-08:00",
            "description": "<p> ... </p>",
            "published": "2012-11-30T07: 56: 42Z",
            "author": "...",
            "author_id": "...",
            "tags": "tennis vintage photo"
        }
    ]
}
```

To access the URL of the photo, you need the following expression:

```
pictureElement.photoUrl = pictures.items[i].media.m
```

You can gather the photo URL, as well as other information such as date and description, into a handy data structure—the *pictureElement* object of the sample above.

Adding pictures to the user interface

To display the retrieved pictures, you can use a Windows 8 *ListView*. In *default.html* you already have a *DIV* element bound to the *ListView* component. The next step consists of binding the *ListView* to a data source and defining an item template.

Because you just want to display pictures, the HTML item template can be simple, as shown below:

```
<div id="picturesItemTemplate"
     data-win-control="WinJS.Binding.Template" style="display: none;">
    <div class="listItem">
        <img id="picture" data-win-bind="src: photoUrl" alt="" />
    </div>
</div>
```

The *src* attribute of the *IMG* element is bound to the *photoUrl* property of the bound data object. You add the template at the beginning of the body for the *default.html* page.

As you did in the first exercise of this chapter, you also define a binding list object at the top of the *flickrApp.js* file:

```
WinJS.Namespace.define("FlickrFeed", { Pictures: new WinJS.Binding.List() });
```

You populate the list during the enumeration of the JSON content.

```
flickrApp.parseFeed = function (json) {
    var pictures = JSON.parse(json);
    for (var i = 0; i < pictures.items.length; i++) {
        var pictureElement = {};
        pictureElement.photoUrl = pictures.items[i].media.m;

        // Add the object to the listview
        FlickrFeed.Pictures.push(pictureElement);
    }
}
```

Finally, you bind the *ListView* to the *FlickrFeed.Pictures* list. In *default.html* you add the following markup:

```
<div id="picturesList" data-win-control="WinJS.UI.ListView"
     data-win-options="{ itemDataSource: FlickrFeed.Pictures.dataSource,
                         itemTemplate: picturesItemTemplate,
                         layout: {type: WinJS.UI.GridLayout} }">
</div>
```

Figure 11-7 displays the output of the application, if all goes well.

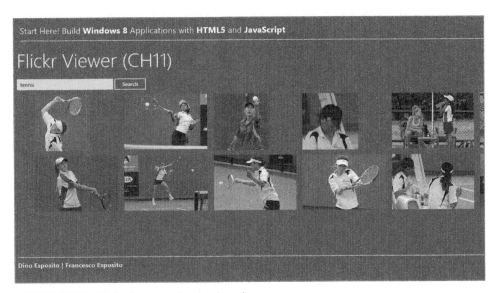

FIGURE 11-7 The Flickr Viewer application in action.

Enhancing the application

As mentioned, JSON is not an exact science. So it's possible to get a JSON string that appears to be invalid. If the *JSON.parse* method can't parse the downloaded text, your application just throws an exception, as in Figure 11-8.

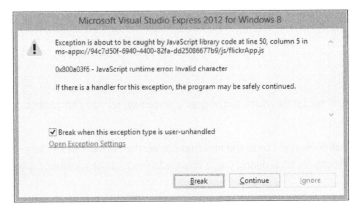

FIGURE 11-8 The Flickr Viewer dealing with invalid JSON content.

Dealing with invalid JSON

When you detect invalid JSON, it's not immediately obvious who might be the source of the problem. The only fact you know is that the parser failed—but why? Was it because the parser has a bug? Or is the JSON provided to the parser invalid? While developing the Flickr Viewer app you faced the error window shown in Figure 11-8 quite a few times, often with no apparent reason. Sometimes, by simply changing the tag the application would work just fine.

When the parser complains about invalid JSON, the first thing to do is to make sure that the JSON content is truly valid. As shown in Figure 11-9, you can validate JSON text by copying it into the following website: *http://jsonlint.com*.

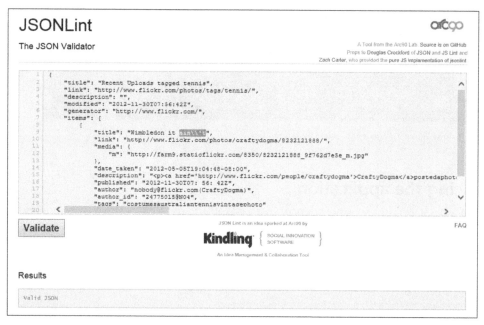

FIGURE 11-9 The JSONLint website.

But how can you grab the text of the JSON you're getting as a response, so you can paste it into the editor of JSONLint?

In Visual Studio, you place a breakpoint right onto the line that parses the content (see Figure 11-10). The breakpoint halts execution on that line, thus giving you a chance to inspect the runtime context.

```
flickrApp.js*  →  ×  default.css      default.html
        function (response) {
            flickrApp.parseFeed(response.responseText);
        },
        function (response) {
            var message = "Error downloading photos.";
            if (response.message != null)
                message += response.message;
            flickrApp.alert(message);
        }
    );
}

flickrApp.clear = function () {
    FlickrFeed.Pictures.splice(0, FlickrFeed.Pictures.length);
}

flickrApp.parseFeed = function (json) {

    var pictures = JSON.parse(json);
At flickrApp.js, line 49 character 5 i < pictures.items.length; i++) {
        var pictureElement = {};
        pictureElement.title = pictures.items[i].title;
        pictureElement.link = pictures.items[i].link;
        pictureElement.author = pictures.items[i].author;
        pictureElement.photoUrl = pictures.items[i].media.m;
        pictureElement.dateTaken = pictures.items[i].date_taken;

        FlickrFeed.Pictures.push(pictureElement);
    }
}
```

FIGURE 11-10 Placing a breakpoint to inspect the content of the *json* variable.

When execution has paused on the breakpoint, you just move your mouse over the *json* variable. A possibly very wide tooltip appears. If the text is fairly long, inspecting it from the tooltip may not be easy. As an alternative, click on the down arrow icon that appears right before the text. When you do that, you are offered a better option: to select a text visualizer (see Figure 11-11).

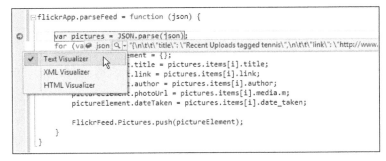

FIGURE 11-11 Inspecting the content of the *json* variable into a comfortable visualizer.

The text visualizer is a plain text editor where you can comfortably inspect the content of the *json* variable—the text you're going to pass to the JSON parser and that is known to generate an "invalid character" exception. You can easily select that text and copy it to the clipboard. To copy the text to the clipboard, you can either type Ctrl+C, or right-click the text and select Copy (see Figure 11-12).

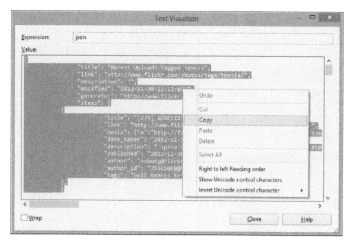

FIGURE 11-12 The text visualizer to copy the JSON text to the clipboard.

With the JSON copied to the clipboard, you can go to the JSONLint website mentioned earlier, paste the text in the editor, and validate it.

Fixing invalid JSON

It turns out that the Flickr web service doesn't always return valid JSON that can be successfully validated against the JSONLint validator. At the same time, any JSON that JSONLint validates is correctly parsed back by the *JSON.parse* function in Windows 8.

One issue you'll discover is that the Flickr service doesn't always handle the single quote character found in some descriptions correctly. For example, consider the following text:

```
Wimbledon it ain\'t
```

This text appears in the description of some photos. To make it pass the JSON validation, you need to double escape the single quote, so the string looks like this:

```
Wimbledon it ain\\'t
```

You can fix this problem quickly and effectively by introducing yet another extension to the *String* prototype. Open the *helpers.js* file again and add this code:

```
String.prototype.doubleEscapeSingleQuotes = function () {
    var theString = this;
    if (theString != null && theString != "") {
        return theString.replace(/\'/g, "\\'");
    } else {
        return theString;
    }
}
```

It is important to note that simply calling the *replace* function doesn't work, because the *replace* function only replaces the first occurrence of the matching string. You need to wrap the string to replace it in a regular expression (as shown below) and explicitly add the *g* qualifier to make it work on the entire string.

```
/string-to-replace/g
```

The code that parses the JSON becomes

```
flickrApp.parseFeed = function (json) {
    var amendedText = json.doubleEscapeSingleQuotes();
    var pictures = JSON.parse(amendedText);

    for (var i = 0; i < pictures.items.length; i++) {
        var pictureElement = {};
        pictureElement.photoUrl = pictures.items[i].media.m;

        // Add the object to the listview
        FlickrFeed.Pictures.push(pictureElement);
    }
}
```

With this added code, you should be able to correctly parse Flickr JSON in every case you've encountered so far.

Displaying a different set of photos

To complete the exercise, you might want to add a second button to clear the currently displayed photos. The function you're going to create is also useful for silently clearing the view when the user starts a new search. Note that without a "clear" step, any new search will just append photos to the existing list.

To add the Clear button, add the following markup to the *default.html* page:

```
<button id="buttonClear">Clear</button>
```

Next, in *flickrApp.init*, you register a handler for the button's *click* event.

```
flickrApp.init = function () {
    document.getElementById("buttonSearch")
            .addEventListener("click", flickrApp.searchClick);
    document.getElementById("buttonClear")
            .addEventListener("click", flickrApp.clearClick);
}
```

And finally, you get to write the code for the handler and to clear up photos.

```
flickrApp.clearClick = function () {
    flickrApp.clear();
}
flickrApp.clear = function () {
    // Zero the length of the list
    FlickrFeed.Pictures.splice(0, FlickrFeed.Pictures.length);
}
```

You also might want to place a call to *flickrApp.clear* method in the download function just before placing the remote call.

```
flickrApp.download = function (tags) {
    // Add tags to the Flickr URL
    var url = flickrApp.Source.format(tags);

    // Clear existing photos (if any)
    flickrApp.clear();

    // Get new photos
    WinJS.xhr({ url: url }).then( ... );
};
```

With this final version, you can run as many searches as you want while displaying only the most recently found photos, which is both less confusing for the user and also improves the overall application performance.

Summary

Being able to access data from a remote location via HTTP is a key feature for nearly every modern application—especially for applications possibly deployed to a mobile device. In a Windows Store application written with HTML and JavaScript, you perform HTTP access using the *WinJS.xhr* object. In this chapter, you saw two exercises that showed how to make a query via HTTP to get remote data, and consume the responses containing RSS and JSON data. Although this chapter didn't exhaust the list of possible HTTP-related tasks, it definitely addresses the most common scenarios.

This chapter concludes the section of the book dedicated to basic aspects of Windows 8 programming. In the next section, you'll enter more advanced territory—dealing with devices and sensors, Live tiles, and publishing. The next chapter is about programming against embedded devices and sensors, such as GPS and webcams.

Chapter 12

Accessing devices and sensors

If you are interested, you never have to look for new interests. They come to you.
When you are genuinely interested in one thing, it will always lead to something else.

— *Eleanor Roosevelt*

Smartphones and tablets owe much of their success to the high quality of their sensors and internal devices. If you go back to the early days of the iPhone, you may recall how astonished people were with the now-mundane Flashlight application. That was essentially a toy app—though it had some practical use. The assortment of devices and sensors you find on modern devices, such as a tablet equipped with Microsoft Windows 8, is so rich as to enable developers to think and build completely new types of applications.

As a Windows 8 developer you have access, even from a JavaScript-based programming environment, to a variety of Windows Runtime application programming interfaces (APIs) that give you control of a range of sensors, including such things as a GPS, a light sensor, an accelerometer, and a compass. In addition, a Windows Store application can gain access to devices both connected to the computer or embedded in it. Typical examples are printers and the webcam.

In this chapter, you'll learn how to use the webcam programmatically, how to print content, and how to work with one of the most useful sensors—the GPS component that returns the current location of the user.

Working with the webcam

Today almost all computers and devices come with a high-resolution webcam. A webcam is typically employed by built-in programs to support video conferencing and video chat. It is also common for applications to leverage the webcam to take instant pictures of the user. From a programming perspective, the webcam is just like any other piece of hardware. As a developer, you learn about its public API, apply the correct calls, and get the behavior you expect. In the 1990s, working with hardware was often a difficult and challenging task. Thankfully, we now live and code in a different century! As an example, in the next exercise, you'll build a Windows Store application that takes instant pictures of the user.

Capturing the webcam stream

As usual, you start by creating a new Windows 8 project using the Blank App template. Next, you create a new *Pages* folder and add common files such as *header.html* and *footer.html,* as you've seen repeatedly in the preceding chapters. Edit the *default.html* and *default.css* files appropriately for this application, as described earlier in this book. (This work is required only to ensure that all applications have a consistent look and feel.)

Setting up the project

More importantly, open up the *default.js* file and add the following bootstrapping code:

```
app.onready = function (args) {
    instantPhotoApp.init();
};
```

You should know by now that the *init* function will be invoked when the application is fully loaded and ready to respond to the user's commands. However, you must create the *init* function. As you've done quite a few times already in past exercises, add a new JavaScript file to the project under the *Js* folder and name it **instantPhotoApp.js**.

The name of the JavaScript file is actually unimportant, in the sense that whatever name you use can work. However, it's probably not a good idea to name a project file after your favorite pet. The convention used in this book is to name the main JavaScript file of the application after the name of the project, plus an *App* suffix.

Here's the initial content of the JavaScript *instantPhotoApp.js* file.

```
var instantPhotoApp = instantPhotoApp || {};
instantPhotoApp.init = function () {
    // To be done
}
```

At this point you should have a working but empty application. You'll add some significant markup to arrange the user interface.

In *default.html*, add the following chunk of HTML code:

```
<h1>Instant Photo (CH12)</h1>
<div class="center">
    <img id="imgPhoto" src="/images/nophoto.png" />
```

```
    <br />
    <button id="buttonShoot" class="horizontalBtn">Take a picture</button>
    <br />
</div>
```

Basically, the webcam application consists of a button that triggers the webcam and an *IMG* element where users will view the captured image. The final preliminary step is to add a handler for the *click* event for the Take A Picture button. Open the *instantPhotoApp.js* file and type the following code:

```
instantPhotoApp.init = function () {
    document.getElementById("buttonShoot")
            .addEventListener("click", instantPhotoApp.takePicture);
};

instantPhotoApp.takePicture = function () {
    // Some more code here
}
```

Now, you're all set and ready to tackle the webcam API.

Checking the webcam capability

Code is not allowed to freely access the webcam without explicit user permission. For this reason, to give your app a chance to successfully use the webcam you must first declare your intention to use it.

As shown in Figure 12-1, double-click the manifest file you have in the project and select the Capabilities tab from the subsequent view.

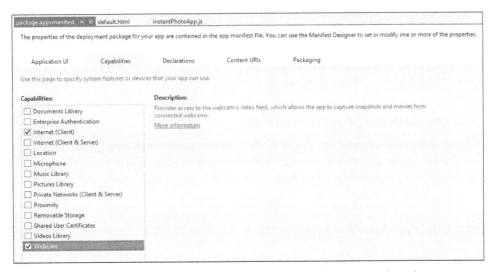

FIGURE 12-1 Enabling the capability that gives your code the ability to access the webcam programmatically.

Note that the single *Webcam* capability is sufficient for the purposes of writing an instant photo application. However, if you were writing an application that uses the webcam to capture a video stream, you would probably also want to add the *Microphone* capability. The *Webcam* capability alone provides access to the video stream, but not to the audio stream.

Configuring the webcam

The Windows 8 API provides a common dialog to deal with the webcam. All you need to do is get an instance of the *CameraCaptureUI* object and then launch it.

```
var dialog = new Windows.Media.Capture.CameraCaptureUI();
```

The *CameraCaptureUI* object deals with photos and video, so it exposes two distinct properties by which you can configure video and photo settings: *photoSettings* and *videoSettings*. For the purpose of this exercise, you'll focus only on *photoSettings*.

The *photoSettings* object offers a few properties to define the size (in pixels) of the resulting image, its aspect ratio, and the file format in which you want to store the image. Here's what you need to do to ensure a 16:9 aspect ratio and store the image bits as a JPEG image.

```
var dialog = new Windows.Media.Capture.CameraCaptureUI();
var aspectRatio = { width: 16, height: 9 };
dialog.photoSettings.croppedAspectRatio = aspectRatio;
dialog.photoSettings.format = Windows.Media.Capture.CameraCaptureUIPhotoFormat.jpeg;
```

If you don't like the JPEG format, you can choose the PNG format instead:

```
dialog.photoSettings.format = Windows.Media.Capture.CameraCaptureUIPhotoFormat.png;
```

In general the JPEG format results in a slightly more compact file that requires fewer resources and less time to transfer over the wire, and it also takes less space when stored on disk. In contrast, the PNG format ensures a somewhat better image quality; the tradeoff is a larger file size—a PNG image is usually nearly double the size of a JPEG image.

Accessing the webcam programmatically

After you have configured the webcam, you're ready to launch the dialog that will guide the user to take the picture. The following listing shows the complete code you need to have in *instantPhotoApp.js* to capture an image. To be precise, the listing below doesn't yet include the code to display the captured image.

```
instantPhotoApp.takePicture = function () {
    try {
        var dialog = new Windows.Media.Capture.CameraCaptureUI();
        var aspectRatio = { width: 16, height: 9 };
```

```
        dialog.photoSettings.croppedAspectRatio = aspectRatio;
        dialog.photoSettings.format = Windows.Media.Capture.
                                  CameraCaptureUIPhotoFormat.jpeg;
        dialog.captureFileAsync(Windows.Media.Capture.CameraCaptureUIMode.photo)
            .then(
                function (file) {
                    // More code here
                },
                function (err) {
                    // User canceled the operation.
                }
            );
    }
    catch (err) {
        // Show some error message.
    }
}
```

As you can see, the core of the capture operation is the *captureFileAsync* method exposed by the *CameraCaptureUI* object. The method takes just one argument that controls whether you want to use the camera to take a picture or shoot a video.

```
dialog.captureFileAsync(Windows.Media.Capture.CameraCaptureUIMode.photo).then(...);
```

The method works asynchronously, so to work on its results you need to arrange a JavaScript *then* or *done* promise that receives the byte stream of the captured image. Figure 12-2 shows the application in action.

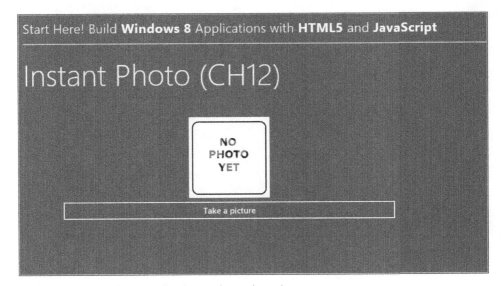

FIGURE 12-2 The webcam application ready to take a picture.

When a user runs the application for the first time, they must provide permission to use the webcam. Figure 12-3 demonstrates a security feature of Windows 8: the user must explicitly enable the application to use the webcam. If the user does not grant permission, then the application won't work.

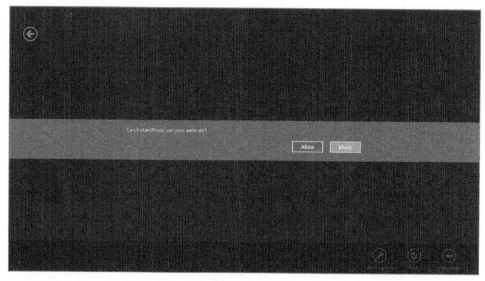

FIGURE 12-3 Granting permission to use the webcam.

Figure 12-4 shows the camera in action after clicking the Take A Picture button.

FIGURE 12-4 The webcam in action.

To actually take a picture, you tap or double-click the screen. Before doing so, users can further tweak the camera options, or even set a timer. The Back button, visible at the top-left corner of the screen, provides a way to return to the application without doing anything. When you click the Back button, the app still considers the operation as completed successfully, except that no file will be passed to the promise methods.

After tapping to take the picture, the dialog gives you a chance to crop the image or retake the picture if you just don't like some aspect of it (see Figure 12-5).

FIGURE 12-5 Selecting a portion of the picture.

Note The webcam displayed by the *CameraCaptureUI* dialog is a full-screen camera. Windows 8 also provides an alternative API that gives you full control over the streaming done by the camera. By using this more advanced API, you can create custom views and apply filters to captured data.

The *captureFileAsync* method returns control to the calling application as soon as the capture operation completes. If a photo was taken, the promise passes an object that references the captured item. Now you need to decide what you want to do with the captured item.

Processing captured items

There are two things you probably want to do with the stream captured by the webcam: display the image for the user and save the image to some permanent location, such as the *Pictures* library.

Displaying the captured picture

The following code shows what you need in order to display the captured picture via an *IMG* element in the main page of the application.

```
dialog.captureFileAsync(Windows.Media.Capture.CameraCaptureUIMode.photo)
    .then(function (file) {
        if (file) {
            var viewer = document.getElementById("imgPhoto");
            viewer.src = URL.createObjectURL(file);
        } else {
            // No photo captured, but no error returned
        }
    });
```

To display a picture in an *IMG* element—the only known way to display pictures in a WinJS application—you need a URL to reference; but the captured item is returned to you as the handle to a Windows 8 storage file. You need to invoke the *URL.createObjectURL* helper function that was specifically created to return a usable URL for blobs, media objects, or streams. Figure 12-6 shows the main interface of the application displaying a captured photo.

FIGURE 12-6 The captured image displayed within the application.

Displaying the captured photo is great, but without some more code, the photo is lost completely as soon as you exit the application. Next you'll make the application a bit more sophisticated, letting it save images as well as take them.

Adding the Pictures Library capability

A Windows Store application runs in a protected environment, often referred to as a "sandboxed environment." That term can mean many things, but for the purposes of this example, it means that the application is not free to access any physical disk location for reading and/or writing.

You've seen in past chapters that a Windows Store application can save any data in its own reserved space. While this option was more than sufficient for the TodoList application you built, it is arguably not a truly viable option for the Instant Photo sample application. The output produced by Instant Photo consists of content that the user likely would want to make accessible to other applications.

To achieve this goal, the best option is to save photos to the *Pictures* folder. Doing that requires you to declare yet another capability. So open up the application manifest again, select the Capabilities tab, and check Pictures Library, as in Figure 12-7.

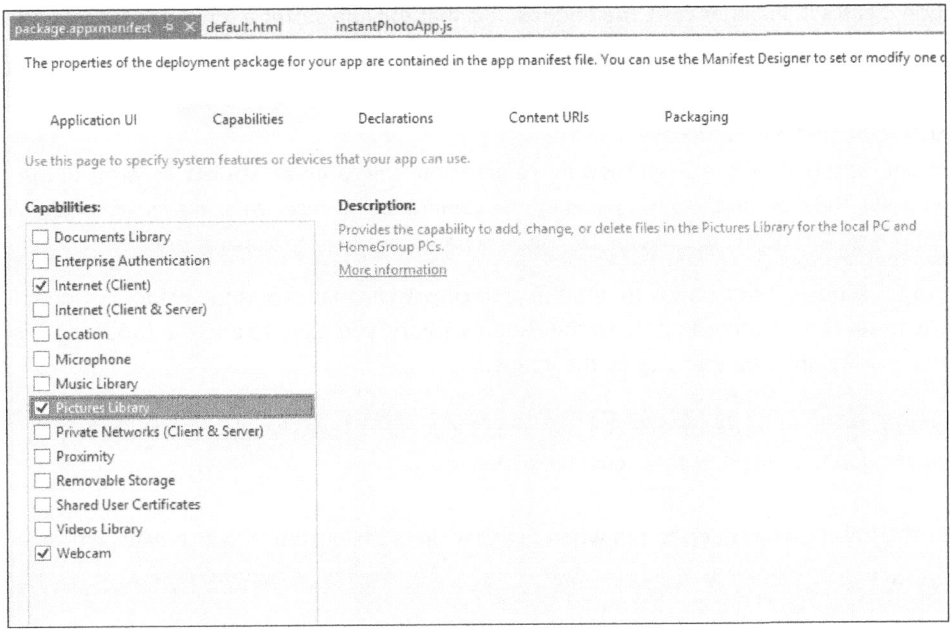

FIGURE 12-7 Declaring the Pictures Library capability.

You may want to let users create a specific subfolder under their *Pictures* folder to hold all the pictures they take with the Instant Photo app. Alternatively, you might want to do that programmatically. That's what you'll do next.

Creating a subfolder for photos

An ideal time to create the *Instant Photo* subfolder is the first time the application is run on a given device. Add the following code to the *init* method in the *instantPhotoApp.js* file.

```
var picturesFolder = Windows.Storage.KnownFolders.picturesLibrary;
picturesFolder.createFolderAsync("Instant Photo",
                          Windows.Storage.CreationCollisionOption.
                          openIfExists)
          .then(function (folder) {
                instantPhotoApp.customFolder = folder;
          });
```

You should save a reference to the newly created folder somewhere so that you can retrieve it later when you actually store the picture. To do that, declare a new global property on the application root object. Edit your *instantPhotoApp.js* file so it begins as shown below:

```
var instantPhotoApp = instantPhotoApp || {};
instantPhotoApp.customFolder = null;
```

The net effect of the code is that any time the Instant Photo application is launched, it checks whether the *Instant Photo* folder already exists within the *Pictures* Library; if it doesn't exist, the application creates it. In either case, the end result is that the app stores a reference to the folder object in the newly created *customFolder* property.

Saving a copy of the picture

The webcam capture dialog box returns a file reference to the captured stream. In terms of the Windows 8 API, the *then* promise triggered by the camera dialog receives a *StorageFile* object. You first encountered this object in Chapter 10, "Adding persistent data to applications."

A *StorageFile* object has a handy method named *copyAsync* that copies the file to a given folder. Therefore, to save the captured photo to the *Pictures* library, you need to add the following line to the *then* promise right after you display the image.

```
// Here file is the storage object returned by the camera capture UI dialog
file.copyAsync(instantPhotoApp.customFolder);
```

Here's the full code you need to run when the user clicks the button to take a new picture:

```
instantPhotoApp.takePicture = function () {
    try {
        var dialog = new Windows.Media.Capture.CameraCaptureUI();
        var aspectRatio = { width: 16, height: 9 };
        dialog.photoSettings.croppedAspectRatio = aspectRatio;
        dialog.photoSettings.format = Windows.Media.Capture.
                                    CameraCaptureUIPhotoFormat.jpeg;
        dialog.captureFileAsync(Windows.Media.Capture.CameraCaptureUIMode.photo)
            .then(function (file) {
                if (file) {
                    var viewer = document.getElementById("imgPhoto");
                    viewer.src = URL.createObjectURL(file);
                    file.copyAsync(instantPhotoApp.customFolder);
                }
            }
    } catch (err) {
        // Show some error message
    }
}
```

Figure 12-8 shows a few photos captured and then safely stored in the *Instant Photo* folder under the *Pictures* library.

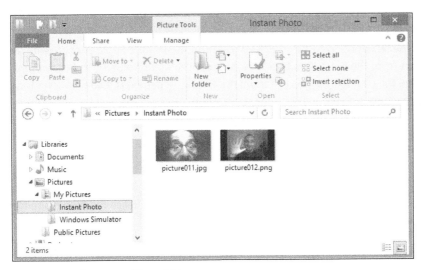

FIGURE 12-8 The *Instant Photo* folder.

Working with the printer

Even though the world is moving toward an increasingly digital and virtual future, printing a document is still an important task that has value despite the environmental considerations of print media. For developers, printing has never been this easy; in prior years, developers had to contend with many different drivers and settings.

Windows 8, however, makes printing as easy as possible. Printing takes only a few relatively standard steps from within JavaScript applications. You should note, though, that JavaScript applications have no access to a subset of more advanced capabilities, such as setting custom options programmatically and printing specific pages.

For basic tasks, though, working with the printer from within Windows Store JavaScript applications is quick and easy. "Basic tasks," means the ability to control the content and template to be printed, and the ability to print context-specific pieces of data.

Here's a new exercise that gives you some experience in printing, using some sample content.

The *Print* contract

In Windows 8, printing is ruled by the *Print* contract. A Windows Store application therefore supports printing by registering for the *Print* contract. The *Print* contract tells the system that the application supports printing, so that when users swipe from the right side of the screen to reveal the Charms bar, they will find the list of available printers. Similarly, you may want to allow users to trigger a printing task from the application's user interface by, for example, clicking a button. When this happens, the charms show up programmatically; the user can then select a printer and print.

Setting up the sample application

Before you focus on specific printing tasks, you need to set up the sample application. Create another Windows Store project from the Blank App template and add the *Pages* folder with *header.html* and *footer.html* files. Define the usual CSS styles in *default.css*. Finally, in *default.js*, add a handler for the application's *onready* event which will initialize the application.

```
app.onready = function () {
    printerApp.init();
}
```

You also add a new JavaScript file named, say, **printerApp.js,** and initialize the global application object, as shown below.

```
var printerApp = printerApp || {};
```

As far as the user interface is concerned, you don't need to do much for this application. You just add a couple of buttons that print different content. Insert the following markup right after the opening tag of the *BODY* element:

```
<div id="main">
    <div data-win-control="WinJS.UI.HtmlControl"
        data-win-options="{uri:'/pages/header.html'}"></div>
    <h1>Print-n-Go (CH12)</h1>
    <button id="buttonPrint1">Print template #1</button>
    <button id="buttonPrint2">Print template #2</button>
    <div data-win-control="WinJS.UI.HtmlControl"
        data-win-options="{uri:'/pages/footer.html'}"></div>
</div>
```

This markup contains an extra feature that you haven't seen in previous exercises. The entire document tree that makes up the user interface is wrapped in a *DIV* element—the *main* element. This surrounding *DIV* element doesn't change the way the user interface looks, but it does make it very easy to hide the entire UI with a single line of code. At this point, if you launch the application you should see something like the image in Figure 12-9.

FIGURE 12-9 The Print-n-Go application.

Registering the *Print* contract

Most of the magic required to print content in Windows 8 happens during the initial phase of an application. In fact, after registering the *Print* contract during initialization, you're nearly all set. Note that application initialization is only the preferred place where you could place the *Print* contract; you could do that later in the application. All that really matters is that you must have the *Print* contract in place before the user can invoke any printing functionality.

As usual for the exercises in this book, you have an *init* method on the main application object. Here's an implementation of the method that registers the *Print* contract:

```
printerApp.init = function () {
    var printManager = Windows.Graphics.Printing.PrintManager;
    var printView = printManager.getForCurrentView();

    printView.onprinttaskrequested = function (eventArgs) {
        var printTask = eventArgs.request.createPrintTask("Print-n-Go", function
                        (args) {
            args.setSource(MSApp.getHtmlPrintDocumentSource(document));
            printTask.oncompleted = onPrintTaskCompleted;
        });
    };
    function onPrintTaskCompleted(eventArgs) {
        if (eventArgs.completion === Windows.Graphics.Printing.PrintTaskCompletion.
                                    failed) {
            printerApp.alert("Failed to print.");
        }
    }
}
```

Registering the *Print* contract essentially means invoking the *getForCurrentView* method on the *PrintManager* system object. The returned view must be further configured with a handler for the requested print task event. In other words, anytime a user requests a print task through the charms, or anytime an app requests print services programmatically, the application must create a print task.

A print task has a name that will reference the job in the printer and is associated with some work aimed at grabbing and formatting the content to print. In Windows 8, you always use a single line of code to reference the code to print. More specifically, from within a WinJS application, you always print the current HTML document displayed to the user. That's just what the line below achieves.

```
args.setSource(MSApp.getHtmlPrintDocumentSource(document));
```

The next point to tackle is how you can ensure that the *getHtmlPrintDocumentSource* always gets the right content from the document's object model.

The printing user interface

Let's put the whole topic of printing the content aside for a moment. The only way to print in Windows 8 is through the print dialog shown in Figure 12-10.

FIGURE 12-10 The print charms.

You select the printer of choice and then see another panel containing a preview of the page that will be printed. As a JavaScript developer, you have no control over that displayed content. You're solely responsible for providing the content to preview and print. The preview window (see Figure 12-11) is generated by the system and requires no extra code beyond the code you saw earlier.

As you can discern from Figure 12-11, if your intended purpose is to print the current content of the screen you don't need to do anything—just bring up the charms print dialog and go. More reasonably, though, you probably want to print only a subset of the content currently displayed on the screen. Doing that requires a few tricks.

In essence, in Windows 8, and from a WinJS-based application, you want to print only some of the HTML content from the currently displayed document. Printing plays by common browser rules, which means that hidden content is not printed, and any visible content can be optionally styled for print.

To print exactly the content you want at a given point, you need to arm yourself with print-only style sheets and some extra code that hides the content you don't want to print, leaving just the content that needs to go to the printer visible.

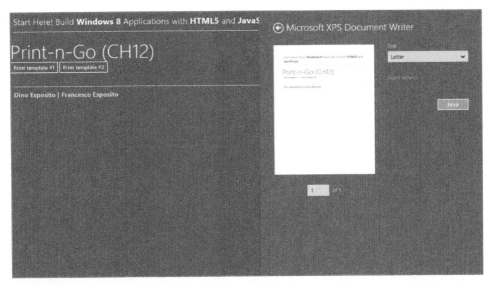

FIGURE 12-11 Preview of the page being printed.

Printing context-specific content

Printing in Windows 8 is purposefully contextual; users expect to be able to print just what's relevant in the current state of an application at any time. This means that in a print-oriented application you will want to keep screen and print content separated, giving you an easy way to switch from one to the other.

Splitting content in subdocuments

In *default.html,* you already surrounded the main content of the page with an outermost *DIV*. The purpose of this outermost *DIV* is to let you split any HTML document into two or more subdocuments: one for regular display and all the others for context-specific print purposes.

For this exercise, suppose you have two print templates to take care of. Add a couple of buttons to print the two templates.

```
<button id="buttonPrint1">Print template #1</button>
<button id="buttonPrint2">Print template #2</button>
```

You define handlers for these buttons in the *printerApp.init* method in the *printerApp.js* file.

```
printerApp.init = function () {
    document.getElementById("buttonPrint1")
.addEventListener("click", printerApp.print1, false);
    document.getElementById("buttonPrint2")
.addEventListener("click", printerApp.print2, false);
    ...
}
```

Finally, in *default.html* add a sibling *DIV* element for each print scenario you intend to support. Here's how:

```
<body>
    <div id="main">
        ...
    </div>
    <div id="print-template1">
        ...
    </div>
    <div id="print-template2">
        ...
    </div>
</body>
```

The user interface goes in the *main* DIV; content you want to be able to print goes in the other *DIV* elements. You now need to ensure that when the application is running normally and not printing, the print sections are hidden. Likewise, you want to hide the application UI content and display the appropriate content when the application is going to print.

The print media

Web browsers have supported screen and print media for a long time. When you author an HTML page, you can link distinct CSS style sheets for screen and print using the *media* attribute on the *STYLE* and *LINK* elements. For example, the following code links the *screen.css* file when the page is being displayed and automatically (and silently) switches to the *print.css* when the page is being printed.

```
<link rel="stylesheet" href="screen.css" media="screen" />
<link rel="stylesheet" href="print.css" media="print" />
```

If you don't specify the *media* attribute, it is assumed to have a value of *all*, meaning that the style sheet will be applied in all cases.

In the current exercise, you want to hide the *print-template1* and *print-template2* sections in screen mode; similarly, you want to hide the *main* section when the page is being printed. You can easily achieve this using the *media* attribute.

To keep it as simple as possible, you'll work with the *STYLE* element. The *STYLE* element allows you to insert style information inline rather than referencing it from an external file.

```
<style media="print">
    #main {
        display: none;
    }
```

```
</style>
<style media="screen">
    #print-template1 {
        display: none;
    }
    #print-template2 {
        display: none;
    }
</style>
```

The result is that the two print templates are hidden in screen mode, whereas the main template is hidden in print mode.

Preparing the document for printing

In a realistic Windows Store application, you may need to have several print templates ready. The *media* attribute doesn't allow you to indicate which print template is turned on so that you can intelligently hide portions of the document you don't need to print. This means that you need some code that is triggered by the user interface to programmatically hide print templates that don't apply to the current context. For example, consider the following markup in *default.html*:

```
<div id="print-template1">
    <h1 id="print-title1">Template #1</h1>
</div>
<div id="print-template2">
    <h1 id="print-title2">Template #2</h1>
</div>
```

When the application is in a state that requires printing the first template, you run the code below:

```
printerApp.preparePrint1 = function () {
    document.getElementById("print-template2").style.display = 'none';
    document.getElementById("print-template1").style.display = '';
    document.getElementById("print-title1").textContent = "Printing template #1";
}
```

Turned on automatically by the browser due to the print *media* attribute, the code hides the second template programmatically when you intend to print the first template. At the same time, the template is populated or updated with fresh content to better reflect the state of the application. At this point, the print template is the only visible part of the document and consequently the only part that will print.

In general, you need to have code similar to the following in order to handle click events on print buttons in your application.

```
printerApp.print1 = function () {
    printerApp.preparePrint1();
    Windows.Graphics.Printing.PrintManager.showPrintUIAsync();
}
printerApp.print2 = function () {
    printerApp.preparePrint2();
    Windows.Graphics.Printing.PrintManager.showPrintUIAsync();
}
```

The *preparePrint1* and *preparePrint2* methods are specular methods that just add printable data to the document subtree and hide unneeded print templates. You define both in the *printerApp.js* file. The *print1* and *print2* methods are invoked from the click handlers of the print buttons in the user interface.

The *showPrintUIAsync* system method is responsible for programmatically displaying the Charms bar for printing—the exact same panel that a user can pop up by swiping from the right edge of the screen. Figure 12-12 shows the print preview when the second template is sent to printers.

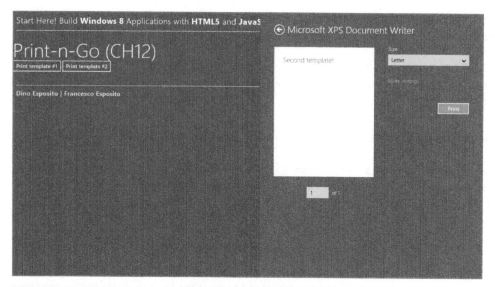

FIGURE 12-12 Gaining control over the content being printed.

Overall, printing from within a WinJS application is a matter of editing the current page so that it only sends out the content you want to print to the browser.

Note Since WinJS applications are essentially browser-based applications, you may think that you can print the old JavaScript way: by calling the *window.print* method. That works, but it is viable only in very simple situations. It is recommended that you use the *window. print* method only if you have a single printing template. After you invoke *window.print* you have no further control over the process and can't update or customize the content being printed.

Working with the GPS system

To round off this chapter, this section shows how you can obtain information about the user's current position. Getting to know the exact (or even approximate) user location is an incredibly valuable piece of information, because it enables you to tailor specific services and information for that user.

Detecting latitude and longitude

Windows 8 devices are equipped with a GPS device that you can query for basic location information, such as its latitude and longitude. Access to the device is wrapped up nicely in an easy-to-use API.

Setting up the project

To get started, you create a new project and follow all the steps as in previous exercises. The user interface can be as simple as in Figure 12-13: just a button and some text elements that display latitude and longitude.

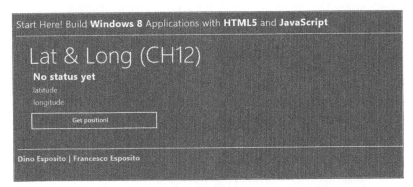

FIGURE 12-13 The main user interface of the geolocation sample application.

The most important step in setting up the project is to add the Location capability in the application manifest. Open the manifest file in the project, select the Capabilities tab, and check Location, as shown in Figure 12-14.

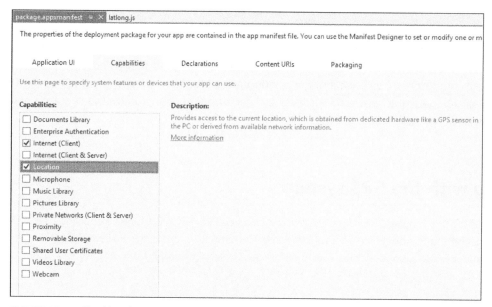

FIGURE 12-14 Checking the Location capability.

The app obtains the location information from the GPS sensor, if one is available on the device. If not, the component infers the user's location information from the IP address that connects the device to the Internet.

Reading geographical position

The code you need to query the location subsystem is shown below. You can copy the following listing straight into the main application JavaScript file for the project, called *latlong.js*.

```javascript
var latLongApp = latLongApp || {};
var geolocator = null;

latLongApp.init = function () {
    document.getElementById("buttonLocation")
            .addEventListener("click", latLongApp.getPosition);
}

latLongApp.getPosition = function () {
    geolocator = new Windows.Devices.Geolocation.Geolocator();
    var position = geolocator.getGeopositionAsync().then(latLongApp.display,
                    latLongApp.error);
}
```

After you have a reference to the geolocation system component, you simply run a query using the *getGeopositionAsync* method. As usual, the method works asynchronously and sets up a promise object that receives latitude and longitude information. Here's the code in the *latLongApp.display* method that displays the raw information to the user:

```
latLongApp.display = function (location) {
    document.getElementById("lat").innerHTML = location.coordinate.latitude;
    document.getElementById("long").innerHTML = location.coordinate.longitude;
}
```

Figure 12-15 shows the final result.

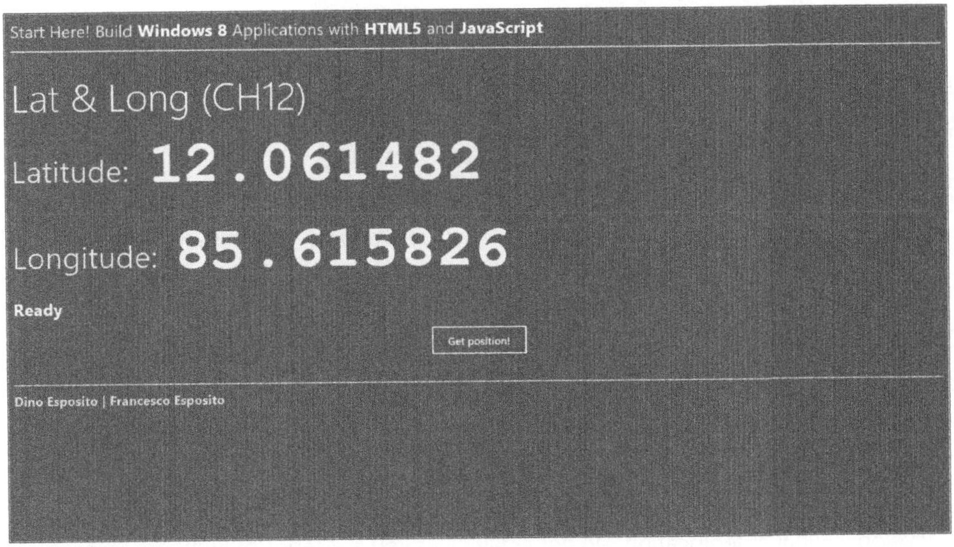

FIGURE 12-15 Raw latitude and longitude numbers shown to the user.

Note that the user may revoke permission to use the location manager at any time by going to the Settings page and acting on the Permission page (see Figure 12-16). Typically, the first time the application is launched on the computer, the system asks the user explicitly to enable the capability; subsequently, it's up to the user to revoke or grant permission for a capability. That same logic applies to the earlier webcam example too.

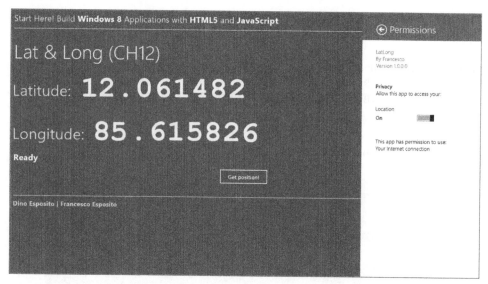

FIGURE 12-16 The Settings page where the user can enable or revoke location permission to the application.

Making use of geolocation data

Geolocation data are quite sensitive, because a user's location can—potentially—reveal where a given individual is at a given time to the entire world. Location is certainly a matter of privacy, but it is also a matter of marketing. For both reasons, Windows 8—as well as other mobile operating systems and web browsers—tends to leave the decision to make location data available up to the user.

As a developer, what a geolocation API generally gives you is a series of numbers that represent latitude and longitude. While latitude and longitude uniquely identify a specific location in the world, they are not always useful to applications. To make them useful, you often need to convert the raw numbers into more human-friendly geographical data, such as city and country?

Adding the Bing SDK to the application

According to the Windows 8 documentation, the object you receive from the call to *getGeopositionAsync* should also contain a property of type *CivicAddress*. As the name implies, this data type is expected to share accurate information about the street, city, and country that corresponds to the pair of latitude and longitude values. However, if you read the documentation carefully and thoroughly, you will also discover that Windows 8 doesn't install any module that can map a geoposition to a civic address. This means that the following code won't throw any exception—but it also fails to give you meaningful data.

```
document.getElementById("address").innerHTML = location.civicAddress.country;
```

It turns out that to map latitude and longitude to a civic address (if such an address exists), you need to reference the Microsoft Bing SDK from your project. A reference to the Bing SDK will also be helpful for visualizing the user's location on a map. First, you need to download the Bing SDK from the following URL: *http://bit.ly/N9NFQN*. Then, to reference the Bing SDK in your project, right-click the References node and select Add Reference. Next, check the Bing Maps for JavaScript item, as shown in Figure 12-17.

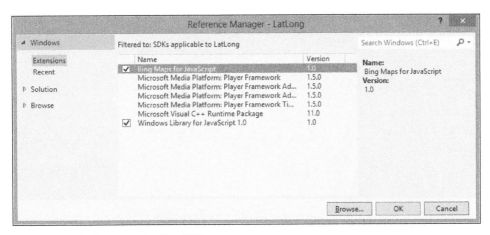

FIGURE 12-17 Referencing the Bing SDK.

Before you can successfully use the Bing SDK, there are a couple of other points to be addressed. The first is to reference the Bing SDK JavaScript file from within your pages. In *default.html*, add the following *SCRIPT* tag:

```
<!-- Bing Map Control references -->
<script type="text/javascript"
        src="ms-appx:///Bing.Maps.JavaScript//js/veapicore.js"></script>
```

The Bing SDK requires some credentials to work. Credentials are the way in which the library tracks users and the use being made of the functions. Bing credentials consist of a key you create after you register on the Bing portal at *http://www.bingmapsportal.com*. Figure 12-18 shows the page you land on after you've successfully registered and created your key for a Windows Store app.

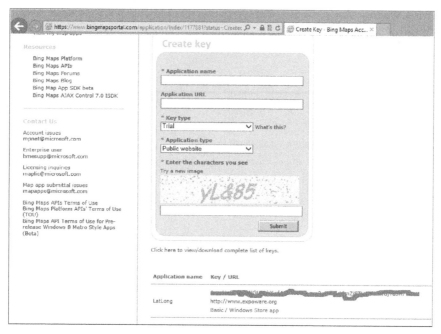

FIGURE 12-18 Getting the key to use the Bing SDK.

Make sure you note the key, because you will need it to use the Bing SDK in your applications.

```
latLongApp.BingKey = "...";
```

You need to initialize the *Bing* library before using it. That's something you might want to do in the application's *init* method. Add the following code to the *latLongApp.init* method:

```
latLongApp.init = function () {
    ...
    Microsoft.Maps.loadModule('Microsoft.Maps.Map', { culture: 'en-us' });
}
```

Now you're all set to display a map and retrieve address information.

Showing the location on a map

Windows Store applications written with JavaScript cannot rely on any built-in components to display a map. However, you can add a *DIV* element to the page and then use the Bing SDK to render the map within the boundaries of that *DIV*. Add the following code to *default.html*—position it as you prefer—for example, just before the footer.

```
<div id="map" style="margin:2px;width:500px;height:400px; border:solid 2px #0ff;">
</div>
```

You might want to explicitly size the *DIV* by assigning a width and height. Explicit sizing prevents the map from covering the entire screen. You'll need some new functions in *latLongApp.js*. Add the following function that prepares the ground for displaying the map:

```
latLongApp.setupMap = function () {
    try {
        var mapOptions = {
            credentials: latLongApp.BingKey,
            mapTypeId: Microsoft.Maps.MapTypeId.road,
            width: 500,
            height: 400
        };
        var mapDiv = document.getElementById("map");
        latLongApp.map = new Microsoft.Maps.Map(mapDiv, mapOptions);
    }
    catch (e) {
        latLongApp.alert(e.message);
    }
};
```

It is key that the *width* and *height* properties match the size of the *DIV* element you plan to use to display the map. You call this new function from within the callback method invoked when the coordinates have been retrieved. The *latLongApp.display* method becomes

```
latLongApp.display = function (location) {
    document.getElementById("lat").innerHTML = location.coordinate.latitude;
    document.getElementById("long").innerHTML = location.coordinate.longitude;

    // Clear the DIV and set up the map object
    document.getElementById("map").innerHTML = "";
    latLongApp.setupMap();

    // Reference the center of the map and set it to the current location
    var mapCenter = latLongApp.map.getCenter();
    mapCenter.latitude = location.coordinate.latitude;
    mapCenter.longitude = location.coordinate.longitude;

    // Set the map view
    latLongApp.map.setView({ center: mapCenter, zoom: 16 });
}
```

What you get this way is already useful, but you can improve it a bit by adding a pushpin to denote the user's location more clearly. Here's how to add a pushpin:

```
latLongApp.addPushPin = function (location) {
    latLongApp.map.entities.clear();
```

```
    var pushpin = new Microsoft.Maps.Pushpin(location, null);
    latLongApp.map.entities.push(pushpin);
}
```

Call the *addPushPin* method at the end of the *latLongApp.display* method.

```
latLongApp.addPushPin(mapCenter);
```

Figure 12-19 shows the result.

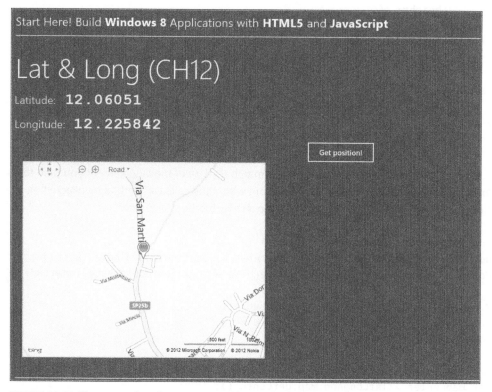

FIGURE 12-19 The current location on a map with a pushpin to denote the exact position referred to by the coordinates.

Getting address information

The final step in the exercise consists of mapping coordinates to more usable information, such as street address, city, and country. As mentioned, this service is built into the native Windows 8 functionality. However, by placing a direct call to the Bing service, you can get a JSON string containing all the details.

Add a new function to the *latLongApp.js* file. This function places a remote call to the Bing service, passing coordinates and getting back detailed civic address information. The URL to call has the following format:

```
http://dev.virtualearth.net/REST/v1/Locations/lat,long?o=json&key=...
```

To invoke the URL, use the *WinJS.xhr* object you first discovered in Chapter 11, "Working with remote data." Here's the code that converts coordinates to an address:

```
latLongApp.convertToAddress = function (location) {
    var url = "http://dev.virtualearth.net/REST/v1/Locations/" +
            location.latitude +
            "," +
            location.longitude +
            "?o=json&key=" +
            latLongApp.BingKey;

    // Invoke the Bing service
    WinJS.xhr({ url: url }).then(function (response) {
        var data = JSON.parse(response.responseText);
        var address = data.resourceSets[0].resources[0].name;

        // Prepare an info-box to add to the map
        var infoboxOptions = { zIndex: 3, title: address };
        var defaultInfobox = new Microsoft.Maps.Infobox(location, infoboxOptions);
        latLongApp.map.entities.push(defaultInfobox);
    });
}
```

The Bing service returns a complex JSON string that, after it's parsed to a JavaScript object, stores the full address to the *name* property.

```
var address = data.resourceSets[0].resources[0].name;
```

You can display the address in a number of ways. For example, you could display it as plain text in the page. Alternatively, you can create an info-box that displays on the map close to the pushpin.

To call the Bing service, you need only the user's latitude and longitude (plus, obviously, your Bing key), so you can call the *convertToAddress* function at any time. In the sample application, however, you might want to place the following call just after the call that adds the pushpin.

```
latLongApp.display = function (location) {
    ...
    latLongApp.addPushPin(mapCenter);
    latLongApp.convertToAddress(mapCenter);
}
```

Figure 12-20 shows the final result.

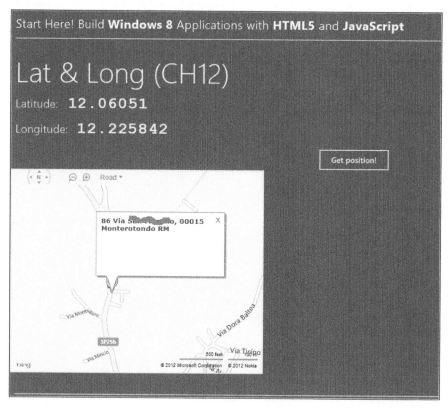

FIGURE 12-20 Showing an info-box with the civic address for the given coordinates.

Summary

Both desktop computers and mobile devices (that is, laptops, tablets, and smartphones) are rich in sensors and ad hoc hardware, which in turn enables developers to write more sophisticated applications that provide a unique perspective to users. The ability to detect the current device position with high accuracy enables personalization beyond the basic content and UI of the application. Other sensors, although not specifically demonstrated in this chapter, can help software to figure out how the device is being used and manipulated or rotated.

Programming Windows Store applications requires that developers become familiar with a range of sensors, such as the GPS sensor that works as a gateway to the surrounding world and hardware. In this chapter, you tackled the webcam, printer, and GPS. More importantly, you explored methods that you can easily apply to other sensors, such as the accelerometer or gyroscope.

In the next chapter, you'll deal with the most characteristic feature of Windows-based devices—Live tiles.

Chapter 13

Adding Live tiles

There are sadistic scientists who hurry to hunt down errors instead of establishing the truth.

— Marie Curie

The Microsoft Windows 8 and Windows Phone user interfaces are characterized by colorful blocks that remind many users of those old-fashioned icons that made earlier versions of Microsoft Windows so popular. However, the new blocks are significantly larger than icons and are displayed side by side under the control of the operating system. The blocks are referred to as *tiles*. The term *tile* mostly refers to the shape and size of the graphical element. Tiles in Windows 8 (as well as tiles in Windows Phone) have an additional and fairly interesting capability: they can display tailored information generated by the application appropriate for the needs of the user who installed the application. Such tiles are referred to as *Live tiles*.

An icon is a static image that makes it quick and fast for users to identify the application. The icon, though, never changes on its own to reflect the current state of the application. A Live tile, on the other hand, is a sort of an application appendix that passes some content to the operating system, which then displays that information to the user even when the application is offline or not running.

From a developer's perspective, dealing with Live tiles requires becoming familiar with a new application programming interface (API), and the concept of an *application notification*. In this chapter, you'll work through an exercise that adds Live tiles to the TodoList application you built in previous chapters.

What's a Live tile anyway?

Figure 13-1 shows the Start screen of a Windows 8 machine. Each block in the user interface represents an installed application. While a Live tile can be active and kept up to date, in most cases (such as when the application is offline) the tile is just a newer and snazzier version of the plain icons used in previous versions of Windows. In Figure 13-1, all the tiles are static and show only the application's logo and name.

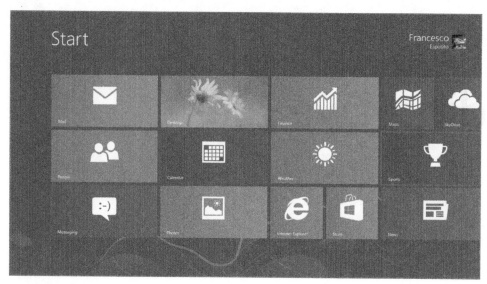

FIGURE 13-1 Tiles in the Start screen of a Windows 8 machine.

Tiles in action

Users can operate on tiles in much the same way they can operate on icons in earlier versions of Windows. Specifically, the user can move tiles around, group them, make them larger or smaller, and enable or disable live notifications. In the end, tiles are just updated icons, restyled and enriched with the ability to receive live notifications from the underlying application.

Moving Live tiles around

Windows 8 creates a new tile for each installed application and pins it to the Start screen. It is then up to the user to unpin the tile from the Start screen if they don't want to see its tile, or even uninstall the application altogether. Figure 13-2 shows the context menu that appears when a user right-clicks a tile.

As Figure 13-2 shows, the available operations are: unpin the application from the Start screen, uninstall the application, change the size of the tile, and toggle live notifications from the application on or off.

FIGURE 13-2 The context menu of a tile.

Just as with icons in Windows 7 and earlier versions, users can move tiles around and organize them in a horizontally scrolling list. Unlike icons, though, in Windows 8 tiles can't be grouped into folders. Moving tiles couldn't be simpler; all a user needs to do is drag tiles around using the mouse or a finger on a touch-enabled device (see Figure 13-3).

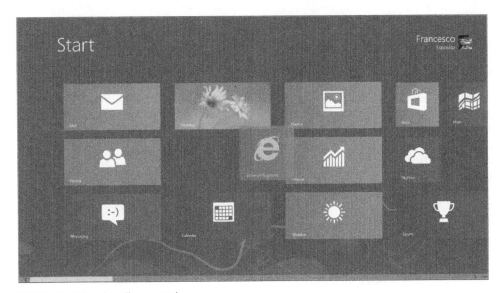

FIGURE 13-3 Moving tiles around.

Resizing tiles

Tiles can be of two sizes: small or large. A small tile is a square box of 130 x 130 pixels; a large tile is about twice that wide. In Figure 13-3, the Microsoft Internet Explorer tile being moved is a small one; the Mail tile in the top-left corner is an example of a large one.

Tiles for custom applications are always created as small tiles; the size can be changed only by the user, through the context menu. Resizable tiles are a challenge for developers who want to add notifications to their applications. As you'll see later in the exercise, you should plan to use different graphical templates for small and large tiles.

Unpinned applications

In Figure 13-2, you saw the Unpin From Start menu item. That option lets users remove a given application from the Start screen. Note that *unpinned* is not the same as *uninstalled*. Unpinned simply means removing an application from the list of applications visible in the Start screen, whereas uninstalled means that the application has been fully removed from the device.

To retrieve an unpinned application later, simply swipe from the bottom of the device (or right-click outside of any tiles). In doing so, you bring up a context menu with a button that gives you access to the full list of installed applications, which includes unpinned applications (see Figure 13-4). Another option is to start typing the name of an application from the Start screen; the UI will limit the display to only those applications whose names match the typed characters.

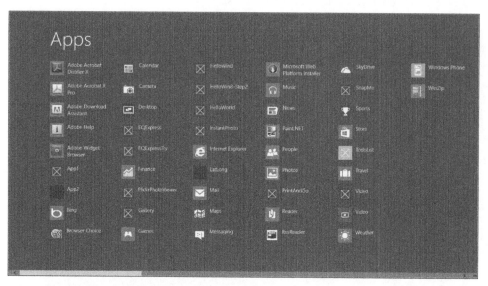

FIGURE 13-4 The list of all installed applications.

Creating Live tiles for a basic application

The most interesting aspect of dealing with tiles is making them live, via support for programmatic notifications. To approach the task of turning tiles into Live tiles in a simple way, you'll first build a new sample application that displays some static text in its tile. Next, you'll proceed with a more sophisticated example where the text displayed reflects the data and state of the application itself.

Preparing the application

Create a new Windows Store application using the usual Blank App template and add the usual *header.html* and *footer.html* files in the *Pages* folder. You will also need to add a few new styles to the *default.css* file and add a JavaScript file named **tilesDemoApp.js** after the application. In addition, it is key for you to add the following line to the *default.js* bootstrapper code.

```
app.onready = function (args) {
    tilesDemoApp.init();
};
```

Here's the initial content of *tilesDemoApp.js*:

```
var tilesDemoApp = tilesDemoApp || {};
tilesDemoApp.init = function () {
    // More code goes here
};
```

The *default.html* page should look like the code below:

```
<!DOCTYPE html>
<html>
<head>
    <meta charset="utf-8" />
    <title>Simple Tiles Demo</title>

    <!-- WinJS references -->
    <link href="//Microsoft.WinJS.1.0/css/ui-dark.css" rel="stylesheet" />
    <script src="//Microsoft.WinJS.1.0/js/base.js"></script>
    <script src="//Microsoft.WinJS.1.0/js/ui.js"></script>

    <!-- TilesDemo references -->
    <link href="/css/default.css" rel="stylesheet" />
    <script src="/js/default.js"></script>
    <script src="/js/tilesdemoapp.js"></script>
</head>
<body>
    <div data-win-control="WinJS.UI.HtmlControl"
        data-win-options="{uri:'/pages/header.html'}"></div>
```

```
    <h1>Simple Tiles Demo (CH13)</h1>

    <div data-win-control="WinJS.UI.HtmlControl"
         data-win-options="{uri:'/pages/footer.html'}"></div>
</body>
</html>
```

So far, so good, but nothing in the application yet adds life to the default static tile.

The notification object

To add live capabilities to tiles, you need to create a *notification*. In this context, a notification is an instance of the *Windows.UI.Notifications.TileNotification* object. When you instantiate the notification object you pass some data that identifies the layout you want for the content within the tile. You should create the notification object only once in the application's lifecycle. However, you can subsequently update the tile's content as many times as needed depending on the logic of the application. The notification object acts as a bridge between the application and the system; once created, the notification remains in place for some time even if the application is terminated or offline.

Creating an application notification

To add Live tiles to an application, you go through three steps. First, you choose the layout of the tile text. Next, you add application-specific data to the layout. Finally, you create a notification object from the template and add it to the system's list.

Windows 8 comes with a long list of tile templates. You find them in the *Windows.UI.Notifications. TileTemplateType* enumeration. Each member of the enumeration refers to a different layout with a few placeholders for text and/or images. A frequently used tile template is the following:

```
Windows.UI.Notifications.TileTemplateType.tileSquareText02
```

The template consists of two rows of text that are automatically styled to look like the title and subtitle of some item. The first line of text is aligned at the top of the tile and displays with a larger font. The second line wraps to the bottom and is rendered with a smaller font.

A tile template is ultimately an XML string; as a developer, however, you don't have much exposure to the details of the XML. All you need to do is get the content of the template and work on it to replace some elements. Here's the code you need to add to the startup code of your application. You open up the *tilesDemoApp.js* file and add the following code:

```
tilesDemoApp.init = function () {
    var template = Windows.UI.Notifications.TileTemplateType.tileSquareText02;
    var xml = Windows.UI.Notifications.TileUpdateManager.
              getTemplateContent(template);

    // More code goes here
}
```

The XML content returned to you depends on the selected template. For the template chosen here, the template contains two *text* elements to be filled up with the text you want to display on the tile. Add the following code to add application-specific content to the template.

```
tilesDemoApp.init = function () {
    var template = Windows.UI.Notifications.TileTemplateType.tileSquareText02;
    var xml = Windows.UI.Notifications.TileUpdateManager.
            getTemplateContent(template);
    var textElements = xml.getElementsByTagName("text");

    // Fill up text placeholders in the tile template
    textElements[0].innerText = "Title";
    textElements[1].innerText = "This is the subtitle";

    // More code goes here
}
```

Finally, you need to register the tile with the operating system so that the content can be properly displayed from the Start screen. A few more lines of code should then be added to the *init* function in the *tilesDemoApp.js* file. Here's the final code you need to have in the *init* function:

```
tilesDemoApp.init = function () {
    var template = Windows.UI.Notifications.TileTemplateType.tileSquareText02;
    var xml = Windows.UI.Notifications.TileUpdateManager.
            getTemplateContent(template);
    var textElements = xml.getElementsByTagName("text");

    // Fill up text placeholders in the tile template
    textElements[0].innerText = "Title";
    textElements[1].innerText = "This is the subtitle";

    // Create and register the notification object
    var liveTile = new Windows.UI.Notifications.TileNotification(xml);
    Windows.UI
        .Notifications
        .TileUpdateManager.createTileUpdaterForApplication().update(liveTile);
}
```

You first create a new notification object from the template XML and then add it to the system's list of Live tiles for the installed applications. For each currently active Live tile, the system maintains an updater object that is responsible for periodically displaying up-to-date content in the Start screen. Figure 13-5 shows the Live tile of the sample application as it shows up on a Windows 8 machine.

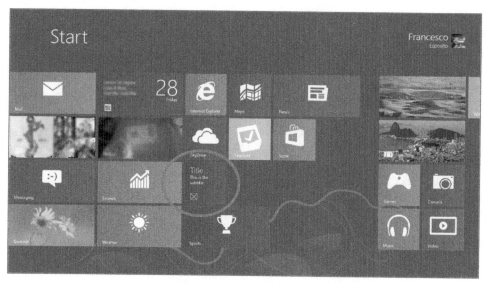

FIGURE 13-5 The Live tile for the sample application in action.

Regardless of the template you choose, the original application's logo is still displayed at the bottom of the tile. The rest of the tile is at your disposal and can be filled up according to the template.

Adding Live tiles to an existing application

In the end, adding a Live tile to the application is not really a hard task. All that it takes is a few calls to a system provided API. The challenge comes when you try to add Live tiles to a real-world application. In this case, the hardest part of the job is deciding which data goes to the Live tile, how you retrieve that, how often you update it and, of course, picking up the most appropriate template. In addition, you also might want to support both large and small tiles so that you serve your users a true Windows 8 experience.

Bringing back the TodoList application

In Chapter 10, "Adding persistent data to applications," you completed an exercise aimed at creating a persistent version of the TodoList application. The final version of the application was able to create, edit, and delete tasks; each task was saved to the roaming folder thus ensuring that the application's settings could be uploaded to the cloud and shared with another copy of the same application installed on a different PC or device.

In this exercise, you'll take over from there and extend the TodoList application of Chapter 10 with Live tiles.

Preparing the ground

You make a copy of the project from Chapter 10 and name it **TodoList-Local**. You might want to rename project files to reflect the number of the current chapter. You might also want to tweak the content of the *default.html* page for pure graphical reasons. So open the *default.html* file in the text editor within Microsoft Visual Studio and edit the following line:

```
<h1> TO-DO List (CH13) </h1>
```

Now you should be ready for refreshing your memory of the application and making plans for Live tiles. Figure 13-6 shows the main user interface of the application—nearly the same as in Chapter 10. Figure 13-7, instead, shows the default tile that Windows 8 creates for the application.

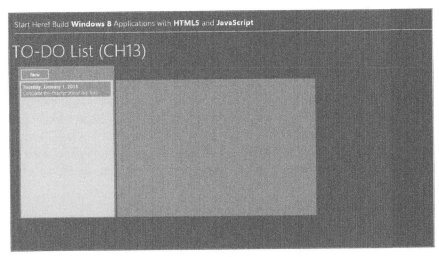

FIGURE 13-6 The basic application to be extended with Live tiles.

FIGURE 13-7 The default tile of the TodoList application.

As a user, when you right-click a tile you see a context menu with the options available. When Live tiles are not active, no special option is made available. Windows 8 detects if the application supports Live tiles and adds an extra button to the context menu to turn live updates on and off.

Identifying project files to edit

As you may have noted with the previous basic exercise, adding Live tiles support to an application only requires a bit of code. Subsequently, the only project file you should focus on, as far as Live tiles are concerned, is *todolist.js*. Live tiles, in fact, have no impact on the overall user interface of the application, nor do they affect the application's manifest or require special permissions.

However, just because the Live tiles management code is sort of standalone code, it can be easily isolated to a distinct file which is then called back from the main script file of the application. So in the rest of the exercise, you'll be focusing on the creation of a new JavaScript file and, maybe more importantly, on the most appropriate template and content to display.

Implementation of Live tiles

Live tiles exist as a way for developers to present useful information to users without requiring them to even open up the application. Live tiles serve as a reminder about the features or content of the application, and they also tend to make your application more frequently used. For Live tiles to be successful, they should present useful information about the application in a timely and attractive manner. For this reason, the choice of the tile template and the selection of data to display is key.

Preparing the ground for Live tiles

You add a new JavaScript file to the project. Let's call it **liveTiles.js**. To start out, you also add the following code to the newly created file:

```
var liveTilesManager = liveTilesManager || {};
liveTilesManager.enable = function (listOfTasks) {
    // More code goes here
}
```

In addition, you should reference the *liveTiles.js* file from within *default.html*. Therefore, you open *default.html* in the Visual Studio editor and add the following line:

```
<script src="/js/livetiles.js"></script>
```

Now you're ready to add some more significant code to the Live tiles manager.

Choosing the tile templates

Windows 8 comes with a long list of predefined templates for tiles. You find predefined templates for both large and small tiles. Essentially, a tile template is a short piece of XML data that wraps up the information to show. Typically, a Live tile consists of images and one or more lines of text. To learn more about the available tile templates, you can pay a visit to the following URL: *http://msdn.micro-soft.com/en-us/library/windows/apps/hh761491.aspx.*

Most of the time, the tile contains a title and a subtitle possibly split over multiple lines. Several templates, however, exist that also add an image.

The choice of the template should also take into account the size of the tile and the fact that the user may be willing to change the size of the template on the fly by simply acting on the context menu of the tile. For the purpose of this exercise, you choose the following templates—for the large and small tiles, respectively.

```
Windows.UI.Notifications.TileTemplateType.tileWideText01
Windows.UI.Notifications.TileTemplateType.tileSquareText02
```

The former template is made of four lines of text styled differently. The first line displays with a larger font, whereas the lines that follow use regular font size, display on different lines, and do not wrap text. The latter template is for small tiles and is made of one header string rendered in larger font. The header string is followed by a second string of text rendered with regular font and wrapped over a maximum of three lines.

To enable the chosen tile templates, you add the following code to the *liveTiles.js* file:

```
liveTilesManager.enable = function (listOfTasks) {

    // Prepare template for LARGE tile
    var templateLarge = Windows.UI.Notifications.TileTemplateType.tileWideText01;
    var xmlLarge = Windows.UI.Notifications.TileUpdateManager.getTemplateContent
                     (templateLarge);
    var textElementsLarge = xmlLarge.getElementsByTagName("text");

    // Prepare template for SMALL tile
    var templateSmall = Windows.UI.Notifications.TileTemplateType.tileSquareText02;
    var xmlSmall = Windows.UI.Notifications.TileUpdateManager.getTemplateContent
                     (templateSmall);
    var textElementsSmall = xmlSmall.getElementsByTagName("text");

    // More code goes here
}
```

As you learned in the previous exercise, a tile template consists of multiple *text* elements. In the code, variables *textElementsLarge* and *textElementsSmall* are arrays of XML nodes that refer to the text elements in the two XML templates.

The next step consists of populating these *text* elements with data that belongs to the running application.

Selecting data to display in tiles

The TodoList application is entirely based on a list of tasks; each task has its own description, due date, and priority. A Live tile for TodoList will likely display the latest task or perhaps the next task to be completed. The *liveTilesManager.enable* function receives the list of current tasks and decides which information to display.

In this exercise, you will pick up the first task and display its description and due date. For this to happen, you add the following code to the *liveTiles.js* file. More precisely, you add this code to the bottom of the *liveTilesManager.enable* function.

```
// Grab application's information for the tile(s) to display
var featuredTask = listOfTasks.getAt(0);

// Add data to the tile(s)
textElementsLarge[0].innerText = "TO DO";
textElementsLarge[1].innerText = featuredTask.description;
textElementsLarge[2].innerText = "";
textElementsLarge[3].innerText = "due by</b>: " + featuredTask.dueDate.
                                 toLocaleDateString();

textElementsSmall[0].innerText = liveTilesManager.getDueDateCompact(featuredTask);
textElementsSmall[1].innerText = featuredTask.description;
```

You also need to add the code for the *liveTilesManager.getDueDateCompact* function. This function is a utility function that simply formats the due date in an *mm/dd/yyyy* format. The function goes at the end of the *liveTiles.js* file.

```
liveTilesManager.getDueDateCompact = function (task) {
    var date = task.dueDate;
    var day = date.getDate();
    var month = date.getMonth();
    month++;
    var year = date.getFullYear();
    var x = month + "/" + day + "/" + year;
    return x;
}
```

Combining small and large template together

Although it is not strictly required, any Windows Store application should consider supporting both small and large tiles. So far, you configured both tiles independently; however, this is not enough. Windows 8 requires that large and small tile templates are combined together in a single template. This must be done programmatically. Here's the code you need to append to the *liveTilesManager. enable* function:

```
// Combine together small and large templates
var node = xmlLarge.importNode(xmlSmall.getElementsByTagName("binding").
            item(0), true);
xmlLarge.getElementsByTagName("visual").item(0).appendChild(node);
```

The net effect of this code is appending the small template to the large template. Now you're ready to create the notification object from the template and register it with the system. You therefore add the following code:

```
// Create the notification object
var tileNotification = new Windows.UI.Notifications.TileNotification(xmlLarge);
Windows.UI.Notifications
        .TileUpdateManager.createTileUpdaterForApplication().
            update(tileNotification);
```

In summary, you are now all set as far as the creation of the tiles is concerned. The remaining point is connecting the application with the tiles.

Connecting tiles and application

The application's tiles are updated whenever the application hits some code that updates the notification object. The frequency of these updates, and the content displayed, depend on the application. As far as the TodoList application is concerned, the notification object is created upon startup and updated every time a new task is edited, deleted, or created. This ensures that fresh data is always displayed to the user as a reminder even when the application is not running.

Given the structure of the TodoList application, the best place to invoke the *liveTilesManager.enable* function is from within the *populateTaskList* function that you find defined within *todolist.js*. You locate the function and modify it, as shown below:

```
TodoList.populateTaskList = function () {
    var promise = new WinJS.Promise(function (complete) {
        var tasks = new Array();
        var localFolder = Windows.Storage.ApplicationData.current.roamingFolder;
        localFolder.getFilesAsync()
                .then(function (files) {
                    var io = Windows.Storage.FileIO;
                    files.forEach(function (file) {
                        io.readTextAsync(file)
                            .then(function (json) {
                                var task = TodoList.deserializeTask(json);
                                tasks.push(task);
                            })
                        })
                        .then(function () {
                            var tasksList = new WinJS.Binding.List(tasks);
```

```
                        tasksList = tasksList.createSorted(function (first,
                            second) {
                            return first.dueDate > second.dueDate;
                        });
                        var listview = document.getElementById("task-listview").
                            winControl;
                        listview.itemDataSource = tasksList.dataSource;

                        // Notification
                        liveTilesManager.enable(tasksList);
                    });
                });
            })
        });
        return promise;
    }
```

Compared to the original version of the *populateTaskList* function, there are two main changes to note. The first change is the obvious call to the *liveTilesManager.enable* function which turns on Live tiles. The second change refers to the promise object that wraps up the entire body of the function. The promise object is not strictly required but helps in case of further development. Having *populateTaskList* return a promise gives you a chance to concatenate the behavior of *populateTaskList* with other behavior via the *then* and *done* methods.

Figure 13-8 shows the large Live tile of the application.

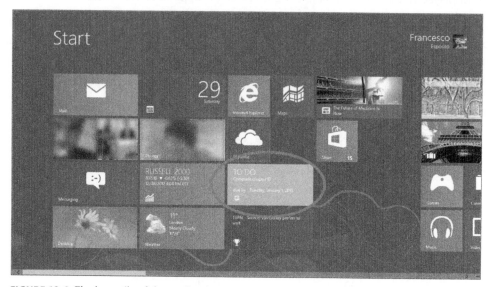

FIGURE 13-8 The large tile of the application.

Figure 13-9, instead, shows the small tile. As you can see in Figure 13-9, now the context menu of the application's tile also includes buttons to turn on and off live notifications.

FIGURE 13-9 The small tile of the application with its context menu.

More advanced features of Live tiles

The two exercises discussed in the chapter show basic features of Live tiles and are enough to get developers started. However, the feature list of tiles doesn't end here. In particular, you can add an expiration to notifications so that Live tiles are automatically turned off when a given time is reached. This is particularly useful when the application needs to display data in the form of reminders. In addition, you can associate the content of tiles with background agents so that the content is updated in the background even when the application is not running. A background agent is a piece of code that doesn't have a user interface but runs periodically under the control of the operating system. By using a background agent, an application can retrieve data asynchronously and push updates to the tiles even without displaying its own user interface.

Summary

In this chapter, you learned about Live tiles. Live tiles are a unique feature of Windows 8 that applications can use to display information to the user right from the Start screen. Any Windows Store application is assigned a tile upon installation; by using some ad hoc code, you can give life to the tile and make it receive and display application information.

In the first exercise, you configured a sample application feeding a small tile with canned data. Next, you extended the TodoList application from Chapter 10 and added small and large Live tiles to display the details of the latest task. The user has a lot of control over tiles: at any time the user can switch between small and large tiles and even turn off live notifications entirely.

With this chapter, you completed the tour of Windows 8 programming and you are now ready for publishing an application to the Windows Store.

Chapter 14

Publishing an application

Success is the ability to go from one failure to another with no loss of enthusiasm.
— Winston Churchill

For many years, the process of publishing a Microsoft Windows application was limited to building a setup program—possibly with the aid of an ad hoc framework. The setup program, in the end, looked a lot like a smart script through which you copy files in the target folder, arrange databases, configure the system, and create a shortcut on the desktop. More importantly, the setup program could be distributed directly by the author with no sort of intermediation. The author was also responsible for advertising the application.

Mobile platforms such as iOS and Windows Phone approached the problem of distributing applications in a different way. The platform owner—Apple for iOS and Microsoft for Windows Phone—makes itself responsible for distributing applications and for giving applications a bit of extra visibility by creating a central store. This approach has been taken also for Microsoft Windows 8 native applications that are, in fact, known as Windows Store applications.

In Windows 8, applications that use the native user interface—those applications you practiced with throughout the book—can only be distributed through the store. The main reason for this choice is to ensure that available applications are of good quality, work well on the devices, and are devoid of security vulnerabilities and bugs. Microsoft ensures an application is good for the store at the end of a certification process; as you can guess, this comes at a cost. The cost is a 30 percent share of the price for paid applications. For free applications, there's a limitation on the number you can upload and a flat rate beyond the threshold.

In this book, you learned how to build Windows Store applications by taking advantage of the several new application programming interfaces (APIs) available. Now it's about time you close the circle and learn what it takes to publish a finished application to the store.

Getting a developer account

So, Windows 8 users can only install new Windows 8 applications from the Windows Store. But who can upload such applications? The answer is that every Windows 8 developer must obtain a developer account from Microsoft, which entitles them to publish applications. Without a valid developer account, your dazzling application will never be installed except on the computer where you developed it.

> **Note** Windows 8 comes with two main areas of functionality. One is the classic Windows user interface that allows you to install any application, either manually or through a provided setup program—just as in any previous version of Windows. The other is based on the modern Windows 8 user interface. To install any of these applications, you need to get and install them from the Windows Store.

Registering as a developer of free applications

To register as a Windows 8 developer, from the Microsoft Visual Studio Store menu, choose the Open Developer Account item and then follow the on-screen instructions (see Figure 14-1).

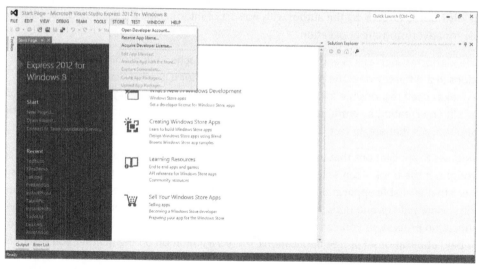

FIGURE 14-1 The Store menu to create a developer's account.

Clicking the Get A Developer License For Windows Store Apps link takes you to the Windows 8 Dev Center, where you click the displayed button to register as a developer (see Figure 14-2).

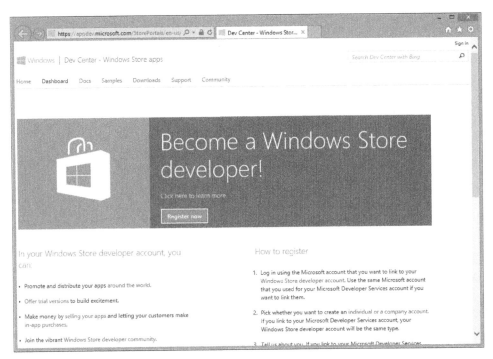

FIGURE 14-2 Click to start the registration process.

If you already have a Windows Phone developer account, you can associate that to Windows 8 instead of completing a new registration. However, if you want to keep distinct accounts for Windows Phone and Windows 8, then you need to provide distinct Windows Live IDs. Of course, if you are a new Windows 8 developer, you just enter a Live ID and proceed.

Account information

When creating a new developer account, you should be aware of which type of account you want to create: personal or business (see Figure 14-3).

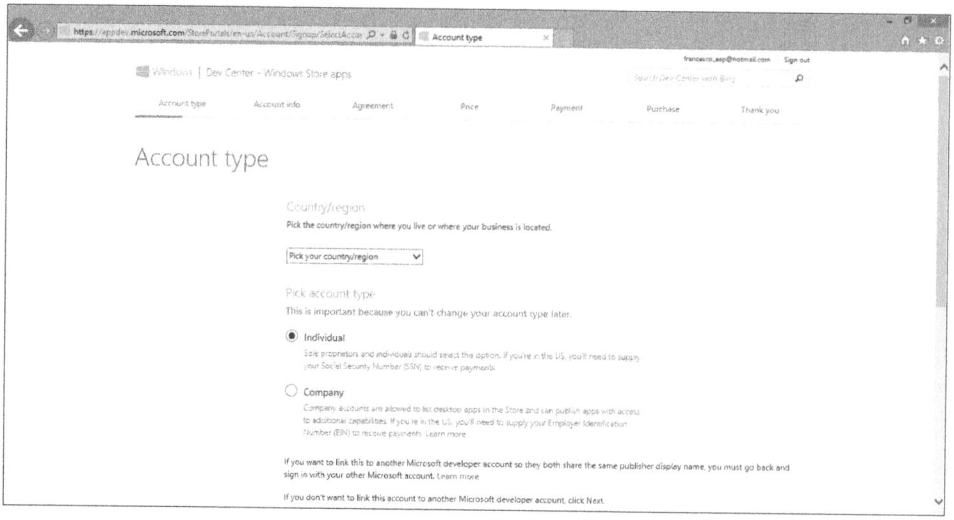

FIGURE 14-3 Do you want an individual or a company account?

Note that you can't switch from one type of account to another. To create a company account, you need to provide Microsoft with a lot more documentation about the company and its executives. On the other hand, a company account lets you have multiple administrators—and even create and publish applications for internal company use. However, if you're just practicing with Windows 8 and want to upload one or two applications for which you are the sole developer, an individual account is just fine.

You proceed by entering your personal information, including your full name and address. Next, you choose your display name. The display name is important, because it is the name that Windows 8 will show as the author of the application. The display name of any app publisher must be unique; when you suggest a name the Windows 8 Dev Center site provides real-time verification as to whether the name you have chosen is available or already taken (see Figure 14-4).

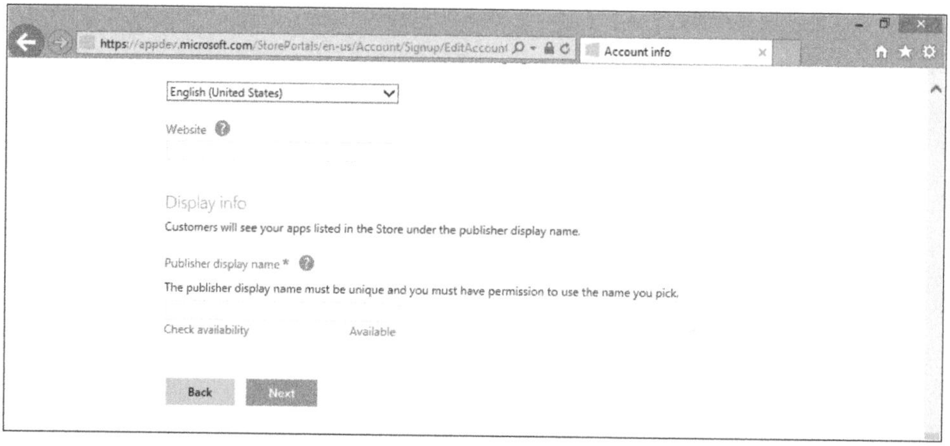

FIGURE 14-4 The publisher's name must be unique.

Payment details

Whether you want to create a personal or business account, you must be a registered Windows 8 developer. Unfortunately, registration is not free. You must pay to be a Windows Phone or iOS developer, and you must pay a yearly fee to be a Windows 8 developer as well. At the time of this writing, the registration fee for individuals is $49.00. For companies, it is $99.00 (or an equivalent amount in other currencies).

After choosing your display name, you will see the contract that's being signed between you and the Windows Store. You'll also see a summary page detailing what you get in return for your money (see Figure 14-5). If you decide to proceed, you will be asked to enter your credit card information to pay the fee. If you have a promotion code, you will enter it at this time.

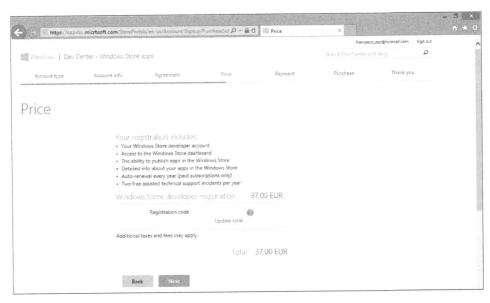

FIGURE 14-5 The checkout screen.

Registering as a developer of paid applications

Figure 14-6 shows the final screen you see after you have successfully completed the registration process. At this point, you're all set to start publishing free applications. If you intend to publish paid applications, however, you'll need to complete some extra steps.

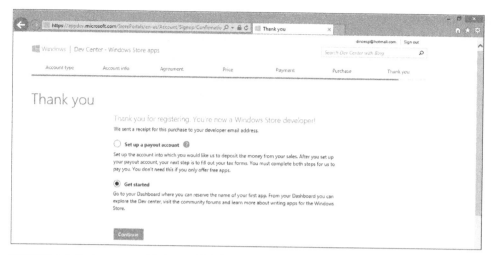

FIGURE 14-6 You're now enabled to publish free applications to the Windows Store.

From the Microsoft perspective, the fundamental difference between free and paid user applications is that in the latter case, Microsoft needs to pay you when people buy your applications. Consequently, before your app can be published to the store, Microsoft needs to make sure it knows how to pay you later.

You must provide two separate blocks of information: bank details, so that money can be safely wired to you, and tax information, to satisfy internal revenue service (IRS) reporting requirements. The banking information may vary depending on the country you live in, but most of the time it requires only an international bank code and an alphanumeric string (the IBAN string) that identifies your account.

As far as taxes are concerned, you may need to fill out an electronic form, which is different for US residents and non-US residents. The details of this step may vary from country to country, but for the most part there should be no need to mail paper documents. Dealing with taxes and banks is usually an annoying procedure, but in this case it doesn't take too long—and hopefully happens only once. For more information, you can refer to the instructions at the following link: *http://bit.ly/PrOrbW.*

Steps required to publish an application

All Windows Store applications go into the same catalog; therefore, each application must have a unique name.

Choosing a name for the application

Choosing a name is therefore an important step; if you have a very specific name in mind, then you should plan to reserve it in advance. If the name you like is already taken, you have no other option than to choose a different name!

Reserving an application name

You can reserve a name for your future application at any time by clicking the Reserve App Name option in the Store menu of Visual Studio (see Figure 14-7).

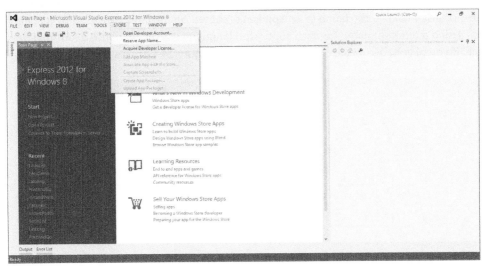

FIGURE 14-7 Starting the procedure to reserve the application's name.

To reserve the name, type the name of the application; if the Windows Store detects no conflicts, you will get a positive response, as shown in Figure 14-8.

FIGURE 14-8 The name T-List has been reserved.

Note that after a name has been reserved, you are the only person who can use it. Name reservations are valid for one year; however, if you don't publish an application under that name within a year of making the reservation, the Windows Store will release the name and others can use it.

Localizing an application name

There are some situations in which the application has a name that is "neutral" to spoken languages. In such cases, you won't ever want to change the name regardless of how many languages you localize the application for. This is, however, a very special situation. More likely, you might want to translate—or just change—the name of an application based on the language used by its intended audience. Using a different name for each supported language is a recommended (not mandatory) approach. If you plan to use localized names, the page in Figure 14-9 shows how to proceed.

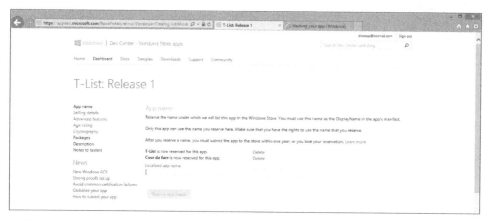

FIGURE 14-9 Choosing localized names.

After reserving the name, you can start packaging the application.

> **Note** As mentioned, if the name is truly important for the application, then you should first reserve the name and then start developing the application.

Packaging an application

The packaging step consists of creating a single container with all the files that make up your application. Before you start packaging, you should ensure that the application is feature-complete and contains no bugs or vulnerabilities.

Compiling in Release mode *store logo.png*

A finished Windows Store application is an application that needs no further changes to the code and has defined files for the various logos and the splash screen. In addition, you might also want to have some screenshots ready that help advertise the application in the Windows Store. Pay attention to the file: that will be your application's icon in the Windows Store.

When everything is ready, you first compile the application code in Release mode. When you compile an application, you usually choose between two modes: *Debug* (the default) and *Release*. Both modes produce a valid executable file; however, the Debug mode pads the executable file with extra information used for debugging purposes. After your application is bug-free and feature-complete, there's no longer any need to keep the debug information. Compiling in Release mode gives you a more compact (and even slightly faster) executable that doesn't include unnecessary internal debugging symbols.

Preparing the app package

After you have an executable compiled in Release mode, you can proceed with the creation of an app package. You create an app package by clicking the Create App Packages item in the Store menu (see Figure 14-10).

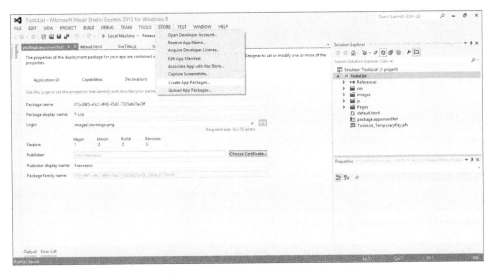

FIGURE 14-10 Start the process of creating an app package.

Package creation requires several steps, during which Visual Studio displays a few forms for you to fill out. The first form is shown in Figure 14-11. This form requires you to enter the name of the published application. The form lists any reserved names you may have; you can just select one or run the wizard to reserve a new name at this time.

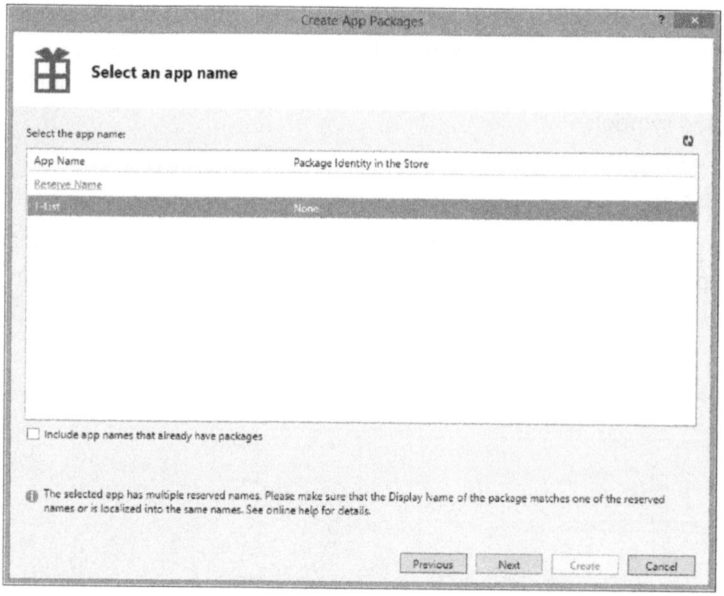

FIGURE 14-11 Setting the name of the application.

In the next step, you choose the destination folder on the local disk where you want to save the package. Keeping track of this folder is important, because you will need it to upload the package to the Windows Store at the end of the packaging process. You also need to select at least one target platform from the form shown in Figure 14-12.

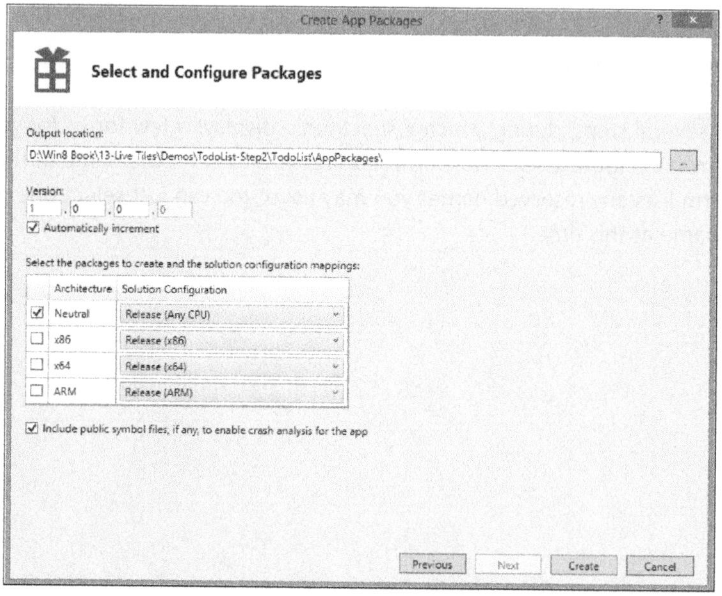

FIGURE 14-12 Choosing a target Windows 8 platform.

The *target platform* refers to the hardware architecture of the machines that may run your application. To ensure the widest possible audience for your application, you should generally choose to compile for all platforms.

> **Important** The point here is that the Windows 8 operating system runs on a variety of different hardware configurations, most typically 32-bit machines (x86), 64-bit machines (x64), and devices such as a tablet with an ARM architecture. To make it clear, if you fail to tick the ARM checkbox, then your Windows Store application won't be able to run on a Windows 8 tablet running WinRT.

When you push the Create button in the form shown in Figure 14-12, Visual Studio runs a process that creates a valid package for the Windows Store application. During this process, Visual Studio launches the application and performs several tests on it. If everything checks out, you will see the dialog box shown in Figure 14-13.

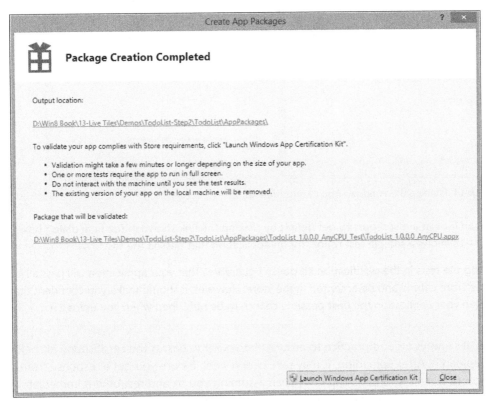

FIGURE 14-13 The app package has been successfully created.

Having an app package ready doesn't mean that you're done. The application is not yet ready to upload to the Windows Store. You have only created the package in a format that the Windows Store can accept. There's no guarantee that your application, as-is, will be accepted and published to the store. Your application must still be certified before it can appear in the Windows Store.

Any application submitted to the Windows Store for publication needs to pass a number of additional tests. If the application crashes during any of these tests, or fails the tests in any way, the Windows Store will reject the application, providing you with documentation about the app's misbehavior and some guidelines on how you can go about fixing it.

The Windows App Certification Kit

To avoid a rejection, or more precisely, to reduce the likelihood that your application will be rejected, you can run the same battery of tests that Microsoft runs on applications locally, before you submit your app to the store. Those tests are available to you through the Windows App Certification Kit. As shown in Figure 14-13, you can click on the Launch Windows App Certification Kit button at the bottom of the window and run the same tests locally that your application will be subject to after you submit it. Figure 14 shows the two-step process.

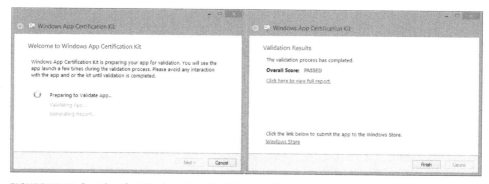

FIGURE 14-14 Running the Windows App Certification Kit.

You can look at a test report to get details by clicking the link shown in the final dialog box. Figure 14-15 shows a sample test report for an application that passed the tests.

Passing the tests in the certification kit doesn't *guarantee* that your application will pass all Windows Store criteria and be accepted in the store. However, it should make you confident that you have given your application the best possible chance to be published when you upload it.

Note It's always a good practice to ensure that your app passes the certification kit before you upload it. After uploading, it may take over a week before you get a response from Microsoft. If the response is negative, even assuming you fix and resubmit it immediately, it will take at least another week before your application can be published.

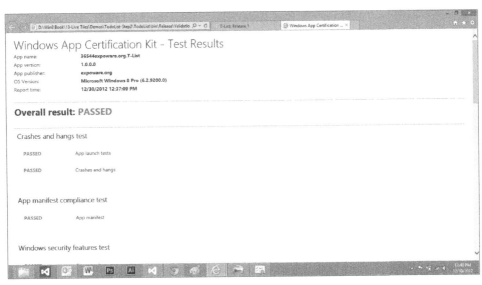

FIGURE 14-15 A sample report of the standard tests for a successful app.

Uploading the application

The final step in getting the application published is to send the package to Microsoft. You do this by clicking Upload App Packages from the Visual Studio Store menu. As soon as the package transfer begins, you will see a page similar to Figure 14-16.

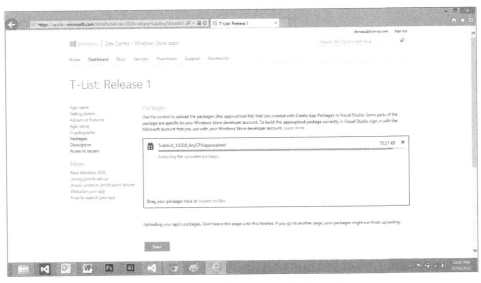

FIGURE 14-16 Uploading the package named T-List to the Windows Store.

After it has reached the Windows Store servers, you need to properly describe your application package and get it ready for final testing. So at this stage, you enter the description that you want users to see, and any keywords that may help them to find your app in the store (see Figure 14-17). This is also the place where you can add screenshots to help sell your application to potential customers.

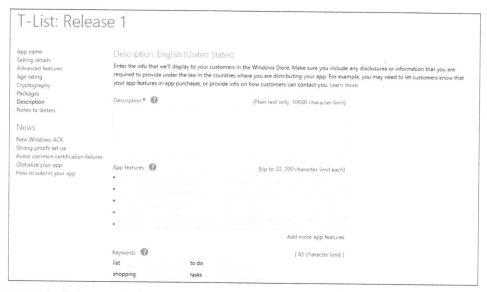

FIGURE 14-17 Entering the description and keywords for your application.

The application will go through several tests before publishing. Some tests are automated (for example, the tests in the certification kit); other tests will be run by a person. You may enter some information to help that person better understand and verify your application's behavior. As in Figure 14-18, adding notes for testers is the final step before you actually submit the application for certification.

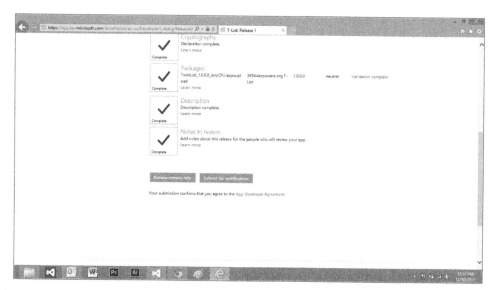

FIGURE 14-18 All has been done; the app is ready for certification.

After you submit your application for certification, the related package is queued for the automated tests. Automated tests are related to security and technical compliance of the application. They are analogous to the certification tests you (should) have already run locally, and because they're automatic, you'll know whether your app passed or was rejected within only a few hours. If something goes wrong, you receive a prompt notification.

The most delicate part of the certification process is checking for content compliance. This task is completed by a person, and may take up to seven days. After passing this test, the application goes into Release mode. When you entered the application description, you were also given the chance to decide about the release procedure. Application release can happen as soon as the application has passed all tests, or at your earliest convenience. After the application is approved and you're ready to publish it, the package moves to the signing phase, where its binary code is signed with a key to prevent tampering and is then put on the output queue to become visible on the Windows Store servers.

Sideloaded applications

The scenario described so far is likely the most frequent. However, there's another scenario that needs to be addressed briefly. What if you don't want to publish the application to the store, but just make it available to a well-known customer or customers?

Publishing an application to the Windows Store, whether a free or paid application, gives every owner of a machine equipped with Windows 8 a chance to download and install your application. This is desirable in most cases, but not in all cases.

Therefore, Windows 8 offers a different way to distribute applications, known as *Enterprise Sideloading*. Not all Windows 8 machines are configured to support sideloaded applications, so by taking this track, you are limiting your target audience to only owners of the Enterprise edition of Windows 8. More basic versions of Windows 8 don't support sideloaded applications—only approved applications that are downloaded and installed from the store. However, even basic Windows 8 machines can support sideloaded applications by purchasing ad hoc keys on a per machine basis.

In addition, for application sideloading to work, the target machines must be part of a domain that enables the policy to "Allow all trusted apps to install."

Summary

Overall, you have three options for writing applications that run on a Windows 8 machine. The first is to write Windows desktop applications that also run on earlier versions of Windows. But if you were doing that, the entire content of this book would be useless to you. In fact, you would write such applications against the .NET Framework using C# or Visual Basic as the primary programming language.

The second alternative is the main thrust of what this book has covered: writing Windows Store applications that take advantage of both Windows RT and the Windows 8 modern UI.

These applications, though, are usually intended for distribution through the Windows Store in an unrestricted way. This means that after you have made the application available to the Windows Store, any Windows 8 user can get and install it. Finally, the third option is to create sideloaded applications. A sideloaded application is a Windows 8 modern UI application, such as those described in this book, that you can install on machines set up so they have special capability of accepting trusted applications. It is key to note that a sideloaded application is in no way different from a Windows Store application; it's the target environment that must be configured differently, so that machine can install applications from locations other than the Windows Store, such as via email or from a CD or DVD.

This book covered Windows 8 development with HTML5 and JavaScript from an initial "Hello Windows 8" application all the way through to publishing a completed free or for-sale application. If you made it to this point and completed all the exercises, you're in a position to start publishing some great Windows 8 applications. All the best!

Index

Symbols

W

About the authors

Dino Esposito, a long-time trainer and top-notch consultant, is the author of many popular books for Microsoft Press that have helped the professional growth of thousands of .NET developers and architects. Dino is the CTO of a fast-growing company that provides software and mobile services to professional sports, and currently is also a technical evangelist for JetBrains, where he focuses on Android and Kotlin development, and is a member of the team that manages WURFL—the database of mobile devices used by organizations such as Google and Facebook. Follow Dino on Twitter at @despos and on *http://software2cents.wordpress.com.*

Even though he's still a teenager (he's only 15), **Francesco Esposito** has accumulated significant experience with mobile application development for a variety of platforms, including iOS with Objective C and MonoTouch, Android via Java, Windows Phone, and even BlackBerry. He wrote most of the code for IBI12—the official multi-platform app for the Rome ATP Masters 1000 tennis tournament.

When not writing apps, hanging out with friends, or practicing water polo, he likes going to school, where his secret goal is to achieve the highest marks ever so he can get a scholarship to Harvard or just buy his own Surface tablet.

Now that you've read the book...

Tell us what you think!

Was it useful?
Did it teach you what you wanted to learn?
Was there room for improvement?

Let us know at http://aka.ms/tellpress

Your feedback goes directly to the staff at Microsoft Press,
and we read every one of your responses. Thanks in advance!

 Microsoft

CPSIA information can be obtained at www.ICGtesting.com
Printed in the USA
LVOW020935170613

338888LV00001B/1/P